Trading Stories: Experiences with Gender and Trade

Edited by Marilyn Carr
and Mariama Williams

COMMONWEALTH SECRETARIAT

Commonwealth Secretariat
Marlborough House
Pall Mall, London SW1Y 5HX
United Kingdom

Published by the Commonwealth Secretariat
Edited for publication by Tina Johnson
Designed by Wayzgoose
Printed by The Charlesworth Group

Photo credits: p. 64 Robin Hammond/Panos Pictures; p. 88 Rebecca Nduku/Commonwealth Secretariat; p. 116 G.M.B. Akash/Panos Pictures; p. 124 Andy Johnstone/Panos Pictures; p. 172 Sanjit Das/Panos Pictures; p. 184 Phytotrade Africa; p. 208 Rebecca Nduku/Commonwealth Secretariat; p. 232 SEWA Trade Facilitation Centre

Copies of this publication may be obtained from:
The Publications Section
Commonwealth Secretariat
Marlborough House
Pall Mall, London SW1Y 5HX
United Kingdom

Tel: +44 (0) 20 7747 6534
Fax: +44 (0) 20 7839 9081
Email: publications@commonwealth.int
www.thecommonwealth.org/publications

A catalogue record for this publication is available from the British Library.

ISBN: 978-0-85092-873-0 (paperback)
ISBN: 978-1-84859-044-1 (downloadable e-book)

Contents

Figures

Tables

Foreword

Gender equality is a key factor for equitable pro-poor growth and sustainable human development. Trade, as an important aspect of globalisation and a major source of growth and development, can have major implications for gender equality. Yet gender analysis has not been integrated either into the substantive areas of trade policy and agreements or into non-trade concerns, such as food security, public health and labour standards, that have increasingly formed part of the negotiating framework for trade. The processes of globalisation and trade liberalisation are presumed to be gender neutral; they often ignore the fact that gender inequalities within society and the economy mean that trade policies do not have the same effects on women and men. Contributing to these differential impacts are gender differences in roles and responsibilities in the household, in the composition of a country's workforce and key export industries, and in access to resources – material, financial, technological and social.

Understanding these inequalities leads to the conclusion that incorporating gender analysis into trade policy research, formulation and implementation will enable trade policy-makers to strengthen the potential outcomes of their work towards the ultimate goals of pro-poor growth and sustainable development. To that end, the Commonwealth Plan of Action for Gender Equality 2005–2015 encourages member governments and commits the Commonwealth Secretariat to take various actions, including ensuring that trade and general macroeconomic policies are designed to promote women's empowerment and do not cause adverse gender impacts, and promoting the integration of gender analysis in trade policy and negotiation of trade agreements. These commitments are reflected in the Commonwealth Secretariat's Strategic Plan 2008–2012.

In 2004, when the Commonwealth Secretariat published *Chains of Fortune: Linking Women Producers and Workers with Global Markets*, we were concerned to ensure that the benefits of globalisation, actual or potential, were enjoyed by women as much as by men. The case studies that were brought together demonstrated how women producers and workers in the informal economy (who in many parts of the world comprise the majority of the economically active population) could contribute much more to the growth of output and exports if they were enabled to do so.

This new publication, *Trading Stories: Experiences with Gender and Trade*, is part of a wider Commonwealth Secretariat programme that has worked systematically to build capacity at national and regional level with the key government ministries and private sector institutions involved in trade policy formulation, implementation and negotiations. Twenty case studies focus on the gender impact of trade frameworks such as the General Agreement on Trade and Services and sanitary and phytosanitary measures, and on best practice models that link women with global markets, including fair trade, organic, niche and mainstream markets. By bringing together these case studies into one accessible publication, *Trading Stories* is an invaluable contribution to the Commonwealth's commitments on gender equality, pro-poor growth and sustainable development, and a much-needed addition to a growing resource base that will advise and assist trade policy-makers and other stakeholders. Previous Commonwealth publications in this area include not only *Chains of Fortune*, but also *Gender Mainstreaming in the Multilateral Trading System* and *Gender and Trade Action Guide: A Training Resource*.

This book is the result of a collective effort by many groups and individuals. We would like to thank all the contributors for their inputs, former colleagues Sarojini Ganju Thakur and Fatimah Kelleher for their work on the project as it developed, and in particular the editors, Marilyn Carr and Mariama Williams, for their ongoing commitment to its completion. In addition, we would like to thank those who have reviewed the text and suggested revisions and improvements, as well as the production team, who have turned it into a finished publication.

We would also like to acknowledge the financial support of the UK Department for International Development, who funded the project.

Caroline Pontefract
Director, Social Transformation Programmes Division
Commonwealth Secretariat

Acronyms and Abbreviations

ACGD	African Centre for Gender and Development
ACP	African, Caribbean and Pacific
ADASC	Anti-dumping and Subsidies Commission (Jamaica)
AfT	Aid for Trade
AGOA	African Growth and Opportunity Act
APEC	Asia-Pacific Economic Cooperation
ASAFE	Association pour le Soutien et l'Appui à la Femme Entrepreneur (Cameroon)
ASCENT	Asian Centre for Entrepreneurial Initiatives (India)
ATC	Agreement on Textiles and Clothing
BNP	Bee Natural Products Ltd (Uganda)
CAFRA	Caribbean Association for Feminist Research and Action
CARIBCAN	Caribbean-Canada Trade Agreement
CARICOM	Caribbean Community
CBI	Caribbean Basin Initiative
CBO	community-based organisation
CCIMA	Chamber of Commerce, Industry, Mines and Crafts (Cameroon)
CDDASA	Customs Duties (Dumping and Subsidies) Act (Jamaica)
CEDAW	Convention on the Elimination of All Forms of Discrimination against Women
CEEWA	Council for the Economic Empowerment of Women in Africa
CIB	Coffee Industry Board (Jamaica)
CITU	Centre of Indian Trade Unions
CMA	Common Monetary Area
CMT	cut-make-trim
COMESA	Common Market for Eastern and Southern Africa
CSME	CARICOM Single Market and Economy
DANIDA	Danish International Development Agency
DFID	Department for International Development (UK)
EAC	East African Community
EC	European Community
ECLAC	Economic Commission for Latin America and the Caribbean
ECOWAS	Economic Community of West African States
EPZ	export processing zone
EPZA	Export Processing Zones Authority (Kenya)
EU	European Union

FAO	Food and Agriculture Organization
FCEM	Femmes Chefs d'Entreprises Mondiales
FDA	Food and Drug Administration (USA)
fob	free on board
FTAA	Free Trade Area of the Americas
GATE	Greater Access to Trade Expansion
GATS	General Agreement on Trade in Services
GATT	General Agreement on Tariffs and Trade
GDP	gross domestic product
GNAEP	Greater Noakhali Aquaculture Extension Project (Bangladesh)
HACCP	Hazard Analysis and Critical Control Point
IATP	Institute for Agriculture and Trade Policy
ICT	information and communications technology
IFAD	International Fund for Agricultural Development
IFC	International Finance Corporation
IITC	Inter-Institutional Trade Committee (Uganda)
ILO	International Labour Organization
IMF	International Monetary Fund
IOIA	International Organic Inspectors Association
IT	information technology
ITA	Ministerial Declaration on Trade in Information Technology Products
ITPF	Information Technology Professionals Forum
ITU	International Telecommunication Union
JAMPRO	Jamaica Trade and Investment Company
JLA	Jamaica Livestock Association
JOAM	Jamaica Organic Agriculture Movement
KSG	Kenya Sugarcane Growers
KWBA	Kitgum Women Beekeepers Association (Uganda)
KWSFA	Kenya Women Sugarcane Farmers Association
LCAWU	Lesotho Clothing and Allied Workers Union
MDG	Millennium Development Goal
MFA	Multifibre Arrangement
MTS	Multilateral Trading System
MuB	manufacturing under bond
NAADS	National Agricultural Advisory Services (Uganda)
NAFTA	North American Free Trade Agreement
NAMA	Non-Agricultural Market Access
NGO	non-governmental organisation
NIFT	National Institute of Fashion Technology (India)

NLDP	National Leather Development Programme
NTFP	non-timber forest product
OECD	Organisation for Economic Co-operation and Development
OWIT	Organization of Women in International Trade
PDA	personal digital assistant
PEAP	Poverty Eradication Action Plan
PRSP	Poverty Reduction Strategy Paper
QAP	quality assurance programme
SACU	Southern African Customs Union
SEWA	Self Employed Women's Association (India)
SFA	Special Framework of Assistance
SIP	Swazi Indigenous Products
SME	small and medium-sized enterprise
SPS	sanitary and phytosanitary
SSOQ	Shrimp Seal of Quality Programme (Bangladesh)
STATIN	Statistical Institute of Jamaica
STFC	SEWA Trade Facilitation Centre (India)
SUCAM	Sugar Campaign for Change (Kenya)
TAC	Toehold Artisans Collaborative (India)
TBT	technical barriers to trade
TRCB	trade-related capacity building
TRIPS	Trade-Related Aspects of Intellectual Property Rights
TTWU	Tailors and Textiles Workers Union (Kenya)
TUNADO	The Uganda National Apiculture Development Organization
UEPB	Uganda Export Promotion Board
UNITES	Union for Information Technology and Enabled Services (India)
UNCTAD	United Nations Conference on Trade and Development
UNDP	United Nations Development Programme
USAID	United States Agency for International Development
USO	universal service obligations
UWI	University of the West Indies
VAT	value added tax
WTO	World Trade Organization

Introduction

Marilyn Carr

In most developing countries, women producers and workers in the informal economy play a key role in providing the food and income that enable their families to exist. The impact of economic globalisation and trade liberalisation on these women has varied according to who they are, where they are, which sector they are involved in and how they are integrated into global production systems. While some women have lost markets and jobs or seen a decline in working conditions, others have been able to find new markets for their products and new jobs on favourable terms.

The literature on gender and trade generally falls into two major categories: the first looks at the impact of trade policies on women and men, and how gender issues affect the outcome of these policies; and the second looks at the differential access of women and men to export promotion strategies and programmes, and how this affects the strategies' success.

The gender impacts of trade policy

Looking at the impacts of trade policy on women and men – and at the ways in which gender issues affect the outcome of trade policies and programmes – it can be seen, as noted above, that there are both winners and losers. In some cases, export-led growth has resulted in the increased inclusion of women workers in the global economy – albeit on questionable or undesirable terms and with uncertain sustainability. In other cases, the liberalisation of trade and investment has resulted in the destruction of domestic enterprises or paid jobs due to: (a) the steep rise in cheap imports/services on the market; (b) unequal terms of competition for local natural resources; and (c) changing technology and skills requirements.

Export-led manufacturing has undoubtedly led to the creation of many thousands of jobs for unskilled women – especially in south-east Asia and, while wages and working conditions have been questioned, it has enabled many young women who have not worked before to be included in the labour force on terms that are not optimal, but possibly better than alternatives elsewhere in the domestic economy. However, several factors are now having an impact on the situation of women working in export-led industries.

One of these is that markets for labour-intensive products are becoming flooded and highly competitive. As a result, one of two corporate strategies has been adopted, neither of which is helpful in improving the terms of inclusion for women workers in the global economy. One strategy is for multinationals to try to maintain or increase their market share in existing industries by undercutting competitors – usually by cutting labour costs in a race to the bottom. In this case, women become trapped in downwardly mobile positions and economies exhibit 'immiserising' growth.[1] The other strategy is for multinationals to diversify into different types of products that yield higher profits in less crowded markets. In this case, the new industries are usually more technologically sophisticated and demand higher skill levels, which men have greater opportunities than women to acquire. As a result, unskilled female workers are excluded from the latest and more technology-intensive phase of globalisation in which there is a switch from working 'harder' to working 'smarter' (Carr and Chen, 2004).

Another factor affecting female workers in export-led industries is increased vulnerability. In global supply chains they are particularly prone to the effects of financial crises and economic recessions. These can result in the closure of export-linked factories or in industrial restructuring, resulting in factory workers being forced to work from home with much lower incomes and without any form of security or benefits. Changes in trade policy and removal of preferential treatment measures, such as the phasing out of the Multifibre Arrangement (MFA), also result in restructuring and loss of jobs and security for women workers.

The patterns experienced in the manufacturing sector are replicated in the agricultural and services export sectors. While Africa has largely been excluded from export-led industrialisation – mainly because it is more abundant in land than in unskilled labour – it has become incorporated in global value chains of a different type: those involving non-traditional agricultural exports such as fresh fruit, vegetables and cut flowers aimed mainly at the European market. Women account for up to 90 per cent of the workforce in this fast growing sector in which large corporations dominate the commodity chain and women work on large-scale 'factory farms' at very low wages, in poor working conditions and without benefits of any sort – in much the same way as women work in labour-intensive manufacturing global value chains.

The same is true for exports of services, with large numbers of young women being recruited into the emerging institutions of the digital economy – for example, call centres – that provide new opportunities for inclusion, but on terms that discourage long-term, permanent contracts and unionisation. Data entry has so far been a promising source of employment for women, although technological changes could lead to redundancies if workers lack the necessary training and skills to adapt; however, it is also becoming a 'footloose' industry, exhibiting many of the characteristics of the 'race to the bottom' phenomenon found in export-led manufacturing industries (Carr and Chen, 2004).

While trade liberalisation has created job opportunities for some women, it has resulted in the destruction of jobs and incomes for others. For example, the construction industry has traditionally employed thousands of unskilled women in many developing countries. Under the existing World Trade Organization (WTO) regime, the essential requirement of global tendering has facilitated the entry into the domestic market of many large international companies using capital-intensive technologies. These displace the women who used to be employed in digging and carrying bricks. National governments have often responded by assisting local companies to compete through upgrading their technological capabilities – a move that leads to still further labour displacement (Jhabvala and Kanbur, 2002).

Women's traditional enterprise activities have also suffered as a result of import competition following increased trade liberalisation. In India, following the influx of cheap soya-based cooking oil from the Americas, an estimated 3 million jobs are thought to have been lost as a result of the closure of small oil mills producing mustard seed oil (Shiva, 2000); and in southern and eastern Africa, the spread of foreign-owned supermarkets is having an impact not only on local retailers, but also on small-scale food producers, who have to make investments and adopt new practices if they are to avoid exclusion from their traditional markets (Weatherspoon and Reardon, 2003). Without support from government and other agencies, thousands of traditional women's enterprises are in danger of disappearing.

Women and export markets

A second category of literature looks at the ways in which women and men have differential access to export promotion strategies and programmes, and the extent to which constraints on women's involvement affect the success of these programmes. Again, there are winners and losers. When women have access to support programmes, they are able to contribute to increasing exports, as well as benefiting themselves by linking up with the lucrative export markets opening up as a result of trade liberalisation. When barriers to entry have prevented them from taking advantage of new economic opportunities, gains from globalisation and trade liberalisation fail to be distributed as evenly as they should be and goals in terms of poverty reduction are less likely to be achieved.

In some cases, self-employed or own account workers are being absorbed into global production systems, often against their will and on terms that are not entirely favourable to them. For example, many forest dwellers who earn a significant part of their income from gathering and selling non-timber forest products such as mushrooms, honey and medicinal plants can only access markets – even domestic ones – through a long chain of intermediaries in which they have little or no power to influence the terms of their engagement (Carr, 2008). Without the assistance of local and international non-governmental organisations (NGOs), government departments and social entrepreneurs, own account workers such as these have little chance of being able to link up with export markets on their own terms. Fortunately, there are now many more examples, including those in this book, of interventions that have resulted in increased control and returns for women through better organisation and access.

Filling a gap in the literature

In general, the literature on gender and trade is short of case studies that highlight in a very practical way the issues involved and the strategies that have been implemented in an attempt to address them. The collection of case studies in this book – ten studies on the impact of trade on women and ten on linking women with export markets – seeks to fill this gap.

While there is obviously some overlap between the two sets of case studies, the first focuses mainly on the way in which trade policies can and do have a negative impact on women unless gender issues are taken into consideration by policy-makers and/or efforts are made to assist women to overcome negative effects through implementation of complementary support measures. The second set focuses more on the ways in which women producers and workers can be directly helped through government and other agencies to access export markets and become integrated into global value chains on their own terms and with a greater share of control and returns.

References

Carr, M (2008). *Gender and Non-timber Forest Products: Promoting Food Security and Economic Empowerment*, International Fund for Agricultural Development (IFAD), Rome.

Carr, M and Chen, M (2004). 'Globalization, Social Exclusion and Gender', *International Labour Review*, 143 (1 and 2).

Jhabvala, R and Kanbur, R (2002). *Globalization and Economic Reform as Seen from the Ground: SEWA's Experiences in India*, MIT Press, Cambridge, MA.

Shiva, V (2000). *Stolen Harvest: The Hijacking of the Global Food Supply*, Zed Books, London.

Weatherspoon, D and Reardon, T (2003). 'The Rise of Supermarkets in Africa: Implications for Agrifood Systems and the Rural Poor', *Development Policy Review*, 21(3).

PART ONE
The Impact of Trade on Women

1 Introduction to Part One

Mariama Williams

Trade agreements and gender

The work of gender advocates has shown that power imbalances based on gender influence the distribution of output, work, income and wealth in the economy. Gender norms and cultural gender biases influence the behaviour of economic agents, affecting their ability to respond to market signals such as price changes that come with adjustments in measures such as tariff reductions. Therefore, it is important to understand the gender dynamics at play in each country and how women and men are affected by the design, implementation and outcomes of trade policy. This is also critical to our understanding of, and approach to, the role of trade in the national and global economy. Ultimately, as argued by Çağatay (2003), gender relations are not something outside the economy in some realm of 'preferences', 'aptitudes' and 'traditions'; they are continually being reformulated and permeate all economic decision-making and activities.

Gender advocates have therefore increasingly and convincingly insisted on a much more complex and nuanced review of the issues. Such an approach seeks to shift the focus from simply looking at the flow of goods and services to paying greater attention to the links between trade and the spheres of production and reproduction – 'the care and development of people and their capacity to work' (Çağatay, 2003). Focusing on these linkages opens up the issues of the division of labour in society between women and men, paid and unpaid work and its contribution to the market, access to resources, intra household distribution of income and resources, and the conditions under which male and female entrepreneurs conduct their businesses. It also explicitly allows for an examination of the informal and household economies, and the contribution of these to trade, growth and sustainable development.

Many of the factors affecting women's overall empowerment and control over economic and financial resources relative to men, including microfinance, are well known. These include: gender inequality around differential access to social and physical goods; gender gaps in education, income, time use and leisure; and gender-differentiated roles and responsibilities in the household, community and labour markets. In the literature discussing the Millennium Development Goals (MDGs), these factors are clustered in terms of their implications for women's capabilities, access to resources, opportunities and security. Empirical research has also located these gender-differentiated dynamics across a broad range of human social and economic activities, including agriculture, services, manufacturing, water and energy distribution and use, transportation and disaster management.

At the sectoral level, agricultural liberalisation has implications for women's and men's access to food (food security), livelihoods and rural development. Services liberalisation affects access to water, health care and electricity, which are essential for social reproduction. The agreement on Trade-Related Aspects of Intellectual Property Rights (TRIPS) affects access to affordable medicines, genetic resources and technologies that are critical for women's and men's health, functioning and capabilities. TRIPS also has implications for the ownership, production, transfer and protection of indigenous, traditional and community-based knowledge, which is critical to both the overall economic and social empowerment of women and men, as well as for long-term economic development.

Part one of this book seeks to explore the short- and long-term effects on gender equality objectives and on women's and men's economic and social empowerment of changes in sectoral and national trade policy that have been generated by bilateral, regional, inter-regional, plurilateral or multilateral negotiations. Ten case studies covering a variety of Commonwealth developing countries are presented. Each study explores changes in the trade environment on a particular sector or through a particular trade provision, such as the agreements on agriculture, services or non-agricultural market access.

The case studies are not original; they are drawn from the available literature in the public domain. Some are from long and comprehensive country studies, while others are compiled from a number of short and targeted sectoral studies. In each case, the contributor has sought to fine-tune and pinpoint, as clearly as possible, the specific gender dimensions by tracing out the differential impacts on women and men. Each contributor has sought to update the case study as much as possible to explore actions taken to assist and promote the economic empowerment of women. Attempts have also been made, as far as possible, to impose a uniform format, but some case studies vary because of the data available for the sector or country.

Organisation of the studies

The case studies are arranged in four broad groupings that attempt to isolate the different types of trade regulation and trade development in use in the current policy environment.

The first group highlights the issue of import liberalisation, primarily through the reduction of tariffs, on developing countries. In 'A Bitter Pill to Swallow: The Effects of Tariff Reductions on Sugar in Kenya', Yves Conze and Mariama Williams examine the issue of the liberalisation of imports in the agricultural sector by highlighting the unintended consequences of changes in Kenya's tariff level and structure on its sugar industry. The second case study, 'Profits Fly the Coop: Gender Impacts of Trade Liberalisation on the Jamaican Poultry Industry' by Carol Narcisse, draws heavily on a much wider and more comprehensive study, *Gender Analysis of Liberalization in the Jamaican Economy* by Women's Edge Coalition (Wyss and Whyte, 2004), to highlight the pervasive impacts of liberalisation in the poultry industry on food security, livelihood and rural development in Jamaica.

The second group of case studies examines the issue of preferences gained or lost. The four studies show in dramatic ways what can happen when protection on a commodity is withdrawn, making it open to competition from all comers. 'Can it be Mended? Kenya and the MFA Phase-out' by Paul Kamau and 'Knitting it Together: India and the MFA Phase-out' by Pramod Dev explore the impacts in Kenya and India respectively of the phase-out of the Multifibre Arrangement, which was subject to a ten-year phase-out of import quotas on textiles and apparel between January 1995 and January 2005 under the WTO Agreement on Textiles and Clothing (ATC). In Kenya, this led to widespread downsizing by firms and consequent lay-offs and casualisation of labour contracts. India, on the other hand, had a significant percentage share in the global textiles and clothing trade, a well-developed value chain and strong domestic markets. Indian firms were, therefore, much better able to stand up to full competition. Initially, the country even experienced some acceleration in growth; and although over time it experienced some downturn, this did not have the same devastating effects as in Kenya. However, women in both countries experienced a similar decline in their welfare, as firms attempted to deal with the new competitive environment by laying off workers and casualising labour.

'A Stitch in Time? AGOA and Lesotho's Clothing Sector', compiled by Mariama Williams and Marilyn Carr, highlights the case of Lesotho, where losses in the textiles sector due to the MFA phase-out were offset by the granting of preference under the African Growth and Opportunity Act (AGOA). Initially, AGOA seemed to have a dynamic effect on Lesotho's garment industry. However, changes in AGOA regulations in 2007 required manufacturers to source their raw material fabric inputs from the USA or AGOA countries. The authors explore what the impacts of this have been for women workers in the jeans sector.

'Slipping on a Peel: The Effects of Changing Trade Regimes on the St

Lucia Banana Industry' by Carol Narcisse explores the impact of the loss of unilateral preference on a product, bananas, that is central to economic activity and income generation. This loss is due to the reconstruction of European Union (EU) historical preference schemes to African, Caribbean and Pacific (ACP) countries as a result of new multilateral trade rules and a trade policy environment governed by reciprocity. For the small developing island of St Lucia, the growth and trading of bananas was a critical pathway for poverty eradication, as well as the economic advancement of women, and the loss of preferred access to EU markets proved to be devastating on both fronts.

Trade in services has only recently been brought under the scrutiny of multilateral trade discipline through the General Agreement on Trade in Services (GATS). The third group of case studies explores the issue of services liberalisation. Such services are as varied as health care, education, banking and information technology. While cross-border trade in traditional products (e.g. apples or cars) are regulated by price and non-price mechanisms, service liberalisation is not so much focused on tariff and non-tariff barriers; rather, it emphasises the dismantling of domestic regulations and elimination of prohibitions on foreign service providers. Such restraints on cross-border trade in services may include artificial barriers to entry and exit, rules that discriminate against foreign operators and occupational licences.

The two case studies presented here explore the gender impacts of two quite different aspects of services. 'Moving Forwards, Falling Backwards: GATS and the Migration of Skilled Professionals from the Caribbean' by Carol Narcisse draws attention to the temporary movement of nurses and teachers, primarily from poor countries to richer ones. While this may have certain advantages for both the worker who migrates and the receiving economy, in as much as it may lead to a higher income and economic advancement for the former and better health-care services for citizens of the latter, it generally means a vital loss in professional services in health care and education for the women, men and children left at home. While this case study puts the spotlight on the Caribbean, it also makes references to Africa and Asia, which experience similar dynamics.

'Digitalising It: Women and Trade in ICT in Developing Countries' by Mariama Williams and Carol Narcisse spotlights how the liberalisation of trade in information and communications technology (ICT) affects women. Aspects of this growing area are currently covered under the GATS, but for the most part the provision of interest is the plurilateral agreement on information technology (IT), which is only applicable to its signatories. It is also clearly linked to the TRIPS agreement. At the same time, most developing countries are in some process of liberalisation of their telecommunications and other ICT sectors, because many of them are parties to bilateral and regional trading arrangements. ICT has the potential to accelerate growth in developing countries. It can also be a tool for the rapid empowerment of women, in situations where women are able to gain access to and control over the many widely proliferating ICT products. But, as the case study shows, this potential progress can be stymied by the nature and scope of ICT rules and regulations put in place locally and nationally, even though these are proscribed by multilateral and regional liberalisation processes.

The fourth and final group of case studies attempts to grapple with the complicated and controversial areas of trade-related health and safety regulations and their impact on female and male workers and entrepreneurs in developing countries. Both studies focus on the impact of the EU ban on the export of fish products – one from the Asian and the other from the African point of view. 'Packaged to Perfection: The SPS Agreement and Aquaculture in Bangladesh' by Marilyn Carr and Sanae Ito puts the spotlight on the gendered impact of sanitary and phytosanitary (SPS) regulations on the Bangladesh shrimp sector, which faced an EU SPS-inspired ban in 1997. This had implications for the poverty reduction strategy in the country, as it tended to force a trade-off between two types of fish farming production techniques that had quite different export growth and poverty reduction potential. SPS and other non-tariff barriers impose a heavy direct cost (in terms of lost revenue in the case of an outright ban on exports) and further costs involved in upgrading and implementing new standards of food and related safety protocol such as Hazard Analysis and Critical Control Point (HACCP).

Like Bangladesh, Uganda also faced a ban on exports of fish to the EU. In 'Sitting on the Docks: The SPS Agreement and the Fish Industry in Uganda', May Sengendo tries to unravel the impact on women of the three bans placed on the industry between 1997 and 2000. These resulted in the closure of many domestic enterprises in fishery and related sectors and the loss of many jobs for the poor women and men they employed, with long-term implications for poverty eradication and women's empowerment.

The lessons that are drawn from these case studies aim to provide guidance to policy-makers and development practitioners on the sort of mitigating and compensatory actions that are necessary in order to lessen the negative impacts of changes in trade policy regimes or instruments, mechanisms and processes on women's employment, entrepreneurship, and informal and household sector activities. The lessons also highlight pathways for enhancing the positive benefits of trade intensification on women's overall economic and social empowerment.

References

Çağatay, N (2003). 'Economic Growth, Gender Inequalities and Poverty Reduction', Office of Development Studies, United Nations Development Programme (UNDP), New York.

Wyss, B and Whyte, M (2004). *The Effects of Trade Liberalization on Jamaica's Poor: An Analysis of Agriculture and Services*, Women's Edge Coalition, Washington, DC.

Import Liberalisation

2 A Bitter Pill to Swallow: The Effects of Tariff Reductions on Sugar in Kenya

Yves Conze with Mariama Williams

> *'The people making these rules should come to the ground and see how we live. We are very bitter. We are sad and we are stranded because we don't know what tomorrow will have for us. Will they come to help us when we are dead?'*
>
> Co-founder, Kenyan Women Sugar Cane Farmers Network

Background

Kenya has been East Africa's most industrialised country since its independence from Britain in 1961. It has also developed the reputation of being the regional hub for trade and finance as a consequence of a conscious and proactive development agenda. It is a member of the East African Community (EAC) and the Common Market for Eastern and Southern Africa (COMESA) and a partner in the Lomé Convention/Cotonou Agreement (2000) with the EU.

Kenya's gross domestic product (GDP) is estimated at US$31.42 billion and its per capita GDP at US$1,600 (2008).[2] The economy grew on average by 3.2 per cent a year between 1975 and 2001, although growth has slowed in the last few years. The structure of the economy is such that services were estimated in 2007 to generate 59.5 per cent of GDP, followed by 23.8 per cent for agriculture and 16.7 per cent for industry. Agriculture, despite its relative low output, still employed 75 per cent of the population of 85 million and was the largest contributor of foreign exchange to the balance of payments.

Change in trade policy

Trade has played an important role in the economy, although the country initially embarked on import substitution by erecting tariff walls in order to protect its infant industry. This policy has been in reverse since the 1980s, when Kenya introduced structural adjustment measures such as de-control of prices and removal of subsidies on fertilisers, transport and fuel. The country has moved from import substitution to trade liberalisation with its Sixth Development Plan (1989–93). Further liberalisation occurred with the implementation of commitments under the WTO (1995), EAC (1996 and 2000) and COMESA. Kenya also signed up to the African Growth and Opportunity Act and the Cotonou Agreement.[3] The net results have been complete price deregulation on major products, the elimination or lowering of a number of tariff bands, the unrestricted import and export of goods, deregulation of crops overseen by the marketing boards, the removal of subsidies and currency devaluation. Over time, Kenya has experienced economic stagnation, a worsening poverty index and a breakdown of the socio-economic structure.

The strongest impact of import liberalisation has been on the sugar sector. Following a joint complaint from Australia, Brazil and Thailand, the WTO ruled in 2005 that the EU sugar regime was in breach of WTO regulations (Poulton and Tyler, 2007). With unlimited import of goods, Kenya experienced a 50 per cent increase in imports of sugar between 1995 and 2001, resulting in shrinkage of the local sector by 79 per cent and lay-offs totalling over 32,000 workers (ActionAid Kenya, 2005).

ActionAid Kenya research shows that both producers and consumers have suffered from high prices and loss of income due to trade liberalisation. This finding contradicts the popular belief that such liberalisation brings benefits to consumers in the form of cheap prices. Instead, even in periods of high spikes of import surges, consumers paid almost 50 per cent more for sugar than previously. However, the economic and social status of the various players allowed them to take different defensive and offensive actions in order to mitigate the negative impacts of trade liberalisation. For example, as noted in the ActionAid Kenya study, millers were able to take a more proactive stance to try to ensure market share. They undertook more branding of their sugar and were also able to diversify into different products. Farmers and communities living in the sugar belt, however, had very few ways to cope effectively with import surges.

The sugar sector in Kenya

The production of sugar plays an important role in Kenyan society. It serves as a cash crop for many small farmers, especially in the western and Nyanza regions. Sugar production is labour intensive and offers employment to many of the over 8 million people (28 per cent of the population) who live in these areas. Providing a higher mean income than other sectors, sugar production also helps to promote regional and rural economic development.

Aside from its impacts on farmers, the decrease in sugar production has affected a number of other sectors with which sugar is interlinked, such as input supply, manual weeding, cane and sugar transport, sugar milling factories, agro-chemical industries (Kisumu Molasses Plant and the Agro-Chemical and Food Company), equipment suppliers and molasses distribution. This web of interconnection of economic livelihood sources contributes to sugar's role as a stabilising variable in both the regional and national economy.

Kenya has 'six operational sugar-milling factories ... and over 200 jaggaries with capacities ranging from 1 ton to 30 tonnes of sugarcane per day', the latter producing jaggery sugar which is used in the production of white rum (ActionAid Kenya, 2005). Liberalisation of sugar has led to one mill closing and two others (Muhoroni and Miwani) going into receivership. The net impact is the dislocation of over 60,000 households, with the likely impact extending to over 150,000 households (ActionAid Kenya, 2005). The industry is suffering greatly. Between 1995 and 2004, the sector experienced a decline in employment and wages of over 70 per cent.

Liberalisation under COMESA and the WTO allowed import volume to grow from 65,816 metric tonnes to 171,308 metric tonnes in just two years between 1996 and 1998, and this quadrupled to 249,336 metric tonnes in 2001. No industry can be expected to survive this onslaught. The local producers were also victims of their own inefficiency in terms of production costs. According to experts, it costs US$450–600 to produce a tonne of sugar in Kenya, but only US$250 per tonne in other COMESA countries such as Malawi, Mauritius and Sudan. In addition, Kenyan sugar competes against the world number one and two producers, Brazil and Thailand. The struggling Kenyan sugar industry has been exposed to intense competition as EU sugar reform led to sugar normally bound for the EU being diverted to the Kenyan market instead.

The increase in imports led to a drastic fall in domestic prices and in the income of small farmers, thus reducing the availability of cash for school and other discretionary expenses. Consequently, the region suffered from both direct and indirect effects. As noted in the ActionAid Kenya (2005) report:

> Western and Nyanza region farmers grow beans, maize and vegetables for subsistence. Income from sugarcane gives them the economic power to buy food when the subsistence crops fail. In addition, income from sugarcane is also used for buying more quality food for nutritional purposes. In the long run, lack of timely payment for sugarcane therefore leads to nutritional problems as well as food inaccessibility.

The cash value of sugar in the region extends far beyond the immediate needs of the small farmer. Any monoculture region or society is subject to the full repercussions of a collapse in price resulting from exogenous shock.

This is reflected in the severity of the collapse of the social structure in the sugar belt. Since sugarcane farming is a sort of 'social collateral' in the provisioning of schools and hospitals, decline in the sector is felt in those areas as well. According to NGOs such as ActionAid, schools, hospitals and individuals used to extend credit on the premise that repayment would come with the harvesting of the cane. However, with the contraction in the sugar industry, the entire credit system came to a halt.

The regional and national governmental apparatus is also heavily dependent on sugar for revenue. When the sector contracted, there was a twofold hit on government revenue: loss of domestic taxes and loss of foreign exchange. This in turn negatively affects social service provisioning in the region.

ActionAid Kenya (2005) notes that:

> In the case of Kenya, the sugar milling factories served a larger function; they acted as quasi government and private social security by providing certain services such as health services and support education services. Miwani sugar factory before its collapse supported 3 primary schools, a secondary school, and a hospital with a capacity 110 beds. Also Mumias sugar factory supports a primary school, a secondary school and a health centre. This is common with all milling factories as shown in the study findings. Therefore, the domino impact is clearly greater than originally anticipated ....

The collapse of the sugar sector has other repercussions, as the remaining mills tend to discriminate more openly in favour of contract farmers, who together account for about 88 per cent of the total area farmed for sugarcane. Mill owners have facilitated the Outgrowers Association of contract farmers by helping to finance the crop and taking payment later (SUCAM, 2008 cited in CI Network, 2009). Small cane farmers argue that the millers' actions cause delay in the harvesting of their own crops, thus contributing to crop loss and lower profit margins. They also complain that the millers exploit them by charging high prices for fertilisers and other services, making cane growing unprofitable (IATP, 2005).

Associated with the collapse of sugar are school drop-outs, increased prostitution, crime, HIV and AIDS and poverty (IATP, 2005). According to Persis Koskei of the Kenyan Sugar Cane Growers Network, 'children have dropped out of school and many now work in the sugar fields, while the nursing home that used to serve the community, an essential facility in an environment as harsh as sugar farming, has also subsequently closed' (quoted in Geneen, 2006). The growing HIV and AIDS prevalence rates complicate the social distress in the sugar belt. The National AIDS and Sexually Transmitted Diseases Control Programme reports 40–50 per cent prevalence of HIV infection among adults around Kisumu, compared to a national average of 8 per cent (Ambwer, 1999).

Gender dynamics in the sugar belt

Women in the sugar belt in Kenya are more likely to be poor than men. This is largely due to their lack of rights and control over productive resources and their lack of legal protection. As elsewhere in sub-Saharan Africa, women have low levels of asset ownership and poor access to credit and are highly concentrated in agriculture. The majority of subsistence farmers are women (69 per cent), and this is the group whose members are most likely to be poor in Kenya (Omiti *et al.*, 2002).

Ruth Oniango of Kenya's Rural Outreach Programme argues that women in the rural areas operate in a 'a culture where men own assets and control investment, government training programmes [are] run by and for men, and even international aid assumes farm labour will be done by men' (Alsop, 2008). Moreover,

> The women and children would be the ones tilling and toiling away and then the men go and collect the money ... The challenge is that, given our own socio-cultural traditional setup, women don't own the land. They depend on the men ... Give a woman 20 shillings. If you go home with her the following day, you will find what the 20 shillings did. But if you give it to a man and you go to his home, it will be like he never met you.

According to ActionAid Kenya (2005), female-headed households are actively involved in sugarcane production. The study notes that female producers enjoy less favourable terms due to cultural and ethnic practices that place women at a disadvantage. The report goes on to point out that most women producers had no legal title to their parcels of land and therefore most of the grower and miller institutions still do not recognise their ownership. Many women are also denied credit and their representation in grower institutions is marginalised. Furthermore, the gender division of labour in the sector means that women normally do the physically demanding work of planting cane, weeding and applying fertilisers (ActionAid Kenya, 2005).

A study of the gender patterns in sugarcane-producing and non-sugarcane producing households in Kenya by Kennedy and Coghill (1988) found that though household incomes are significantly higher in the former, the percentage of female-controlled income is significantly lower. Further, it was noted that the childcare patterns of women from sugarcane- and non-sugarcane-producing households do not differ significantly, because sugarcane-producing households tend to use more hired labour (ibid.). However, this does not mean that the women in the sugar belt have a lot of leisure time. They have less than their counterparts in the Philippines, for example. According to Kennedy and Garcia (1992), sugarcane farmers in Kenya and the Philippines share at least three common features: the shift from maize to sugar cane production; the significantly higher mean income of sugarcane farmers than that of non-cane producers; and 'in both cases, the largest share of the work day for women is accounted for by home production activities – getting water, fuel-wood, cleaning, etc.'. Nonetheless, unlike the Philippines, data from Kenya show a low response of the body mass index of women to increasing income. A likely explanation for this is that in the Philippines women have better access to basic services, whereas in Kenya, 'time allocation data reflects the poorer overall infrastructure and the implications this has for women's time' (Kennedy and Garcia, 1992). Kenyan women must devote a significant amount of time to fetching water and fuel-wood. Because of these factors women in Kenya spend twice as much time on home production as do women in the Philippines.

Given their marginal position both in society and cane production – and their multiple roles as workers, service suppliers, and household and community managers – women faced a difficult situation as a result of the import surge in the sugar sector. A number of reports argue that women have also suffered disproportionately from the surge in food imports as a result of trade liberalisation.

With the closing of sugar companies such as Miwani, 'farmers now face the rising costs of taking their harvest further afield' (Geneen, 2006). Reaching the state-owned Chemelil Sugar Company takes over three times as long as it used to take to get to Miwani. Researchers noted that some farmers, especially women, cut their cane only for it to dry on the field due to lack of transport and roads to the nearest mill (Koskei, cited in Geneen, 2006).

Measures taken to help women cope with or take advantage of policy change

Attempts to introduce measures, policies and projects to reverse the decline in the sugar sector and to protect livelihoods have been undertaken at multiple levels.

Local NGOs and private sector organisations

Women have organised themselves into the Kenya Sugarcane Growers (KSG) Network and the Kenya Women Sugarcane Farmers Association (KWSFA) to undertake advocacy on their issues. The KSG Network has appealed to the government and the private sector to help revive the sugar industry by providing incentives to local farmers, reducing taxes imposed on sugar and reviving collapsed companies such as Miwani. It has also taken on board wider issues that are critical to women's empowerment. For example, it is lobbying for support to ensure that the constraints posed by lack of education in their community are dealt with. This point is reinforced by Persis Koskei, a 53-year-old woman sugar farmer, who argues that 'We need to educate ourselves about our market, to know what the people want so that we should be able to diversify our farming' (cited in Geneen, 2006).

KWSFA, which is allied with the Sugar Campaign for Change (SUCAM) and ActionAid, focuses on addressing equality issues. These organisations promote the education of women in the sector, both generally and with specific regard to marketing conditions. They are also lobbying the government to stop the dumping of imported sugar and to offer financial support for better roads and improved access to water for irrigation and household use.

At the level of the broader civil society, SUCAM was launched in 2001, with the support of ActionAid, as an independent lobby and advocacy coalition to advocate for the rights of sugarcane farmers. It also advocates for gender and food security. In addition, the organisation promotes the idea that because population growth has drastically reduced the space for growing cane, sugarcane farmers should embrace block farming and allow space for food crop production. It calls for women and youth to be involved in decision-making in the industry (CI Network, 2007)

There have been a number of consultations under the auspices of the National Consultative Workshop on Sugar on import surges. These brought together a cross-section of key stakeholders in the sugar industry, including producers, farmers' associations, sugarcane farmers' unions, research institutions, the media, academia, sugar importers, industrial users of sugar, sugar millers, Kenya Sugar Board officials, NGOs and suppliers of equipment to the sugar sector (ActionAid Kenya, 2005). There was no specific mention of women's organisations.

The participants at the meetings determined that:

> ... sugar must be treated as a special product (SP) and accorded higher status and level of protection due to its special and multiple attributes as an industrial ingredient in the manufacture of many other products, a major source of food for the Kenyan population, source of energy both new and renewable, environmentally friendly features when compared to fossil energy, contributes greatly to the rural development and cultural social economy through provision of hospital, education, sporting infrastructure in Kenya.

Activists also argue that the Government must endeavour to guarantee loans to cane farmers at affordable interest rates and, where necessary, write off their debts. They advocate that reforms must include improving the efficiency of the sugar extraction process in factories, as well as consideration of the life and food needs of the over 6 million people who are so dependent on sugarcane for their livelihoods.

The Outgrowers' Association calls for tax cuts on fertilisers, chemicals and farm machinery to increase growers' profits.

National

The immediate response of the Government, as it sought to deal with complaints from the major stakeholders, was to seek the intervention of COMESA for safeguard measures to stop the import surges. This was granted initially for a period of one year and later extended for a further four years with a scheduled expiry date of 2012. The Government also sought a remedy under the WTO safeguard framework. There was no specific gendered approach to this issue at the policy level.

Ultimately, due to a number of inherent problems with the administration of safeguard provisions and the problem of illicit imports of sugar, none of these solutions provided an effective remedy to the problem of the import surge in the sugar sector. Currently, the COMESA safeguard protection is administered by the government-led Sugar Safeguard Committee, which is mandated to facilitate sector reforms. It is responsible for providing leadership with respect to privatisation of state-owned firms, adoption of bio-energy, and research on varieties and sugarcane prices based on quality, infrastructure development and poverty reduction initiatives (CI Network, 2007).

In 2008, the Cabinet approved the privatisation of five state-owned sugar companies, and identification of the consultant for this is ongoing.

Regional

Regionally, although this is not gender-specific, COMESA, under its safeguard clause, allowed Kenya to impose a quantitative restriction on sugar coming into its market as follows:

(a) A quota of 200,000 tonnes annually on sugar imported from COMESA countries. This is to meet the shortfall between domestic production and local consumption. Of the quota, 89,000 tonnes is for domestic white sugar and 111,000 tonnes is for industrial refined sugar.

(b) Application of a maximum tariff of 123 per cent, made up of 100 per cent tariff, 16 per cent value added tax (VAT) and 7 per cent Sugar Development Levy (ActionAid Kenya, 2005).

The problem with the tariff is that it is linked to the value of the imported sugar, which may be determined by the cost of production in the exporting country or the price at the place of purchase of the imported sugar. Whatever the cost or price, in most cases it is lower than the one prevailing on the domestic scene.

International

KWSFA officials argue that 'the World Trade Organization should also be involving farmers from the grassroots, especially women in the trade negotiations as the agreements usually cause us more harm than good' (IATP, 2005). There is therefore need for an effective WTO safeguard rule that advocates that sugar should be treated as sensitive. Kenyan civil society advocacy with the Government is seeking protection for the sugar sector by identifying it as a special product in negotiations on agricultural liberalisation.

In the context of existing WTO agreements, there is a specific safeguard for agriculture and a set of three more prominent General Agreement on Tariffs and Trade (GATT) safeguards: anti-dumping, countervailing and emergency safeguards. However, these are not friendly to developing countries such as Kenya. The special safeguard mechanism under the Agreement on Agriculture (which is the simplest to use) is only available to 36 countries and for a limited number of commodities.

Two general GATT safeguards (anti-dumping and countervailing measures) involve overcoming a challenging hurdle of procedural requirements. Their domestic implementation requires significant financial and human resources. A few developing countries are just beginning to establish national institutional frameworks. The emergency safeguard is easy to administer but requires financial compensation for the trading partner affected by actions taken by a country to protect its economy. This makes it almost impossible for poor developing countries to make use of the safeguard.

Lessons learned

The key lessons emerging from the sugar sector experience for national level stakeholders and policy-makers are at least fourfold. First, it is important to diversify economic activities as much as possible in order to end the over-dependence of a majority of the population on one critical sector. As noted by SUCAM, diversification is crucial to broadening the income bases of farmers. Second, the capacity of citizens needs to be built through education in order to enable them to adapt to economic change. Third, it is extremely important to provide and maintain basic social services such as education, health care, roads, water and sanitation. The existence of free compulsory basic and elementary education would have been of great help to the families so negatively impacted by the crisis in the food sector. Government should also develop basic social safety nets that can support citizens in times of upheaval. Fourth, food security must be the driving force behind economic and trade policy.

There is a need for better institutional and administrative mechanisms at government level to deal with issues of imports and their potential injury to the domestic economy. Further, better safeguards (simple to use and effective mechanisms) are needed within both COMESA and the WTO framework. The Government, civil society and international organisations should also pay attention to the underlying gender dynamics in the economy in the design and implementation of poverty reduction strategies and trade agendas.

References

ActionAid Kenya (2005). 'Impact of Sugar Import Surges on Kenya', Vol. 1, Nairobi, September.

Alsop, Z (2008). 'Kenya Farmers Reap Profits Sown by Joined Hands', *Women's e-News*, 23 November, http://www.womensenews.org/article.cfm/dyn/aid/3830

Ambwer, H (1999). 'Health: AIDS Epidemic Hits Kenyan Sugar Industry', Inter Press Service (IPS), Wednesday, 31 March.

CIA (2008). *The World Factbook*, Central Intelligence Agency, Washington, DC.

CI (Communication Initiative) Network (2009). 24 April, http://www.comminit.com

CI Network (2007). 'Sugar Campaign for Change (SUCAM)', The Communications Initiative Network, http://www.comminit.com/en/node/134620

Commonwealth Secretariat (2004). *The Cotonou Agreement: A User's Guide*, Commonwealth Secretariat, London.

Geneen, T (2006). 'Kenyan Farmers Call for Market Access', ActionAid, http://www.actionaid.org/main.aspx?PageID=323

IATP (2005). 'Kenyan Sugar Farmers a Worried Lot', Institute for Agriculture and Trade Policy (IATP), http://www.iatp.org/tradeobservatory/headlines.cfm?refID=77806

Kennedy E and Garcia, M (1992). 'Body Mass Index and Economic Productivity', in James, WPT and Ralph, A (eds), 'The Functional Significance of Low Body Mass Index', Proceedings of an IDECG Workshop, FAO Headquarters, Rome, Italy, 4–6 November, http://www.unu.edu/Unupress/food2/UID10E/uid10e0b.htm

Kennedy, ET and Cogill, B (1988). 'The Case of Sugarcane in Kenya: Part I: Effects of Cash Crop Production on Women's Income, Time Allocation, and Child Care Practices', Working Paper 167, Women in International Development, Michigan State University, June.

Omiti, J, Owino, W, Otieno, W and Odundo, P (2002). 'Poverty Reduction Efforts in Kenya: Institutions, Capacity and Policy', Discussion Paper No. 033/2002, Institute of Policy Analysis and Research, Nairobi, Kenya.

Poulton, C and Tyler, G (2007). 'All-Africa Review of Experiences with Commercial Agriculture', background paper for the Competitive Commercial Agriculture in Sub–Saharan Africa (CCAA) Study, World Bank, Washington, DC, http://sitere-sources.worldbank.org/INTAFRICA/Resources/257994-1215457178567/Ch12_Oil_Crops.pdf

3 Profits Fly the Coop: Gender Impacts of Trade Liberalisation on the Jamaican Poultry Industry

Carol Narcisse

Background

Like many other developing countries, Jamaica has increasingly liberalised its agricultural imports, opening up to competition from cheaper, often subsidised, products. This process has resulted in displacement of the products and livelihoods of local farmers in major areas of agricultural production. Although poultry farming has held its own in the local market – and is faring better than other sectors such as sugar, bananas and dairy – the industry is significantly affected by cheap imports of chicken parts, in addition to facing other challenges such as high energy and feed costs, as well as the effects of hurricanes and other weather risks.

Despite the competition from imports, local poultry producers still hold greater market share. Of 131,000 metric tonnes of raw poultry consumed in 2007, 106,000 came from local suppliers and 25,000 was imported (Best, 2008). This favourable picture reflects the situation of the main commercial producers. These are large entities that rely on contract farmers, a vertically integrated network of family farms that raise chickens (provided by the contractor) and supply the major processors. These farms have production contracts in which the quality and quantity of broiler inputs and the compensation that is received are determined by the contracting firm.

Under this system the grower invests land and housing facilities, labour and operating expenses such as repairs and maintenance. The contract farmer receives chicks, regular technical and veterinary services, and training. The contract is on a flock-by-flock basis and renewal is determined by satisfactory management of the investment that the contractor makes (Jamaica Broilers Group of Companies, n.d.). The investment made by the farmer is significant – in most cases traditional growing facilities are being replaced with modern units using tunnel-ventilated houses. Prospective farmers must prepare infrastructure to the contractor's specifications, which in the case of one contractor, for example, is a minimum size operation of four 16,000 sq ft tunnel ventilated houses costing US$140,000 each. While building and equipment purchase is facilitated by the contractor, farmers must access their own financing through an approved lending institution. In addition to the capital investment, the contract farmer is required to have an individual who is trained in agriculture residing on site, with sole responsibility for managing day-to-day operations.

Contract farming therefore requires a substantial investment, which often excludes women, who generally have less collateral. Of 72 contract farmers associated with one of the two largest contractors, only ten are women and in most cases they acquired ownership on the death of their spouse (Daly, 2009). Women in the poultry industry are therefore mainly small-scale producers whose operations are most at risk from the negative impact of weather shocks, rising prices for feed and cheaper imports. Despite the barriers to scaling up operations, small-scale poultry production is nonetheless a significant contributor to the industry, accounting for some 35 per cent of total poultry meat produced in the island (USAID Jamaica, 2007).

Economic background

Jamaica has historically had an open, dependent economy with serious long-term problems: decreased public revenues, high public wages, increased foreign competition, exchange rate instability, large-scale unemployment and underemployment, and weak access to international financial markets.

Poverty levels stood at 14.8 per cent in 2006 and, though registering a substantial drop to 9 per cent in 2007 due to factors such as construction related to the Cricket World Cup, the rate is likely to rise again in the wake of successive development crises – food, fuel and the current global financial crisis.

Women are a particularly vulnerable group in Jamaican society. Their unemployment rate (13.8%) is almost twice as high as men's (7.4%). Women make up 60 per cent of the unemployed labour force (STATIN, 2007) and have access to less than half the earned income of males (UNDP, 2007). A significant percentage of household heads (46.7%) are women. In the capital (Kingston Metropolitan Area) female household headship is 55.2 per cent; in other towns it is 43.2 per cent and in rural areas 41 per cent. With women's lower level of access to earned income, the data show that male-headed households outstrip female-headed ones in consumption expenditure. Female-headed households are larger and more concentrated in the poorest quintile: 45 per cent have no partner but have children, compared to 7.1 per cent of male-headed households (STATIN and the Planning Institute of Jamaica, 2006).

In addition to high levels of unemployment and household headship without a partner but with children and other dependents, women have fewer employment options and mobility than males. Agriculture has been a key occupational area for women, whether as farmers or traders of farm produce, and small-scale, backyard poultry production has been an area they have dominated (see Box 3.1).

Box 3.1 Women and backyard poultry farming

Poultry production is a predominately female activity that grew from being the fifth largest category of agricultural work for women in 1993 to the third largest by 2001. Women accounted for more than half of all poultry workers in 1993 and 2001, while they accounted for only between 20 and 24 per cent of all agricultural workers.

One reason that women may have entered the sector is that there are few start-up costs, and women traditionally have more difficulty gaining access to credit or loans to launch other farming ventures. With backyard poultry farming, the initial costs are low and, with the activity being done in one's backyard, it is something that women can do at home and in combination with their childcare and other household responsibilities. In fact, many women do this to make extra money to support their children or, if they do not have other paid employment, to support their families.

The backyard farmer tends a few chickens, often as one of multiple ways of earning a living. The backyard farmer pays for a hen house, lights, feed, equipment to deliver water and food to the birds, and the costs of the chicks themselves. They typically will sell poultry in the local market to outlets such as local workplace cafeterias, hotels and restaurants.

Although backyard poultry farming enables women to combine paid and unpaid work, it is not a particularly lucrative venture. According to Dr Michael Witter of the University of the West Indies: 'The typical poultry farmer has 10,000 chickens, kids in school and a little house. She works but she works on the margins. One slip can cause immense problems for her.' For the backyard chicken farmer, the situation is even more precarious. While the contract farmer obtains medicine and other chemicals (although not hormones) from the company, the backyard farmer cannot afford this. She will buy food for her chickens, but often cannot afford to purchase medicine. As a result, her chickens have a higher mortality rate. Since she has fewer chickens, each one represents a larger investment, and subsequently a greater economic loss if one dies.

Source: Wyss and Whyte, 2004.

With smaller operations and no guaranteed outlet for the chickens produced, women in backyard poultry farming are likely to be disproportionately affected by changing trade policies that require them to compete with cheap and often subsidised poultry products.

Changes in trade and economic policy

The process of trade liberalisation has spanned over three decades in Jamaica. Witter (2004) describes how it began with the stabilisation agenda of the International Monetary Fund (IMF) in the late 1970s and then accelerated in the 1980s with the World Bank's structural adjustment programmes. He goes on:

> In the 1980s too, the United States Agency for International Development's (USAID) loan programmes played a supporting role to the IMF and the World Bank by way of the cross-conditionality of the financial programmes that were enshrined in what was called the tri-Partite approach (1987) to Jamaica's adjustment process. In the 1990s, the trade liberalization process was continued with the reform of the common external tariff of CARICOM; the pressure to comply with the World Trade Organization's (WTO) international trade regime; the restructuring of trade relations with Europe ... and the commitments taken in the context of the process to establish the Free Trade Area of the Americas (FTAA).

The premise of trade liberalisation is the creation of a 'level playing field'. However, as Witter (n.d.) explains

> As part of that liberalization ... comes the removal of taxes and the removal of special concessions to local producers. The philosophy behind that was ... that markets know best, and if we remove the protection, our producers would be made more competitive as a result of competition with external, more efficient producers. But these producers also turn out to have subsidies, which are mysteriously allowed to remain in place ... In reality we had to buy into what is called a level playing field policy when there was no level playing field.

The specific policy changes that were part of the process of liberalisation included the following (FAO, 2003):

- Elimination of all quantitative import restrictions and the use of reference prices;
- Reduction of tariff rates over a 5-year period (3–7 years for some products) with no tariff to exceed 100 per cent after reductions;

- Elimination of general food subsidies;
- Removal of credit subsidies and adoption of market-related credit terms;
- Deregulation of several commodity boards, e.g. the Cocoa Industry Board, Coffee Industry Board, Sugar Marketing Board and Citrus Industry Board;
- Divestment of land and publicly owned enterprises.

In addition, other liberalisation policies adopted at the macroeconomic level had an impact on the sector – for example, the abolition of foreign exchange controls. The resulting devaluation of the Jamaican currency has meant higher import costs for an agricultural sector that is heavily import dependent.

Trade policy and the poultry industry

Though faring better than the sugar, banana and dairy industries, which have been severely affected by trade liberalisation, the poultry industry has had to contend with import surges of low-priced chicken parts especially, from the USA (Singh *et al.*, 2005). Both backyard and contract farmers are affected by the cheaper, imported meat, the latter because the contracting firm reduces the number of birds placed in the field when demand declines.

In its research on trade liberalisation and poverty in Jamaica, the Women's Edge Coalition (Wyss and Whyte, 2004) provides to date the most definitive account of the challenges to the poultry industry posed by competition from cheap, subsidised imports (see Box 3.2). While the report presents the scenario up to 2003, the local controversy that ensued from the granting of permits for imports at a lowered tariff in 2008 indicates the continuing relevance of the findings.

Despite the passing of the Safeguard Act, successive governments have reduced tariffs on imported chicken meat, especially in peak periods of consumption such as holidays. Such a relaxation of the import restrictions occurred in December 2008 – supposedly to satisfy demand during the Christmas season. The Government granted permits for the importation of 625,000 kg or 25 containers of leg quarters at a duty of 40 per cent, down from 260 per cent. The Minister said this was to facilitate affordable prices for the consumers, while still allowing local producers to compete.

As usual, this occasioned protests from major producers, who contended that there was no shortage and that the imports would threaten the livelihood of chicken farmers. The Minister defended the decision by saying that the Government was concerned that any shortage of chicken during the period would lead to additional price increases over what had already taken place, creating hardship for consumers.

Box 3.2 Challenges to the poultry industry from subsidised imports

Poultry is a popular food item in Jamaica. It is less expensive than pork or beef and is considered healthier, particularly the white meat. From 1996–2000, chicken production increased 40 per cent and local production was able to satisfy 60 per cent of the demand. The remainder, primarily lower-cost chicken necks, backs and leg quarters, was imported from the USA. Under the WTO, Jamaica granted high levels of market access to imported agricultural products. It had already gone a long way in liberalising imports prior to the launch of the WTO, reducing its import duties from as high as 200 per cent to 40 per cent for agricultural goods. Lowering import duties makes it less expensive for other countries to export food and other products to Jamaica. Jamaican officials may have believed that trade liberalisation would enable them to import cheaper food for low-income consumers, pressure inefficient farmers to leave the sector and make other farmers more competitive.

In 1994, the USA exported just over US$13 million of poultry meat and edible offal to Jamaica, but by 1998 this had almost doubled to US$25.2 million before returning to roughly US$13 million in 2001. In the early 1990s, the USA adopted aggressive marketing strategies to sell poultry products internationally. One strategy involved exporting leg quarters to Jamaica at prices well below costs of production. It claimed the practice was not dumping, since the leg quarter prices in Jamaica were no lower than those in the USA. This was because, based on American consumers' preference for white meat over dark meat, US producers were selling leg quarters at only about 40 to 60 per cent of production costs, while they sold breast meat at four times the cost of production. In this way, they covered their costs.

Poultry producers in Jamaica were particularly riled because while they were struggling to compete with lower-priced US chicken products, exports of Jamaican poultry were barred from the USA under sanitary and phytosanitary (SPS) measures that were required by the WTO. The SPS rules barred Jamaican poultry on the grounds that the country had not demonstrated that Newcastle disease, a viral disease affecting chickens, had not occurred in the country during the past 50 years. Producers appealed to the Jamaican Government to enact measures to protect the local industry. They requested that the Government raise the WTO bound tariff rate to the ceiling that Jamaica had set of 100 per cent for chicken, which was the only remedy available to the country under its WTO

Box 3.2 (continued)

commitments. This would mean that a 100 per cent tax would be levied on imported chicken, making the price close to that of local producers. However, policy-makers were reluctant to act as the Government was bound by an IMF agreement not to raise tariffs at all. Wealthy members of the poultry sector continued to lobby for the local market to be protected, and in 2001 the Government passed the Safeguard Act,[4] which allows Jamaica to use temporary tariffs or quotas to restrict imports of a product where there is clear evidence that increased imports have caused or threaten to cause serious injury to the domestic industry and it is in the public interest to impose these measures.

Source: Adapted from Wyss and Whyte, 2004

Impacts of trade policy changes on women

The backyard farmer is the most vulnerable of the suppliers of chicken to the local market. Though often supplying the immediate market of her community, she is also competing with the cheaper imported meat. While there is little data on the number of farmers who have had to go out of chicken production due to increased competition from imports,

> ... anecdotal evidence suggests that nearly half of the 'backyard' farmers may have left. Some analysts have suggested that the backyard farmers moved into other enterprises such as working in the market selling vegetables while others may have moved to tourist areas to find work. Rural women, who are the majority of these 'backyard' producers, were most affected by the trade policies. (Wyss and Whyte, 2004: 25)

Measures taken to help women to cope with or take advantage of policy changes

National

While no national programmes have specifically targeted women, there have been general measures that would benefit women in the industry. For example, the Safeguard Act in 2001 increased import duties from 86 to 260 per cent for poultry products (Wyss and Whyte, 2004), which helped protect local poultry farmers, including small-scale producers who are mostly women.

However, in July 2003 Robert Levy of Jamaica Broilers still had reason to suggest that Jamaica and other Caribbean countries needed to reduce their imports of chicken from 25 per cent to 15 per cent. Levy noted that Caribbean countries as a whole granted high market access for chicken in comparison with Mexico, which imports 5 per cent of its poultry, and Brazil, which imports less than 1 per cent (Wyss and Whyte, 2004).

Prior to the passing of the Safeguard Act, the Government enacted the Customs Duties (Dumping and Subsidies) Act (CDDASA) in 1999, which sets out the general investigation process and provides for the imposition of anti-dumping and countervailing duties against dumped or subsidised goods. CDDASA established a statutory body called the Anti-dumping and Subsidies Commission (ADASC), whose function is the implementation of the provisions of the Act (FAO, 2003).

Additionally, a number of agricultural support services are provided by the Government in order to enhance competitiveness and develop the agricultural sector generally. These include research and extension, the development of technology, human resources and marketing, plant quarantine/produce inspection and veterinary services.

The Government also provides income tax exemption for up to ten years for farmers with approved farmer status. Agricultural production inputs are exempted from general consumption tax payments and farmers are eligible for a 20 per cent duty concession on the importation of farm vehicles.

The Jamaica Livestock Association (JLA), a civil society organisation, advocates for the interests of poultry farmers by lobbying against unnecessary importation of poultry products and regulating importation in times of shortages, for example following hurricanes. During such economically challenging periods, the JLA has, for example, imported eggs for distribution through farmers to retail outlets until production returned to normal. The JLA supplies, at competitive prices, all the requirements of independent poultry farmers – from day-old chicks and feeds to feeders, laying boxes, mesh wire, health-care products and medications. The Association's Field Representatives keep in touch with farmers, giving them the advice they need to make their business profitable (JLA, n.d.).

International

A review of programmes supported by international agencies that benefit women in agriculture generally and in poultry specifically suggests that these programmes have been relatively small in scale and have been:

- In response to weather shocks (hurricane damage, etc.), with support being given to rebuild coops, restock, etc.;

- Related to efforts to improve the income-generating capacity of rural and/or urban women in specific pilot communities, with backyard poultry farming as one of the strategies.

Lessons learned

The overarching lesson to be drawn from the analyses is that trade is not gender neutral. In agriculture, as in other areas of the economy, women and men come to the market with different material capacities and needs. These affect their relative position and vulnerability within a given sector. Effective policy-making, monitoring and evaluation require that these differences be identified and that specific and appropriate remedies be implemented.

As stated by the Women's Edge Coalition:

> ... the reality of free trade has not always lived up to the rhetoric, particularly for the poor. ... In particular, trade's effects on women, who are more likely than men to be poor, must be carefully examined. For, if trade is to lift up the poor, then there should be positive benefits for women living in poverty for whom a small increase in income could have an enormous impact on their quality of life. (Wyss and Whyte, 2004: 1)

And they concluded, among other things, that:

> The WTO agreements affected Jamaica's small producers and limited the ways in which the Government could respond to an influx of cheap, imported goods.
>
> The state has a legitimate role in developing policies for the public good as well as in regulating goods – for example, ensuring food safety and the safety of new drugs. International trade commitments should be consonant with other international commitments on development, gender equality, and economic, social, and cultural rights. Moreover, international trade commitments should enhance Jamaica's national laws and policies that are designed to increase economic development within the country.
>
> Jamaica's economic and social crisis has many factors, but it is clear that the WTO commitments that Jamaica has undertaken have hindered the ability of the state to act in the public interest. As a small island economy, Jamaica is already vulnerable to the exigencies of external forces. Jamaica must be able to maintain needed flexibility to act in the interest of the public.
>
> Jamaican women, particularly women living in poverty, have a great stake in the outcome of trade negotiations. Trade negotiations can either create new opportunities for women which will enable them to support

> their families and invest in their children's future or instead, trade may create the narrowest range of poverty-waged jobs for women while reducing the ability of the Government to legislate in the public's interest. (ibid.: 75)

As Wyss and Whyte (2004) point out, Jamaican women have consistently demonstrated 'their entrepreneurial zeal, their ingenuity [and] their ability to work hard to support themselves and their families'. What they need are policies to open up sectors where they can compete and laws that promote a balance between work and family life.

References

Best, R (2008). 'CARICOM Poultry Industry: Changing Competitive Environment and Evolving Response', presentation at a forum on Strengthening Agricultural Trade Strategies: Towards a Caribbean Agenda, 6–8 November, Belize City, Belize, http://www.ecdpm.org/Web_ECDPM/Web/Content/Download.nsf/0/B183060314 7E53A1C1257501005C05A8/$FILE/Best_CARICOM%20Poultry%20Industry_ Changing%20Competitive%20Environment%20and%20Evolving%20Response. pdf

Daly, J (2009). Telephone interview by the author of *The Live Production Manager*, Jamaica Broilers Group, 20 April.

FAO (2003). 'Jamaica', in WTO Agreement on Agriculture: The Implementation Experience: Developing Country Case Studies, Food and Agriculture Organization (FAO), Rome, http://www.fao.org/docrep/005/y4632e/y4632e0m.htm

Jamaica Broilers Group of Companies (n.d.). 'Best Dressed Chicken Operations', http://www.jamaicabroilersgroup.com/jabroilers.dti?section=poultrydivision&pag e=fieldops&PHPSESSID

JLA (n.d.). 'About Us', Jamaica Livestock Association website, <http://www.jlaltd. com/about.us.farmers.htm>.

Singh, RH, Rankine, LB and Seepersad, G (2005). 'A Review of Agricultural Policies: Case Study of Jamaica', report prepared for the CARICOM Secretariat, Department of Agricultural Economics and Extension, University of the West Indies (UWI), http://www.caricom.org/jsp/community/agribusiness_forum/agri_policy_ jamaica.pdf

STATIN (2007). http://www.statinja.com/stats.html

STATIN and the Planning Institute of Jamaica (2006). 'Jamaica Survey of Living Conditions 2006', http://salises.mona.uwi.edu/databank/slc2006/survey0/index.html

UNDP (2007). *Human Development Report 2007–2008: Fighting Climate Change: Human Solidarity in a Divided World*, Palgrave Macmillan, New York.

USAID Jamaica (2007). 'Rural Enterprise Development of the Poultry Industry: Bridging the Gap', 30 August, http://jamaica.usaid.gov/en/Article.1084.aspx

Witter, M (2004). 'Trade Liberalization: The Jamaican Experience', prepared for the United Nations Conference on Trade and Development (UNCTAD), http://r0.

unctad.org/ditc/tab/events/nama/docs/Draft_studyjamaica.pdf
Witter, M (n.d.). Interviewed for 'When The Cows Come Home', Life Series article, Lifeonline, http://www.tve.org/lifeonline/index.cfm?aid=1438
Wyss, B and Whyte, M (2004). *The Effects of Trade Liberalization on Jamaica's Poor: An Analysis of Agriculture and Services*, Women's Edge Coalition, Washington, DC.

Preference Gain and Loss

4 Can it be Mended? Kenya and the MFA Phase-out

Paul Kamau[5]

Introduction

The textiles and clothing industry has traditionally been considered one of the first steps up the industrialisation ladder in developing countries that are seeking to move from an economic structure based on primary commodity production to one in which manufacturing contributes an additional source of employment, value-added and exports. It has also been recognised as a major source of formal employment for women with low skills (Weston *et al.*, 2008; Vijayabaskar, 2002). Textiles and clothing production is the largest source of industrial employment in the world, providing jobs for millions of people, the majority of whom have few employment alternatives. Its low skill requirements and large labour absorption potential have made this industry an important source of non-agrarian employment for the rural populace. Moreover, textiles and clothing products constitute the major exports of a number of developing countries.

In Kenya, between 60 and 70 per cent of the approximately 60,000 workers in the textiles and clothing industry are women with generally low levels of education and skills (Kamau, 2007). The industry accounts for 20 per cent of formal employment in the manufacturing sector. In addition, the subsector creates about 150,000 indirect jobs and supports the livelihoods of over 200,000 people, especially small-scale cotton farmers. However, the clothing industry in Kenya faces significant crises. These emanate from continued deterioration in the purchasing power of the majority of the population (reducing effective demand for products), cheap imports and the elimination of quotas following the termination of the Multifibre Arrangement in 2005. Consequently, closures of firms and lay-offs have increased drastically within the industry. Available statistics indicate that nearly 10,000 jobs were lost in the export processing zone (EPZ) alone between 2004 and 2007 due to factory closures and reduced operations. When non-EPZ firms are included, anecdotal sources indicate that approximately 40,000 jobs have been lost since 2004.

The termination of the MFA, which governed global textiles trade under a quota regime from 1974 to 2004, has exposed Kenya to stiff competition in third markets from more established manufacturing economies such as China (McCormick *et al.*, 2006). It has caused a dramatic shift in the world market for textile and clothing, creating winners and losers. While China and India (perceived winners) have achieved breathtaking gains in their garment exports, the industry in less competitive countries such as Kenya (perceived losers) has suffered a major setback, making its sustainability highly uncertain. Increasingly, competitiveness in global garment markets relies heavily on innovative capability and an ability to upgrade. Flexibility in production processes is also critical in maintaining the competitiveness of the Kenyan industry.[6]

The impact of the termination of the MFA on the garment industry in developing countries is now the subject of attention from analysts. This case study contributes to an evolving body of literature by critically examining how the termination has affected female workers in Kenya. It is largely based on 20 in-depth interviews conducted in 2008 among garment workers (helpers, operators and supervisors involved in the direct production of garments). Twelve were female and eight male; half the interviewees worked in EPZ firms, while the other half worked in non-EPZ firms. In addition to the primary data, secondary literature and published data sources were used to supplement the gaps in the interviews.

Structure and growth of the clothing industry

The Kenyan clothing industry is quite diverse in terms of size, ownership, technology and market orientation. It consists of micro, small, medium, large and very large firms that form a pyramidal structure with three tiers.[7] The base of the pyramid is formed by the micro and small enterprises that produce mainly for the domestic market, estimated at about 60,000 firms in 2003 (McCormick *et al.*, 2007). The next tier consists of firms ranging from medium to fairly large that produce mainly for the domestic market, with some forays into other countries within the region. Included here are many of the garment firms established during the import substitution era that have survived liberalisation. The third tier consists of large to very large export-oriented, often foreign-owned, firms. It is estimated that there were 15 such firms in 2000, most located in Nairobi and Mombasa, but by 2003 the number had tripled, mainly in response to the African Growth and Opportunity Act (see below). The majority of these firms operate in the EPZs, and workforce ranges from 200 to 3,000 workers (McCormick *et al.*, 2006).

The clothing industry grew rapidly during the first two decades after independence in 1963, owing to the controls instituted by the Government to protect the industry. However, by the mid-1980s the scope of import substitution policy in Kenya was exhausted. Beginning in 1986, the Government introduced structural adjustment programmes aimed at strengthening the competitiveness of the industrial sector.[8] The policy measures in the programme were aimed at removing the anti-export bias (disincentives to export) inherent in past policies. As a result of trade liberalisation, the clothing industry started to shrink because it could not penetrate and/or retain its share of international markets. In addition, massive dumping of used clothes – known locally as *mitumba* – significantly undermined the growth prospects of the industry (Omolo, 2006). In order to re-invent the industrial sector in the context of trade liberalisation, and in response to the deterioration of export performance, export promotion programmes were established in 1987. These included manufacturing under bond (MuB), EPZ and duty or VAT exemption schemes. The first two targeted new investments, while the third targeted existing manufacturers. These programmes were instrumental in creating an export-oriented garment industry in Kenya.

The EPZ scheme was established in 1990 and became fully operational in 1993. It is covered under the Export Processing Zones Act (Chapter 517), Laws of Kenya, which defines an EPZ as '... a designated part of Kenya where any goods introduced are generally regarded, insofar as import duties are concerned, as being outside the customs territory but are duly restricted by controlled access ...' (EPZA, 2008). The objective of the programme is to promote exports, foreign exchange earnings, transfer of technology and skills, employment creation and enhancement of industrialisation. Incentives for EPZ firms in Kenya include a 10-year tax holiday, unrestricted foreign ownership and employment of expatriates, freedom to repatriate unlimited amount of earnings, and infrastructure support. These firms are also exempted from observing some core labour laws and regulations. For example, until 2003 trade unions could not organise workers in EPZ firms and the Factories Act (Chapter 514) is still not being enforced in the zones. The majority of the EPZ firms were established in response to enormous market prospects presented the US-led AGOA (Phelps *et al.*, 2009). For customs purposes, sales from Kenyan businesses to the EPZs are treated as exports, and vice versa.

For firms in the EPZ for which data are available, employment grew from 5,565 workers in 2000 to a high of 36,348 in 2003, but then started declining in 2005 to reach 28,506 in 2007 (see Table 4.1). Similarly, the number of firms increased rapidly from six to 35 between 2001 and 2003. Beginning in 2004, the number of firms declined, falling to 22 in 2007. However, available evidence suggests that acquisitions and mergers have been very common in the Kenyan garment industry, so that some firms deemed to have closed down continued to operate, but under a different name. This partly explains why even though the number of firms was decreasing, exports and investment declined only marginally. In addition, firms tried to upgrade their production process in order to remain competitive, which could be attributed to the increasing investment between 2005 and 2006.

Table 4.1 Performance of the Kenyan EPZ clothing sector, 2000–2007

	2000	2001	2002	2003	2004	2005	2006	2007
Number of enterprises	6	17	30	35	30	25	25	22
Employment (number)	5,565	12,002	25,288	36,348	34,614	34,234	31,317	28,506
Expatriates (number)	211	282	630	820	753	720	584	460
Exports (US$ million)	30	55	104	146	221	195	207	205
Investment (US$ million)	16	48	88	128	108	132	143	123

Source: Author's computations based on EPZA Annual Reports

While the Kenyan clothing export market is dominated by a few large firms, a majority of which operate under the EPZ programme, there are thousands of micro and small enterprises that mainly produce for the domestic market. The large producers use modern industrial machines and employ a mass production type work organisation, while many of the small firms use simple electric or foot-powered sewing machines. A wide range of goods are produced including jeans, T-shirts, polo shirts, sports wear, shorts, track suits, women's tops and trousers. In addition, firms produce uniforms, baby wear, promotional materials and undergarments.

Most of the firms in the export-oriented sector do not undertake value adding activities such a design or procurement of key raw materials. Instead, such activities are conducted by customers, agents or retailers, who specify the designs and sources of raw materials for the factory to produce a prototype. This is sent to the buyer for approval before an order is confirmed. In a few cases, firms work together with buyers or agents to design a garment product to be produced (Phelps *et al.*, 2009). However, this is more common among firms registered as non-EPZ as opposed to EPZ firms.

Undoubtedly, AGOA has had a critical impact on Kenya's global clothing exports. This non-reciprocal trade agreement between the USA and 38 sub-Saharan African countries covers around 7,000 product lines. The original agreement ran from 2000 to 2008, but was subsequently extended to 2015. Kenya was the first country to become eligible for AGOA preference, in 2001, and it is among the 26 countries that enjoy duty free access related to clothing manufacture. Moreover, as a less developed country, Kenya benefits from a special rule requiring only a single transformation in apparel products (otherwise known as the derogation of the rule of origin), initially intended to run until 2004 but then extended to 2007 and now to 2012.[9] Studies show that the country's clothing exports grew from virtually nothing to US$221 million between 2001 and 2004 (Kaplinsky, 2008; McCormick *et al.*, 2006). More than 80 per cent of clothing exports were destined for the US market under the AGOA preferential scheme. After the decline of Kenya's largely indigenous and local market-oriented clothing industry, which had developed before the 1980s, the industry re-emerged as an export-oriented, foreign-owned industry as a direct result of this scheme (Phelps *et al.*, 2009).

Another factor that contributed to the growth of the country's garment industry was the quantitative restrictions imposed by major importing countries under the MFA. While the quota system was in place, entrepreneurs in countries restricted by quotas found ways to exploit the system. They established factories in countries with a low level of quota utilisation, such as Kenya, and in some instances helped in the countries' industrialisation process. With the removal of quotas, however, it is no longer lucrative to continue producing in these countries, and as a result firms began to close down and consolidate their operations in their parent country. Although Kenya has held on, in other countries the clothing industry stimulated by foreign investors was wiped off the industry map once these investors pulled out.

Effects of MFA termination on working conditions

Following the termination of the MFA, the competition from more established producers, particularly China and India, has become more intense (Kamau, 2007; McCormick *et al.*, 2006). Kenyan firms allege that buyers have become more stringent with their production requirements and lead times as they now have a wider selection of suppliers from whom to source their products. Similarly, the firms are being asked to match cut-make-trim (CMT) prices with those being offered by China, if buyers are to continue sourcing from them. The competitive environment has necessitated a change in production strategies, which have included lay-offs, casualisation of labour contracts, setting targets, and lower wages and piece rate payments in order to meet the requirements of buyers.

Evidence has shown that garment-producing countries have been affected differently by the termination of the MFA, depending on their level of industrial competitiveness, factor endowment and marketing connections. As predicted, there have been job losses in sub-Saharan Africa, with a more detrimental impact in low-income countries, where workers are not able to find other jobs elsewhere when retrenched. Analysts feel that the actual impact of MFA termination has not been felt to its fullest because the major importers – the USA and EU – are exercising safeguards negotiated during China's accession to the WTO. Nonetheless, countries such as Kenya have been gradually losing their market share in the USA (Kamau, 2007).

Downsizing and casualising of employment

Following the MFA termination, demand in the global market became more uncertain and flexible. This meant that firms had to 'flexibilise' the workforce to adjust the numbers employed in the production process according to demand. Given the seasonality of garment production in this industry, it has become extremely expensive for firms to maintain production workers on a permanent basis. Workers – especially tailors, who constitute the bulk of the labour force – are recruited on contractual terms (Phelps *et al.*, 2009). Out of the ten firms in our sample, seven indicated that they had shifted from permanent to contract arrangements since 2004. This appears to be more common in the exporting than in the local (non-exporting) firms.

Most women workers in the industry are engaged on short-term contracts and as soon as an order is completed they are laid off. Whereas male workers are able to secure alternative employment during the off-peak season, women usually opt to stay at home. The casualisation of the labour force also precludes workers from bargaining for social security provisions ordinarily obtained through trade unions.

At the same time, real wages in the industry have been declining since 2005. According to respondents from firms, this was caused by the buyers, who are continuously pushing for lower prices. In response, firms are forced to lower costs of production, the most common being labour (McCormick *et al.*, 2006). The practice has been that firms lay off all production workers when the season is low and then advertise the same positions, but at lower pay. A closer look at the wage rates for different categories of workers in the garment industry indicates that monthly average wages declined, particularly for production workers, between 2003 and 2008 (Table 4.2).

The average monthly wage for garment workers in Kenya has been above the national poverty line, indicating that working in the garment industry on average helps to reduce poverty (Omolo, 2006). In 2003, for instance, a supervisor earned on average US$146, while an operator earned

Table 4.2 Average monthly wages of garment workers in US dollars

	2003	2006	2008
Manager	680	652	675
Other officer	170	175	172
Engineer	237	231	210
Supervisor	146	124	120
Operator	77	70	68
Helper	67	58	55

Source: Author's computation from EPZA Annual Reports

US$77 and a helper US$67. At that time the poverty line in Kenya was estimated as US$43.3 per month in urban areas. Wages in EPZ firms were on average 20 per cent lower than in non-EPZ firms. This is due to the fact that the EPZ firms peg their salaries to the national minimum wage guideline. In 2008, however, while the national poverty line was estimated to be US$46.8 per month, wages in the garment industry fell to approximately $120 for supervisors, $68 for operators and $55 for helpers, a downward trend that started in 2005. Most of the firms attributed the decline in wage rates to the increased competition in both the domestic and export markets caused by the termination of the MFA.

Gender discrepancy in the clothing industry

The gender discrepancy in wage levels for male and female workers doing comparable jobs is small, especially when factors such as age, education and experience are taken into account. In the production section, however, female workers are mainly clustered in lower skilled operations and thus are paid less. In most firms, women work as either operators or helpers. It is extremely rare to find women working as production managers or supervisors, who earn salaries varying from 2–10 times that of the average operator.

According to Phelps *et al.* (2009)

> ... the vast majority (96%) of the workers in the Kenyan EPZ clothing industry are involved in direct production even though there are a sizeable number of white-collar jobs. Many of the key positions are held by male expatriates from the home country of the parent transnational corporation.

Moreover, the majority of direct production workers are on casual or temporary contracts – with implications not just for their job security but also for the nature of labour relations and generation of skills in the industry. This condition has been exacerbated by the increased competition following MFA termination.

Women are an easy target for retrenchment in the industry partly because they are considered to be more compliant than their male counterparts, but also because they constitute a majority of the workers in the industry. One manager in an EPZ firm confided that 'female workers are more efficient in carrying out assembly work and that is the reason why firms employ more women that men in the operation section'. Moreover, when women were retrenched, they were unlikely to take a firm to industrial court or to the union – a common phenomenon with male workers. Male workers, it was argued, resisted retrenchment and might even stage a demonstration in the factory, something that female workers were unlikely to do. Similarly, when retrenched, female workers would not go looking for employment elsewhere outside the industry; so when firms needed them, a majority would return to the factory. A firm was therefore assured of recruiting the same group of workers when it got big orders. Male workers tended to move on and find employment in other sectors, particularly in construction, so that when a firm required more workers it could not be sure that most of them would return to work.

Most of the women interviewed stated that they relied on the salary earned in the industry to support their immediate families as well as their extended families in the rural areas, as illustrated in the three examples below.

> **Jane** was born in 1976 and is married with three children. She has worked as a helper in an EPZ firm since 2005 on a contract basis earning US$73 per month. She said that she sends about $10 to her parents, who live in a rural area, to buy food and farm inputs. From time to time she also supports the education of her siblings by sending them school fees. This is in addition to financing the food and housing budget in her house. (*Worker interview, 5 June 2008*)

> **Magdalene** is 21 years old and works as an operator in a local (non-EPZ) firm earning US$50 per month. She remits about $6.5 every month to her siblings who live in rural areas. In Nairobi, Magdalene shares a small house with two other colleagues who are also single and she walks to work. This keeps her housing and transport expenditure low. (*Worker interview, 14 June 2009*)

> **Helen,** who works in the finishing section of an EPZ firm, said that she supports her family with about US$12 every month. She has one child who stays at home with her parents and therefore she is obliged to remit

some money home to cater for her child and other family members. (*Worker interview, 12 December 2008*)

Women interviewed were concerned about the meagre pay they earned in the industry; they also lack job security. Most of them said that, given that they were unlikely to find employment elsewhere, they and their families were likely to slip into abject poverty if they were retrenched.

Work intensity and conditions of work

Working conditions in the industry have drastically deteriorated since 2005, particularly among the exporting firms. Workers have to put in long hours in order to meet targets set by the firm. This emanates from strict demands by the buyers whereby non-price factors such as short lead times and quality deliveries have become a key consideration in placing orders. Even though the majority of buyers claim to be adhering to ethical sourcing practices, it is reported that they are increasingly demanding high quality garments produced within a relatively short period of time and at the lowest price possible. In order to meet these requirements, workers must be willing to work long hours. In some cases, they put in more than ten hours of work a day, six days a week, with a 30-minute lunch break. It is common practice for workers to leave the factory at 8pm, yet they do not earn any overtime pay.

Apart from the other effects of long working hours, fatigue exposes workers to serious hazards such as inadvertent slipping of fingers or hands into the stitching machines. Female workers, who are also generally expected to play the role of homemaker, are unlikely to perform these duties well. It is therefore not surprising that the great majority of female workers in the industry are young and single. Once they get married, their chances of remaining in the industry get smaller. Firms are reluctant to give maternity leave to female workers, a factor that contributes to most of them leaving employment when they get pregnant.

There have been allegations of gender-based harassment by supervisors and those charged with recruiting female workers. However, our interviews did not find adequate evidence to support this allegation. In some cases, respondents claimed that women were coerced into sexual relationships with supervisors in order to remain in employment, but this allegation could not be confirmed.

Declining unionisation

Most workers interviewed were not members of a trade union which could have represented them when their rights were allegedly violated. According to Omolo (2006), most of the clothing firms blatantly violate laws that protect employees' rights to associate and join a union. Even though trade unions are allowed, the firms discourage workers from joining. A person who admits to being a union member may have difficulty finding employment, and in some cases union membership was used as grounds for firing workers.

The fragmentation of production and casualisation of labour mean that workers are increasingly unable to seek legal redress. When on contract during the peak season, workers who previously unemployed have to stick to delivery schedules agreed by the firms, giving them no time to join a union. In any case, insecure employment prevents trade unions from demanding any kind of social welfare and employment security measures from producers. Because of seasonal employment, workers do not have incentives to join a trade union and instead are willing to work long hours to compensate for off-season unemployment.[10]

If workers do join unions, the management may refuse to deduct union contributions and instead ask those who want to contribute to do it on their own. In an interview with an official of the Tailors and Textiles Workers Union (TTWU), it was alleged that firms were 'playing games' with the union so that they would not get the 51 per cent of unionised workers necessary to oblige the firm to sign a recognition agreement. In one case, the TTWU had obtained membership of more than 51 per cent in a particular firm, but the firm still declined to sign a recognition agreement. Although managers claimed that they did not object to workers joining the union, trade union officials and workers alleged that it was a challenge for workers to join because in practice union members were the first to be fired when retrenchment was effected. On several occasions, workers alleged that union officials were easily wooed by the management when it signed a recognition agreement, and instead of championing workers' interests they were just out to enrich themselves.

It was not possible to confirm most of these allegations, but one thing that emerges is that there is a high level of mistrust between management and trade unions, management and workers and, worse, between trade unions and workers. Perhaps more education by the Government with regard to the roles played by each party might be beneficial. NGOs are unlikely to win the confidence of all stakeholders as they are often perceived to be biased.

Conclusion

As shown by this case study, the clothing industry continues to play a significant role in Kenya's development and poverty reduction agenda. It provides job opportunities for a segment of the population that cannot easily find alternative employment. More importantly, the study shows how women workers support both their immediate and extended families through remittances. This undoubtedly provides an appropriate avenue for poverty reduction. The recent growth of an export-led clothing industry as a result of AGOA and the MFA has had positive effects on the welfare of Kenyans.

However, the end of the MFA in 2005 has altered the landscape. Generally speaking, competition has intensified in both the domestic and export markets, particularly from relatively more efficient producing countries such as China and India. Indeed, as noted earlier, nearly 10,000 workers lost their employment in the export-oriented segment in Kenya during the two years following the termination of the MFA.

Kenyan firms have responded to these challenges with a number of strategies: closure, cost cutting, casualisation of labour contracts and increased efficiency. These actions have had adverse effects on women, who have been the primary victims of lay-offs due to the sheer fact of their numbers. Equally, women are perceived as more complacent than men when it comes to labour issues and are therefore easier to deal with from the firm's point of view. While managers argue that they use women workers because of their aptitude for assembly line production processes, critics say it is mainly because women are less likely to find employment elsewhere in the manufacturing sector and will work under harsh conditions without complaining. They are also unlikely to be members of a trade union, as they are working to feed their families, a characteristic that is not as common among male workers.

Female workers in the clothing industry still hold their employment in high regard, as the majority of them did not have a formal job prior to joining the industry. More importantly, they say that through employment in this sector they have improved their livelihoods significantly. Their earnings have enabled most of them to support their immediate and extended family members, though changing employment conditions are becoming a threat to fulfilling this objective.

It is therefore imperative for the Government to work closely with all stakeholders to ensure that female workers' rights are not violated in the name of increased competition arising from MFA termination. Firms can adopt other survival strategies without hurting the labour force. Perhaps further research into alternative approaches to combating competition needs to be undertaken.

References

EPZA (2008). *EPZA Annual Report for 2007*, EPZA, Nairobi.

Kamau, P (2007). 'The Developmental Impact of Asian Drivers on Kenya, with Particular Emphasis on Clothing and Textile Manufacturing', Final Report prepared for OECD Development Centre.

Kaplinsky, R (2008). 'What Does the Rise of China Do for Industrialization in Sub-Saharan Africa?', *Review of African Political Economy*, 115: 2–22.

McCormick, D, Kamau, P and Ligulu, P (2006). 'Post-Multifibre Arrangement Analysis of the Textile and Garment Sectors in Kenya', *IDS Bulletin*, 37(1): 81–88.

McCormick, D, Kimuyu, P and Kinyanjui, MN (2007). 'Textiles and Clothing: Global Players and Local Struggles', in McCormick, D, Alila, PO and Omosa, M (eds), *Business in Kenya: Institutions and Interactions*, University of Nairobi Press, Nairobi.

Omolo, JO (2006). 'The Textiles and Clothing Industry in Kenya', in Jauch, H and Traub-Merz, R (eds), *The Future of the Textile and Clothing Industry in Sub-Saharan Africa*, Friedrich-Ebert-Stiftung, Bonn.

Phelps, NA, Stilwell, JCH and Wanjiru, R (2009). 'Broken Chain? AGOA and Foreign Direct Investment in the Kenyan Clothing Industry', *World Development*, 37(2): 314–325.

Vijayabaskar, M (2002). 'Garment Industry in India', in Gopal, J (ed.), *Garment Industry in South Asia: Rags or Riches?*, International Labour Organization, New Delhi.

Weston, A, Kamau, P and Bhushan, A (2008). 'The End of the MFA and Informal Work in the Global Garment Industry', report prepared for Women in the Informal Economy Globalizing and Organizing (WIEGO), The North-South Institute, September.

5 Knitting it Together: India and the MFA Phase-out

Pramod Dev

Background: the Indian economy

After almost 200 years of colonisation, India in 1947 remained a poor, agrarian economy and supplier of natural resources. The independence period witnessed the emergence of a mixed economy with pronounced socialist leanings that was trying to grow on all fronts simultaneously. Economic development was envisaged through a centralised and controlled planning process, with the Government as the most important provider of services and employment. An import substitution model was preferred to open trading, and restrictions on imports and private and foreign investment were imposed. High tariff walls were the norm and economic reforms were largely absent. By the late 1980s, the lack of incentives for individual initiative, combined with population growth, had resulted in increasing poverty and an underperforming economy.

There were sporadic efforts at liberalisation in the 1980s; however, they remained largely confined to specific sectors. Major reforms were initiated in 1991 as the economy was under severe strain from low growth and mounting foreign debt. Though liberalisation has been a cautious, phased-in process that is still not complete, increasing exports was adopted as an important strategy and has arguably resulted in considerably reducing poverty, even though the size of the population means that a large proportion of the populace is still poor. Economic growth has not been distributed evenly but has deepened the dual nature of society, with high levels of affluence and poverty existing side by side.

The textiles and clothing sector

Trade in textiles and clothing

The textiles and clothing sector became subject to the general rules of the GATT from 1 January 2005. The Multifibre Arrangement and its successor, the Agreement on Textiles and Clothing, had until then tied import markets to a system of quotas that were distributed among different exporting countries. The quota regime ensured that many of the traditional textiles-producing nations continued to export, despite being inefficient compared to major producers such as China and India. Purportedly, textiles and clothing was one of the prominent sectors where developing countries had the most to gain from multilateral trade liberalisation under the WTO. In fact, the prospect of liberalisation of the textiles and clothing sectors was one of the reasons why developing countries accepted the inclusion of contentious issues such as services and intellectual property rights in the WTO Uruguay Round negotiations (Nordås, 2004).

The textiles and clothing industry in India

The textiles and clothing sector is the second largest provider of employment in India after agriculture. It provides direct employment to almost 35 million people, including a substantial number from the socially excluded classes and women. It contributes approximately 14 per cent to the country's industrial production, 4 per cent to its GDP and 16 per cent to its total export earnings (Adhikari and Weeratunge, 2006). India's share in the global textiles and clothing trade was 4.3 per cent in textiles and 3.3 per cent in clothing during 2006, while its rank in world trade was seventh in textiles and fifth in clothing (Ministry of Textiles, 2008).

There is a well-developed textiles and clothing value chain and a strong domestic market, valued at over US$25 billion. All the major components of the production chain are present in the domestic economy. The industry is also extremely varied in terms of the levels of technology and sophistication, with the hand-spun and hand-woven sector at one end of the spectrum and the capital-intensive, sophisticated mill sector at the other. Major sectors include the organised cotton/ man-made fibre textile mills, man-made fibre/ filament yarns, decentralised powerlooms, woollen textiles, silk, handlooms, handicrafts, jute and textiles exports. The export basket includes a wide range of items: cotton yarn and fabrics, synthetic yarn and fabrics, wool and silk fabrics, made-up articles and a variety of garments. Decentralised powerloom/hosiery and knitting are the largest sectors.

In the period immediately following the phase-out of the MFA, considerable increase in trade was registered. One estimate suggests that exports grew at a rate close to 17 per cent in 2005, while imports grew at about 30 per cent. However, high growth of exports to the major markets of the EU and USA was at the cost of exports to the Asian countries, which fell by 12 per cent. Meanwhile, imports from Asia increased to the tune of 45 per cent in the same year (Dev, 2006).

Exports are concentrated on a few products and markets, with more than 50 per cent being garment and clothing products. Europe and America accounted for almost 70 per cent of export earnings in 2005 and their share in the top five export items, all apparel and clothing products, was more than 75 per cent (ibid.).

However, volatility of export demand and appreciation of the Indian rupee in the following year resulted in export growth being reduced to about 7 per cent. The latest report from the Ministry of Textiles (2008) shows that export growth has further decelerated in the recent period. India has not fared well in the post-MFA phase as compared to its main competitor, China, despite the quota restrictions imposed on the latter in the US market. One major factor responsible for the Indian textiles and clothing sector's inability to optimally utilise market access opportunities is the lack of economies of scale. Small and cottage units that employ fewer than 11 workers constitute 80 per cent of the industry; medium units, employing between 21 and 49 workers, account for 14 per cent; while only 6 per cent of units employ more than 49 workers (Adhikari and Weeratunge, 2006). This prevents firms from gaining competitive strength in the international market.

Impacts on women of changes in trade policy

Economic impact

In the post-MFA period the textiles and clothing export sector became highly price elastic. International competition, mainly with China, resulted in wafer-thin profit margins. This means that to achieve economies of scale, maximum output must be produced at the lowest cost. Since the fixed cost components could not be reduced, the variable cost of wages was targeted by employers. Further casualisation of the workforce and increasing instances of piece rate employment and home-based work have been reported.

The first year of the post-MFA period witnessed increasing demand for women workers in most Indian textiles centres, especially in many garment manufacturing units where low-skilled labour was employed in large numbers. Male workers were rendered unemployed in many parts as companies preferred female workers who were offered lower wages. There are reports of women workers being recruited to keep the core issues of right to freedom of association and collective bargaining out of the textiles sector, as well as to deny legally entitled benefits and keep wages down. Moreover, adolescent, unmarried young women aged 18–25 have been recruited who receive no bonuses and are denied the provident fund, state insurance or other payments to which they are entitled.

Though women earned wages and thus found a level of economic independence, they were often the only members of the family who were earning and thus were forced to take up increased responsibility for looking after the family. Since they worked the late shifts when the demand for workers was higher and overtime was a good source of income, the women often faced social stigma and insecurity as the provision of late night transport was increasingly compromised. In addition, the period of higher employment for women, namely 2005–2006, was also a period of high inflation. This, coupled with job losses by the male family members, meant that the overall income effect was negative and welfare for women workers was lower.

Reduction in export demand due to appreciation of the rupee in 2006 resulted in further reductions in prices and margins. This has accelerated the decentralisation of garment manufacturing. It has become difficult for companies to maintain a large permanent workforce as they did in the pre-MFA period. Workers have been off-loaded on a large scale or employed as daily workers according to need in the factories, making job security almost non-existent in the sector.

In some cases, increasing decentralisation and casualisation of work has resulted in workers being forced to sign under different names in the company registers in order to enable the employers to circumvent the statutory regulations on paying health and employment benefits. These changes have also resulted in the emergence of contractors who recruit and supply labourers according to demand and sometimes switch them on a regular basis from one factory to another. This has enabled the companies to avoid any legal obligation to their workers.

Interviews with workers reveal that employers have resorted to practices such as deducting contributions to provident funds and health insurance premiums from monthly wages of casual and daily wage workers. These workers are not covered by the funds or health insurance, and such deductions are illegal practices employed by the firms or the contractors.

Social and cultural impact

In some cases employers have exploited and reinstated social ills such as the practice of paying a dowry, which remain prevalent in India. In the Tirupur area of Tamil Nadu, for example, many girls are recruited under the *sumangali* (married woman) scheme. Poor unmarried women from far off areas are recruited as contract labour with an assurance to their families of good wages and a lump sum at the end of the tenure to enable them to pay their dowry. They have to work for three years without much contact with the outside world or their families. They face exploitative working conditions and low wages, long hours of work, and physical and verbal abuse. Such workers do not fall under the purview of the provident fund or state insurance coverage. Often the promised lump sum is not paid, as the employers terminate contracts on flimsy grounds.

Discernible human development implications are emerging in the post-quota regime in the textiles and clothing sector. Working conditions have generally deteriorated and occupational hazards and diseases are on the rise. In the New Delhi region, for instance, garment companies have introduced a token system to limit the use of toilets during working hours and have reduced the duration of lunch and evening breaks in order to improve productivity. Moreover, as noted above, female workers are made to work the night shifts, which was not the practice earlier.

The change in patterns of demand in export markets also has a bearing on the human development of the stakeholders. In the case of the branded clothing segment, fashions and designs change frequently, in some cases every two weeks. The new styles are more complex and time-consuming to learn and make. Workers are expected to learn the new styles quickly and produce the same or more output (with minimum defective pieces) than they did with the old designs, compounding their problems with adapting to the new requirements.

Most women who are employed in the textiles and clothing sector have jobs that require low skills, and the opportunities for learning new skills have become limited with the decentralisation of the sector. This not only makes them dispensable but also excludes opportunities for personal development. Many older women workers, who were perceived to be slow, also lost their jobs together with the men, due to the emphasis on efficiency and output. These women did not have the necessary skills to find other jobs and have ended up in menial jobs, remained unemployed or have been lured into prostitution.

A major cultural impact of developments in the post-MFA period is the reinforcement of gender roles in communities, where women are seen as only fit for lesser roles.

Measures taken to help women deal with policy changes

National level

The Government has devised various support and incentive schemes for the textiles and clothing sector due to its importance in export earnings. There is a wide range of legal provisions in both central and state legislation. Stringent labour and factory laws are in place to ensure minimum wages and basic working conditions. However, in practice these laws are applied only to the organised sector and their implementation has been ineffective due to problems with monitoring and the increasing casualisation of employment.

Most schemes are aimed at supporting firms directly by providing funds for technological upgrading, cheaper credit and duty drawback. In sectors such as handloom, handicrafts and sericulture, where the number of women workers is high, budget outlays on development schemes are earmarked especially for women. In the handloom sector, for example, 30 per cent of the budget is set aside for activities to help women weavers. In the handicrafts sector, 10 per cent of the budget is earmarked for women artisans. These schemes include provision of training, employment generation, marketing and publicity, input support, modernisation and upgrading of technology, infrastructure support and welfare measures. In the sericulture sector, subsidy and training schemes are operational and two other schemes – health insurance and the creation of crèches and toilets in the cocoon markets – are in the pipeline (Ministry of Textiles, 2008).

For workers in the organised sector there are provisions for provident funds, health care and basic facilities at the workplace. A rehabilitation fund for textiles workers provides interim relief to those unemployed due to the closure of units. In the unorganised handloom sector, weavers associated with co-operatives and self-help groups are provided with cheaper credit and an option for health insurance. The Government has also tried to implement credit, individual and group life insurance schemes and training schemes for handicrafts artisans through the involvement of NGOs and co-operatives (Ministry of Textiles, n.d.).

NGOs and private initiatives, such as the Self Employed Women's Association (SEWA) and FabIndia, have developed sustained product chains from the artisans to the showrooms. These provide workers and artisans in the unorganised sector with livelihood security and markets. The spread and popularity of these chains have helped in reviving specific skills and traditional crafts by opening up urban and export markets. Since the traditional crafts usually involve manual labour and are home-based, the whole family participates and benefits from sustained demand. Women form an important component of this home-based production. Initiatives like SEWA's emphasise women's empowerment through local collectives and providing markets. The success of such initiatives has inspired the second-tier competitors who have further expanded the market for traditional items. However, while profit margins in these activities are very high at retail level, it is not clear if the increased demand and prices translate into a proportional increase in the revenue of the primary producer.

In the private sector, which is organised and mostly unionised, the laws on basic amenities are generally implemented. However, there is an increasing trend of casualisation and erosion of collective bargaining that usually makes women more vulnerable to shifts in demand for exports. On the other hand, there are specific instances of private companies voluntarily adhering to corporate social responsibility agendas and setting norms on the welfare of workers. In isolated instances, the demands of and monitoring by foreign buyers around adherence to social standards have also resulted in firms providing better facilities on the factory premises for their female workforce.

International level

Most activities of the international community in the textiles and clothing sector have been focused on general welfare aspects such as working conditions and labour standards. International campaigns such as the Clean Clothes Campaign, Ethical Trading Initiative and Jobs with Justice, which emphasise labour standards and working and living conditions, are currently running in India.

The efforts of international organisations such as the International Labour Organization (ILO), United Nations Conference on Trade and Development (UNCTAD) have been mostly concentrated on research to influence policy on the linkages between trade and gender.

Lessons learned

Devising effective support measures to counter the increasing vulnerability of women to changes in the sector is a challenge. Such measures have become all the more necessary in the post-MFA trade regime. Better understanding of the issues is required, and at the moment women's problems are not adequately highlighted in the policy arena.

Lessons for local organisations

- Illegal practices in the sector should be effectively documented and reported to bring visibility to the problems faced by women.
- Impetus should be given to collective bargaining and better advocacy at government level.

Lessons for government

- Effective implementation of health and occupational laws and social security measures is needed.
- Consultation with primary stakeholders and women in particular should be improved to customise support measures.

- The focus in trade policy-making is often limited to the problems faced by the firms, therefore the support measures seldom reach the workers.
- Training and skills enhancement programmes should be initiated and effectively implemented targeting women working in the textiles and clothing sector.
- The low-value product chains are at the heart of the problems faced by the sector. There is a need to encourage upgrading of products through policy and support measures.

Lessons for international agencies

- Advocacy is needed at national government level to improve the condition of women in particular and upgrade the sector as a whole.
- Local organisations should be supported and encouraged to carry out the task of documenting and reporting the practices in the sector.
- The Government should be supported in its efforts around training of workers and technological upgrading of the sector.

References

Adhikari, R and Weeratunge, C (2006). 'Textiles and Clothing Sector in South Asia: Coping with Post-quota Challenges' in BS Chimni *et al.* (eds), *Multilateralism at Cross-roads: Reaffirming Development Priorities*, Wiley-India and Centre for Trade and Development (CENTAD), New Delhi.

Dev, P (2006). 'India's Textiles and Clothing Trade in the Post-MFA Period', Country Trade Tracking Report, submitted to UNDP Regional Centre Colombo.

Ministry of Textiles (2008). *Annual Report 2007–2008*, Government of India, New Delhi.

Ministry of Textiles (n.d.). 'Compendium of Schemes', Government of India, New Delhi.

Nordås, HK (2004). *The Global Textile and Clothing Industry Post the Agreement on Textiles and Clothing*, WTO, Geneva.

6 A Stitch in Time? AGOA and Lesotho's Clothing Sector

Mariama Williams and Marilyn Carr

Background

The Kingdom of Lesotho is a small (30,350 sq km) landlocked developing country in southern Africa. It is completely surrounded by South Africa. The population is about 1.88 million persons (US Department of State, 2009).

According to the *Lesotho Human Development Report 2006* (UNDP, 2007), the percentage of the population living below the national income poverty line has declined from 66 to 56 per cent. Poverty is highest among households headed by women, a large proportion of whom are widows, with an average age of 56 years. This is an important phenomenon since Lesotho, like other countries in the sub-region, is vulnerable to chronic food insecurity.

In terms of trade, Lesotho is best known for its exports of diamonds, wool and mohair to primary export partners such as South Africa, the USA and its partners in the Southern African Customs Union (SACU) (Botswana, Namibia and Swaziland, as well as South Africa), where tariffs have been eliminated on the trade in goods with other member countries. Lesotho also belongs to the Common Monetary Area (CMA), which links it with South Africa and Swaziland in a common currency and exchange control union.

Changes in trade and economic policy[11]

Lesotho's efforts to combat poverty and reduce the levels of infant mortality and maternal deaths are highly dependent on its trade performance. The country is therefore vulnerable to changes in international trade patterns and volumes. Since the mid-1990s, a number of changes in the trade environment have had serious implications for the country's growth and development. These include the phasing out, in 2005, of the Multifibre Arrangement (later called the Agreement on Textiles and Clothing); the appreciation of the South African rand against Lesotho's national currency, the loti, which is pegged to it; and the inception of the US African Growth and Opportunity Act. Since the 1990s, Lesotho's growth has been partly driven by the expansion of the textiles industry, primarily owned by Chinese and South African companies.

The currency appreciation and the rounds of trade liberalisation promoted by the MFA phase-out, together with the entry into force of AGOA, have had a significant impact on Lesotho's textiles and garment sector. The phase-out of the MFA, which had restricted trade in textiles to a subset of countries, opened up the global clothing and textiles market to big, low-cost exporters such as China and India and therefore posed a danger to Lesotho's garment sector. On the other hand, AGOA significantly opened up trade between the USA and 38 designated sub-Saharan African countries, including Lesotho. The Act, which offered eligible countries duty and quota free access to the US market for substantially all products, was originally designed to run for eight years, starting in October 2000 and terminating in September 2008; in July 2004, however, it was extended to 2015.

Countries are deemed AGOA-eligible if they meet criteria that include the establishment of a free market economy, the rule of law, political pluralism, elimination of barriers to US trade and investment, efforts to combat corruption, protection of intellectual property rights, protection of human and worker rights, elimination of child labour and policies to reduce poverty. AGOA eligibility is reviewed annually, based on reports that assess the country's record in adhering to the eligibility requirements. Countries must also satisfy certain preconditions on specific enforcement measures such as the adoption of an effective visa system and related procedures to prevent unlawful trans-shipment and the use of counterfeit documents, and the implementation of certain customs procedures that assist the customs service to verify the origin of export products. These are all to be found in Lesotho.

Of particular benefit to Lesotho is that under a special rule for least developed beneficiary countries it enjoys duty free access for apparel using 'third country' fabric, i.e. fabric originating anywhere in the world. It was originally intended that the rule would expire in 2004, but it was subsequently extended to 30 September 2007 and then to 2012.

AGOA has had a positive impact in terms of a rising inflow of foreign direct investment into the clothing manufacturing sector and subsequent increases in employment. Rising employment has helped to foster growth in both the formal and informal sectors of the economy due to spin off and multiplier effects on direct and indirect services such as road construction, freight transport, security, passenger transport, and the distribution of water and electricity. It has also helped to foster growth in communications services such as telecommunications and courier services. Domestic market areas such as food sales and provision have also been positively affected.

The textiles and garment industry

Textiles and garments have been the source of Lesotho's industrial development since the 1980s when a number of firms fled the apartheid regime in South Africa and opened up businesses there. Since then, the country's apparel manufacturing sector has experienced growth.

The most important single export product is denim jeans, which are produced in eight factories employing 15,000 workers (80 per cent women). By the mid-2000s, Lesotho was producing 26 million pairs of jeans per annum, 98 per cent of which were sold in the USA. The factories are supplied with denim fabric by the local Formosa Mill, which also supplies several other African countries. In addition, the garment industry produces approximately 70 million knitted garments a year in 34 factories that employ 28,000 workers. A number of firms supply services directly to the textiles and garment industry (Bennett, 2006).

Impacts of changes in trade policy on women

Economic impacts

Overall, AGOA has been good for Lesotho. The country's manufacturers are the single largest users of the apparel provisions of the Act. In 2004, they earned US$456 million from exports to the USA and a smaller quantity from the EU, Canada and SACU.

It was expected that exports of knitted garments and related jobs would fall in 2007 when AGOA regulations were due to be changed to require manufacturers to source their raw material fabrics inputs from the USA or AGOA countries. Lesotho had previously benefited, through its least developed country status, from the provision of the Act that allowed African factories to use fabric from Asia. It was therefore feared that this would result in retail giants such as Gap and Kmart, which sourced from Lesotho, diverting their orders elsewhere (Bennett, 2006 and 2008; UNCTAD, 2005). However, this did not come to pass, as the provision was extended to 2012 under the AGOA renewal in 2006. Nevertheless, Lesotho's textiles exports fell by 12 per cent in 2005 and 11 per cent in 2006, with corresponding decreases in employment. This can be attributed to two main factors: the ending of the MFA in 2005, which led to retailers sourcing from other countries; and the massive appreciation in the value of the local currency, which has meant that Lesotho's exports have become relatively more expensive.

Although job losses were very high immediately after the ending of the MFA, when many international buyers switched all or part of their garment procurement to China and India, the recent imposition of anti-China textiles and clothing safeguards by the USA and EU has resulted in some orders drifting back to Lesotho and the reopening of several factories. Lesotho remains the largest single sub-Saharan African exporter of garments to the USA (27 per cent of the total). However, international competition from Asian exporters has resulted in some fall-off in textiles and clothing, cumulating in the loss of over 10,000 jobs between 2004 and 2005. Many of these have not been recovered (UNDP, 2007).

Social and cultural impacts

Despite the benefits mentioned above, the liberalisation of trade in textiles and garments has also had significant adverse gender and social effects. These include problems with wages and working conditions, increased incidence of HIV and AIDS, and worsening water and other environmental challenges.

Wages and working conditions

According to the Lesotho Clothing and Allied Workers Union (LCAWU), the number of people employed in the industry – the vast majority of them women – has fallen to almost half of what it was in 2001 (Davis, 2008). Exports of knitted garments and related jobs can be expected to fall further as the country has no AGOA source of knitted fabric, which will become a requirement for export to the USA when AGOA regulations are changed in 2012.

Even before the downturn, labour organisers complained that workers in the textiles sector were exposed to unhealthy conditions that negatively affected their labour and human rights. This situation seems to have worsened with the downturn, as the LCAWU claims that textiles factories often ignore Lesotho's labour laws (BBC, 2002). Labour organisers contend that workers who spend nine hours a day, six days a week sewing labels on T-shirts, who have helped turn Lesotho into a garment manufacturing powerhouse and an important trading partner of the USA, have not themselves received any significant benefits.

HIV and AIDS

The textiles and garment industry has provided a source of employment and income for thousands of women who have migrated from drought-ravaged rural areas where farming has collapsed. Just as AIDS arrived in Lesotho when its men brought HIV home from South Africa, this second wave of migration is also spreading AIDS, as women exchange sex for the money they need to make ends meet in their new and unfamiliar urban environment. The infection rate in Lesotho is about 28 per cent of working-age adults – exceeding that in South Africa; 57 per cent of those infected are women. This is resulting in more openings in garments factories as on average four workers die each month. Few women factory workers have been tested for HIV, although this is slowly changing (Wines, 2004).

Water and other environmental challenges

With much of the attention of policy-makers focused on the manufacturing sector, agriculture has lagged behind, with the result that the welfare of women and men is at risk due to chronic food insecurity.

Gibbs and Gibbs (2002) argue that as a result of trade liberalisation-led growth under AGOA, Lesotho and its capital Maseru are facing a double challenge to the water supply. First, there is barely enough water to supply the industries and people in Maseru already, and growth will be limited without reform of water policies. Second, waste water from various factories is not being adequately treated and is resulting in increased levels of pollution. A report from the UK Department for International Development (DFID) predicted that as a result of these problems, Maseru could face a crisis that meant that employment would fall from a projected 30,000 to 15,000 in 2008 (cited in ibid.).

The water challenge poses significant constraints on the future development of the textiles and garment sectors, as well as all other economic areas. More importantly, it raises concerns about health and safety and the general welfare of citizens. Food insecurity and water shortages place an additional burden on women in their multiple roles as workers, consumers and caretakers of the household, food production and community sustainability.

Measures taken to help women deal with policy changes

Local and national levels

In order to maintain their competitive position, Lesotho's textiles and garment firms have now started to invest in the training of their staff, which should increase productivity and result in workers being able to earn higher incomes as their firms become more profitable. It is unclear whether women and men will benefit equally from new training opportunities.

In addition, the Government is re-examining the package of incentives that it offers to investors. Currently, the major focus has been on a favourable corporate tax regime (better than that for domestic-focused manufacturers) for spending on infrastructure for textiles and garment facilities. The Government is seeking ways to overcome the vulnerability of the textiles sector to changing international shocks and to develop a long-term strategy for the industry. A key aspect of this should be a better approach to incentives, as well as the evaluation of existing domestic policies from the point of view of poverty reduction, human development and gender equality.

There is evidence of a recognition that the previous strategy of export-led growth in the textiles and garment industry might have come at the expense of the social sector, and there are indications that some attempts are being made to rebalance priorities and concerns. For example, the share of the education sector in the recurrent budget rose from 18 per cent in 2003/04 to 22 per cent in 2004/05 and 25.7 per cent in 2007/08. This is a good omen for refocusing on building the human capital of the country (UNDP, 2007).

The Government's national poverty strategy for 2008–2103 and the Lesotho Strategy for Growth and Poverty Reduction aim to reduce poverty through broad-based economic growth designed to create jobs, generate income and empower citizens to make investment decisions that will increase their quality of life (UNDP, 2007). A 2008 AGOA report also highlights that the Government signed a $362.5 million millennium challenge compact in July 2007. The compact aims to reduce poverty through developing urban and rural water infrastructure, enhancing health-care infrastructure and stimulating private sector development by removing barriers to foreign and local private sector growth.[12] The Government is also paying more focused and proactive attention to HIV and AIDS.

As noted above, unions and civil society in Lesotho are organising to achieve better labour conditions and stricter enforcement of labour laws, including the minimum wage in the manufacturing sector.

International level

Several international NGOs are involved in issues such as working conditions, and HIV and AIDS. For example, CARE is training some factory workers to counsel and educate co-workers about HIV, and some factories allow workers time off to visit counsellors. CARE also hopes to get US retailers involved, using their support for AIDS victims in garment factories as a selling point with consumers at home. The Government has also begun to offer voluntary testing programmes in some factories.

Lessons learned

The growth and development of Lesotho is inextricably intertwined with the fate of the textiles and garment sector, which is extremely vulnerable to external shocks. The current growth dynamics are intimately tied to AGOA, which is expected to come to an end in 2015. As a result, decline is anticipated in the sector in the future. The economy is over-reliant on the South African economy with, for example, recent dramatic losses in remittances from miners who have lost jobs there. The current global financial crisis will also have a further negative impact.

There are a number of lessons for local organisations such as unions, as well as for the Government and the international community.

Lessons for local organisations

In addition to advocacy about working conditions and wages in the factories, unions and other civil society organisations must turn their attention to broader welfare issues such as rural–urban imbalance in infrastructural support, food security and environmental sustainability. In the case of rural–urban imbalance, more funds need to be spent on agricultural modernisation and support for subsistence farmers and food production. This will help to ensure adequate supplies of food for domestic consumption at reasonable prices. Similarly, attention to the management and distribution of water should focus on ensuring the protection of this valuable resource, which is critical for life as well as for agriculture, manufacturing and services.

Lessons for the Government

The key lesson that policy-makers in Lesotho seem to be cognisant of is the need to diversify their export base as well as to shore up the domestic economy. It is clear that preferences alone are not enough. The long-term sustainability of investment linked to preferential and regional trade agreements is questionable and must be grappled with head on and proactively. There is a great need to build domestic markets, enhance the labour force and provide broad-based infrastructural support for agriculture. Over-reliance on a few extremely footloose and foreign-dominated firms in the textiles and garment sector of the economy has been at best a far too narrow growth strategy. Recognition of this has propelled the Government to seek the revival of the diamond sector.

There is also a need to pay attention to the social and environmental impact of trade and development strategies. This is especially true in relation to the use of water for industrial purposes, without any regulations concerning the environmental safety of the overall water system. Ultimately, development strategies must think beyond the cross-border flow of goods and services to the human, social and ecological impacts of these strategies.

Lessons for international agencies

Technical assistance must be more broadly conceptualised and implemented to take into account social, gender and environmental impact analysis. In addition, overseas development assistance needs to be scaled up to improve treatment of HIV and AIDS from a gender and social perspective, as well as to promote human development and gender equality. This is necessary to stem the reversal in social and health indicators that is taking place despite rising trade and growth figures.

The international community needs to make food security a focus in trade growth strategy. The growth of trade in the textiles and garment sector has not been sufficient to deal with the fragile food situation that Lesotho continues to face. A focus is needed on the agricultural sector, including the gender challenges and constraints that hamper subsistence farming and food production.

References

AGOA website, http://www.agoa.gov

BBC (2002). 'US Trade "Exploits" Lesotho Workers', *Business News*, 15 March, http://news.bbc.co.uk/2/hi/business/1875088.stm

Bennett MS (2006). 'Lesotho's Export Textiles and Garment Industry' in Jauch, H and Traub-Merz, R (eds), *The Future of the Textile and Clothing Industry in Sub-Saharan Africa*, Friedrich-Ebert-Stiftung, Bonn.

Bennett, MS (2008). 'Spotlight on Lesotho', *iFashion*, 13 August, http://www.ifashion.co.za/index.php?option=com_content&task=view&id=1013&Itemid=91

Davis, C (2008). 'US-Africa: Trade Soars as Labour Rights Languish', *IPS News*, 11 January, http://ipsnews.net/news.asp?idnews=40761

Gibbs, A and Gibbs, TA (2002). 'Water Supply and Pollution Crisis in Lesotho's Textile Factories: The Problems of Footloose Investment', Centre for Civil Society and the School of Development Studies Report, University of Natal, Durban.

Government of Lesotho (2008). 'AGOA Benefits Lesotho's Economy', http://www.lesotho.gov.ls/articles/2008/AGOA_BENEFITS_LESOTHO.php

Malie, M (2001). Speech by the Minister for Industry, Trade and Marketing, press conference to launch the implementation of AGOA in Lesotho, http://www.lesotho.gov.ls/articles/Speech-%20MITM-%20AGOA.htm

UNCTAD (2005). 'TNCs and the Removal of Textiles and Clothing Quotas', United Nations Conference on Trade and Development, Geneva.

UNDP (2007). 'Lesotho Human Development Report 2006', United Nations Development Programme, New York.

US Department of State (2009). '2008 Human Rights Report: Lesotho', US Department of State, Washington, DC.

Wines, M (2004). 'Women in Lesotho Become Easy Prey for HIV', *New York Times*, 20 July.

World Bank (1998). 'Lesotho's Garment Exports: Attracting Foreign Direct Investment', *Findings: Africa Region*, 103, January.

7 Slipping on a Peel: The Effects of Changing Trade Regimes on the St Lucia Banana Industry

Carol Narcisse[13]

Background

The countries of the eastern Caribbean, with the exception of St Kitts and Nevis, moved out of the production of sugar on account of the significant decline of the industry during the nineteenth century (ECLAC, 2008). Bananas became the main replacement crop from the 1880s. This was so profitable, particularly for smaller producers, who were mainly women, that it was referred to as 'green gold'. The impact of the banana industry soon became very visible on the St Lucian landscape, especially in the rural areas. Small farmers were able to purchase land, build decent houses and improve their standard of living.

From 1975, St Lucia received preferential treatment for the sale of its bananas in the UK under the Lomé Convention, a trade and aid agreement between the then European Community (EC) and 71 African, Caribbean and Pacific countries signed in Lomé, Togo. The Convention was designed to provide a new framework for co-operation between the EC and ACP countries – in particular former British, Dutch, Belgian and French colonies. It had two main aspects: (a) it provided for most ACP agricultural and mineral exports to enter the EC free of duty with preferential access based on a quota system for products, such as sugar and beef, in competition with EC agriculture; and (b) the EC committed ECU[14] 3 billion for aid and investment in the ACP countries.

The Convention was renegotiated and renewed three times, culminating in Lomé IV (1990–1999). Two other important mechanisms alongside the Convention were the Stabex and Sysmin schemes, which provided compensatory finance to ACP states to counteract adverse fluctuations in world prices of key agricultural and mineral exports.

Changing trade regimes

With the emergence of the single European market at the end of 1992, the Caribbean's many smallholder banana farmers argued for the continuation of their preferential access to traditional markets, notably the UK. They feared that otherwise the EU would be flooded with cheap bananas from Central America, with devastating effects on several Caribbean economies. Negotiations led to the EU agreeing in 1993 to maintain this preferential access until the end of Lomé IV, pending possible negotiation on an extension.

In 1995, however, the US Government petitioned the WTO to investigate whether Lomé IV violated WTO rules. The WTO Dispute Settlement Body ruled in favour of the USA, effectively ending the cross-subsidies that had benefited ACP countries for many years. In June 2000, a new trade and aid agreement was reached between the EU and ACP countries. Signed in Cotonou, Benin, and known as the Cotonou Agreement, this set up a system of trade and co-operation pacts with individual nations.

In the region, the Caribbean Basin Initiative (CBI) – a temporary US programme that came into effect in January 1984 – provided several tariff and trade benefits to many Caribbean and Central American countries. However, once the USA had entered into the North American Free Trade Agreement (NAFTA) with Mexico in 1994, CBI countries lost their advantage relative to Mexico, a major competitor in industries such as textiles and apparel. Another regional agreement was the Caribbean-Canada Trade Agreement (CARIBCAN), also initiated in the 1980s, which was established to promote trade and investment and provide industrial co-operation through the preferential access of duty free goods from the countries of the Commonwealth Caribbean to the Canadian market.

Whatever the agreement – Cotonou, CBI, NAFTA or CARIBCAN – the benefits to the Caribbean have been mediated by the challenge of competing in an increasingly liberalised global market and the requirement of reciprocity imposed by the agreements and decisions of the WTO. There has been a declining trend in the region's agricultural exports since the first EU regime change in 1993.

Impacts on the St Lucian economy

CARICOM banana exporters were the most affected by the regime changes because of the small size of their operations and the high cost of production. Efforts to achieve economic diversification and competitiveness have not had the desired impact due to the significant structural deficiencies of the region's economies. The St Lucia Government's 2001 report to the WTO summarises the economic challenges:

> St Lucia has a small domestic market with relatively low levels of economic activity. Because of its small size the country faces structural disadvantages relative to larger economies since it is unable to benefit

> from economies of scale which would be essential if it is to be internationally competitive in the production of goods and services. The absence of a natural resource base further compounds the economic difficulties, as economic diversification efforts are stymied and the country is forced to continue to rely on a few economic sectors. The size of the labour force is also constrained by the small population. The inadequate level of labour supply contributes in large measure to the relatively undiversified structure of the economy. This problem is compounded by the paucity of educational opportunities and facilities, the fact that overseas training is expensive and the brain drain of skilled workers from the country.
>
> (WTO, 2001)

The St Lucia Ministry of Social Transformation, Culture and Local Government describes the country as an economy in transition. This is primarily the result of the changing global environment and the dramatic impacts that these changes have had on banana export earnings, tourism and manufacturing. The economy remains largely dependent and open, with goods and services (both import and export) contributing significantly to GDP. Foreign exchange earnings come mainly from agriculture and tourism, with a smaller contribution from manufacturing. Most of the goods consumed locally are imported. Exports declined during the past decade from 35 to 17 per cent of GDP, while the provision of services increased from 20 to 35 per cent (ibid.).

The St Lucian economy shows significant volatility. The Ministry noted that GDP growth averaged 7 per cent in the 1980s, followed by low rates in the early 1990s (an average of 1.3 per cent between 1993 and 1997), improvements in 1998 (3.07%) and 1999 (3.1%) as a result of growth in construction, tourism and financial services, followed by a downturn in 2000 (0.2%), significant contraction in 2001 (-4.6 per cent) and a marginal recovery in 2002 (0.1%) (ibid.).

The Prime Minister and Minister of Finance, Hon. Stephenson King, in his Budget Address for the 2008–2009 financial year, underscored this tendency to volatility indicating that:

> ... the economy experienced a general slowdown in the growth momentum that had been stimulated by activities associated with Cricket World Cup. Thus from a growth rate of 4.9 per cent in 2006, preliminary estimates indicate that real economic growth decelerated to 0.5 per cent in 2007.
>
> (King, 2008)

In addition to being highly vulnerable to weather shocks, the St Lucian economy has been subject to the vagaries of the various trade agreements described above and the consequent shifts in the competitive status of the country's exports. Between 1992 and 2005, annual export volumes in the banana industry fell from almost 133,000 tonnes to 30,000 tonnes (see Table 7.1). Revenues crashed from US$71 million to $31 million, while the number of banana farmers fell from 10,000 in the early 1990s to 1,800 in 2005.

Table 7.1 Banana exports from St Lucia, 1992–2005

Year	Export (tonnes)
1992	132,854
1993	120,127
1994	90,119
1995	103,668
1996	104,805
1997	71,397
1998	73,039
1999	65,196
2000	70,280
2001	34,044
2002	48,029
2003	34,420
2004	42,000[15]
2005	30,000[16]

Source: Kairi Consultants Ltd, 2007

Impacts of changes in trade policy on women

Robinson (2001) writes that:

> ... the recent sharp increases in poverty and unemployment levels experienced by women throughout the Windward Islands are a direct consequence of the decline in the banana industry ... [shown by] research conducted by CAFRA on the impact of new trade agreements on the living conditions of rural women. Respondents to the survey described life as hard and frustrating, indicating that they had found it difficult to survive and raise their children in living conditions that had worsened ... due to the decline of banana cultivation and prices.[17]

The Food and Agriculture Organization (FAO) also notes that 'a large majority of banana farmers are women, whose livelihoods are already being affected by this decline, with a sharp increase in poverty and unemployment levels affecting women throughout the Windward Islands' (Garcia, 2006).

Even before the declines in banana exports, however, women in agriculture were at a disadvantage due to gender inequalities in access to productive resources. Robinson (2001) points out that a dominant feature of Caribbean households is that approximately 40 per cent are headed by women who are the sole providers of both economic and material well-being and domestic services to the family. According to ECLAC (2005):

> ... notwithstanding significant progress in building productive capabilities among women, there remain significant gaps in assuring women's rights to natural and physical capital such as land, water, housing and transportation. Inevitably, there needs to be explicit recognition that the gender division of labour, in rural and agricultural systems in the Caribbean, has implications for women as primary caretakers at both the household and community levels. Relative to men, these multiple roles impact directly on women's time, nutritional status, mobility and morbidity, as well as the capacity to capitalise on potential opportunities for social and economic advancement.

Moreover, gender-based disparities in the agricultural sector have been exacerbated by an emphasis on the expansion of the large-scale production of export commodities such as bananas:

> Such systems of commodity production have proved discriminatory to women in agriculture. In addition, policy initiatives have tended to emphasise the generation and transfer of technologies suited to better endowed regions, large commercial enterprises and the export agriculture subsector. The link between technology transfer and gender, though not sufficiently evaluated, is recognised to have impacted negatively on women's capacity to participate and benefit equitably from mainstream agricultural development pursuits in the Caribbean. (ECLAC, 2005)

Measures taken to help women deal with policy changes

Measures to mitigate the effects of the declining banana industry have focused on promoting economic diversification and reducing poverty.

Social Recovery Programme

One of the major interventions by the Government was the Social Recovery Programme. This was financed by funds from a Special Framework of Assistance (SFA) established by the EC in 1992 to provide technical and financial assistance to banana farmers from ACP countries to assist them to adapt to the new market conditions.

The programme supported interventions at four distinct levels:

- Competitiveness within the banana sector;
- Diversification within the agricultural sector;
- Broader economic diversification outside of agriculture;
- Social adjustments linked to the contraction of the banana sector.

St Lucia was among the first countries in the Windward Islands to qualify for financial assistance, and the Social Recovery Programme was a crucial component of the SFA there. It started in 1999 and lasted for five years. Costing approximately EC$40 million,[18] its focus was on adult education, housing and sanitation, reproductive health care, recreation and sports activity, child protection measures, care of older persons, skills training, land reform and community empowerment activities. Rural women, children and older persons were specifically targeted (Flood-Beaubrun, 2000).

While no evaluation of the Programme, including no gender impact analysis, has been identified, a House of Commons report (2006a) refers to the SFA that funded the programme as '... a tale of unadulterated woe' and a 'sorry saga'; in another report (2006b) it described how: 'At the first ever International Banana Conference in 2004, the Minister (with oversight responsibility) said, "poorly designed projects and rigid Commission procedures regarding disbursements were flagged as factors contributing to this failure"'.

Further, the House of Commons reports indicate that the SFA allocated relatively small sums overall. As only a percentage of these funds was earmarked for social recovery, it is reasonable to conclude that only a small dent could be made on the structural and systemic problems.

St Lucia Rural Enterprise Project

Interventions by the international community have included the International Fund for Agricultural Development's (IFAD) St Lucia Rural Enterprise Project (1996–2003) (IFAD, 2007). This project, which was co-funded by the Caribbean Development Bank, sought to reduce the over-reliance of farmers on the banana industry and mitigate the risk of worsening terms of trade for bananas. Livestock development was promoted as an option for diversification, especially for resource-poor households that already relied on livestock as a source of income and nutrition. The demand for livestock products was expected to increase, and there was already ample scope for import substitution. The project encouraged farmers to serve not only the local market but also the tourist, regional and extra-regional market.

Project activities targeted rural resource-poor households that met the following criteria:

- Farm families on marginal land not exceeding five acres (at least 50 per cent of the income of these families should be derived from agriculture or related activities);
- Landless farmers who rear livestock;
- Rural woman-headed households and women farmers;
- Unemployed/underemployed youth;
- Rural households in which the annual per capita income falls below EC$3,000.[19]

In its mid-term evaluation of the project, IFAD noted that about 1,497 households would directly benefit from the production component, 923 of which were headed by women; within this total, 765 rural households would benefit directly from livestock interventions. IFAD reports that the total project cost was US$3.9 million. Livestock costs made up 14 per cent of this. The project was to operate nationwide; however, up to the point of the 2002 review, the focus was confined to an area in the south of the country, particularly for the community development and credit activities. Moreover, the review suggests that its overall impact to that point was minimal (see Box 7.1).

The most positive outcomes were in marketing and micro-enterprise development. Ecotourism activities were developed, and 528 people benefited from a fund that supported micro-enterprises in several types of economic activities. New outlets were developed for the output of the production component. Farmer associations, as well as private businesses, have been assisted in the development of trade links, and many initiatives have been undertaken to promote local produce and provide market information.

Lessons learned

The magnitude of the problem of increased poverty and vulnerability caused by the decline in agricultural output and trade requires interventions that are based on accurate baseline data. These should be carefully disaggregated in order to allow for appropriate planning and design and effective delivery, and specifically differentiated to measure the impact on the lives of vulnerable target groups.

The two interventions included here illustrate the following weaknesses in economic and social policy planning and implementation:

- Insufficient evidence-based project planning and design;
- Comparatively low levels of financial investment;

- Weak capacity of state institutions for absorbing project resources and delivering services in a timely and efficacious manner;
- Weak monitoring and evaluation systems and limited measurable impact assessment;
- Absence of a systemic plan and scale-up strategy;
- Lack of integration of projects into a national policy framework.

On this last point, an area where such an integrated policy and programmatic approach could make a significant difference to the prospects for small farmers is in improving linkages between tourism and agriculture. The Caribbean Policy Development Centre (2008: 13) notes that:

> ... seasonality of both crop production in agriculture and tourism's requirements intensifies the case for information systems that correlate visitor arrivals (demand) with harvest schedules (supply), given the lack of storage and processing facilities, tenure and land-use patterns, and a general absence of a business approach to agricultural production and marketing among small farmers.

The report by ECLAC (2005) cited earlier provides insight into some of the key lessons in relation to gender and agriculture. It notes that for most CARICOM countries, the disadvantages of smallness and extreme openness mean that external shocks have an almost instantaneous impact on the micro-economy of households. The reconfiguration of imperatives in this regard affects the decision-making framework not only at international, regional and national levels but also, as importantly, at the level of communities and households.

The report notes that interventions to address the impacts of trade liberalisation tend to be gender blind, failing to take into account such realities as women's limited access to requisite resources and their almost exclusive responsibility for social reproduction, which fetters their potential capacity to take advantage of emerging opportunities in the formal market.

The report rightly recommends more rational and even-handed policy formulation and implementation processes that take due account of gender asymmetries within the economy and the need for due recognition of unpaid work, the care economy, the informal sector and subsistence production that characterise the role of women in rural and agricultural systems throughout the Caribbean.

Box 7.1 Limitations of the St Lucia Rural Enterprise Project

The project relied heavily on the performance of extension services and of other public organisations. Despite the training received by extension officers, staff morale and commitment were low, and little energy was spent on the project. Eventually, the Project Management Unit succeeded in getting the Ministry of Agriculture to assign extension officers to work directly with the project, thus improving the project-beneficiary interface.

Overall, the project struggled with serious delays at the beginning, especially in its production component. There were delays in the implementation of the livestock component. Pure-bred animals were imported, and the infrastructure for the animal breeding programme was completed. The dispersal schemes, with the exception of rabbit rearing, were delayed at first but were eventually initiated.

The plant propagation programme was delayed, but it was expected to deliver benefits before the end of the project's life. Micro-irrigation was even less successful and any tangible benefits were uncertain. The results of the research and extension programmes did not meet expectations. Despite the setbacks, production under the project increased and it is projected to cover the needs of the local market in the near future. Expansion in export markets was underway at the time of the mid-term review.

The performance of the credit component was poor. Staff performance, particularly that of the credit officer, was problematic. Reporting was inadequate and loan delinquency high. Few loans (7.5%) were directed towards livestock development. The loan delinquency rates were far higher than expected at appraisal, albeit lower among women, among whom the average loan size was larger than it was among men.

Impact was limited. Training in business skills was provided to 130 beneficiaries, and as many jobs were created.

Source: IFAD, 2007

References

Caribbean Policy Development Centre (2008). 'Fostering Better Linkages Between Agriculture and Tourism in St Lucia', Caribbean Policy Development Centre, Bridgetown, Barbados, http://www.cpdcngo.org/IMG/pdf/Microsoft_Word_-_St._Lucia_Market_Access_Research_-_pdf.pdf

ECLAC (2005). 'Agricultural Transformation and Gender Considerations in Caribbean Economies', Economic Commission of Latin America and the Caribbean (ECLAC), LC/CAR/R.85, December, http://www.eclac.cl/publicaciones/xml/1/26011/R.85.pdf

ECLAC (2008). 'Impact of Changes in the European Union Import Regimes for Sugar, Banana and Rice on Selected CARICOM Countries', Economic Commission of Latin America and the Caribbean (ECLAC), LC/CAR/L.168, May.

Flood-Beaubrun, S (2000). Statement by the Minister of Health, Human Services, Family Affairs and Gender Relations, St Lucia to the 23rd Special Session of the UN General Assembly, June 2000, see http://www.un.org/womenwatch/daw/followup/beijing+5stat/statments/saintlucia7.htm

Garcia, Z (2006). 'Impact of International Agricultural Trade and Gender Equity: Selected Country Case Studies', in Agriculture, Trade Relations and Gender, Food and Agriculture Organization, Rome, http://www.fao.org/docrep/009/a0493e/a0493e04.htm

House of Commons (2006a). 'Special Framework of Assistance for Traditional Suppliers of Bananas', Select Committee on European Scrutiny Fifteenth Report, http://www.publications.parliament.uk/pa/cm200607/cmselect/cmeuleg/41-xv/4109.htm

House of Commons (2006b). 'Special Framework of Assistance for Traditional Suppliers of Bananas', Select Committee on European Scrutiny Seventh Report, http://www.parliament.the-stationery-office.com/pa/cm200607/cmselect/cmeuleg/41-vii/41vii05.htm

IFAD (2007). 'Saint Lucia: Rural Enterprise Project', International Fund for Agricultural Development (IFAD), http://www.ifad.org/lrkm/region/pl/lc_414.htm

Kairi Consultants Ltd (2007). Trade Adjustment & Poverty in St. Lucia 2005/06; Volume 11 – The Macro-Economic and Social Analysis, submitted to the Caribbean Development Bank, http://www.caribank.org/titanweb/cdb/webcms.nsf/AllDoc/6DF4C2923C0B51E3042573D2004F1EF0/$File/SLUCPAVolII.pdf

King, S (2008). 'From Vision to Implementation: Rallying Our People for Development in an Era of Global Opportunities and Challenges', Budget Address for the Financial Year 2008/2009, 21 April, http://www.pm.gov.lc/budgetaddresses/BudgetAddress2008.pdf

Ministry of Social Transformation, Culture and Local Government (n.d.). 'Social Development and Poverty Reduction', PowerPoint presentation, http://www.oest.oas.org/chilesolidario/documentos/Dia_2/12_St.%20Lucia_Eng.ppt

Robinson, N (2001). 'The Caribbean: Small Island Developing States Caught Between Elephants and Hippos', presentation at a seminar and workshop 'Can

Trade Generate Development for Women?', Copenhagen, 27 October, http://www.kulu.dk/Financing/Seminar/nelciarobinson.htm

WTO (2001). 'Trade Policy Review: St. Lucia, Report by the Government', World Trade Organization (WTO), Geneva, May, http://ctrc.sice.oas.org/trc/SaintLucia/SaintLuciaTP.asp

Service Liberalisation

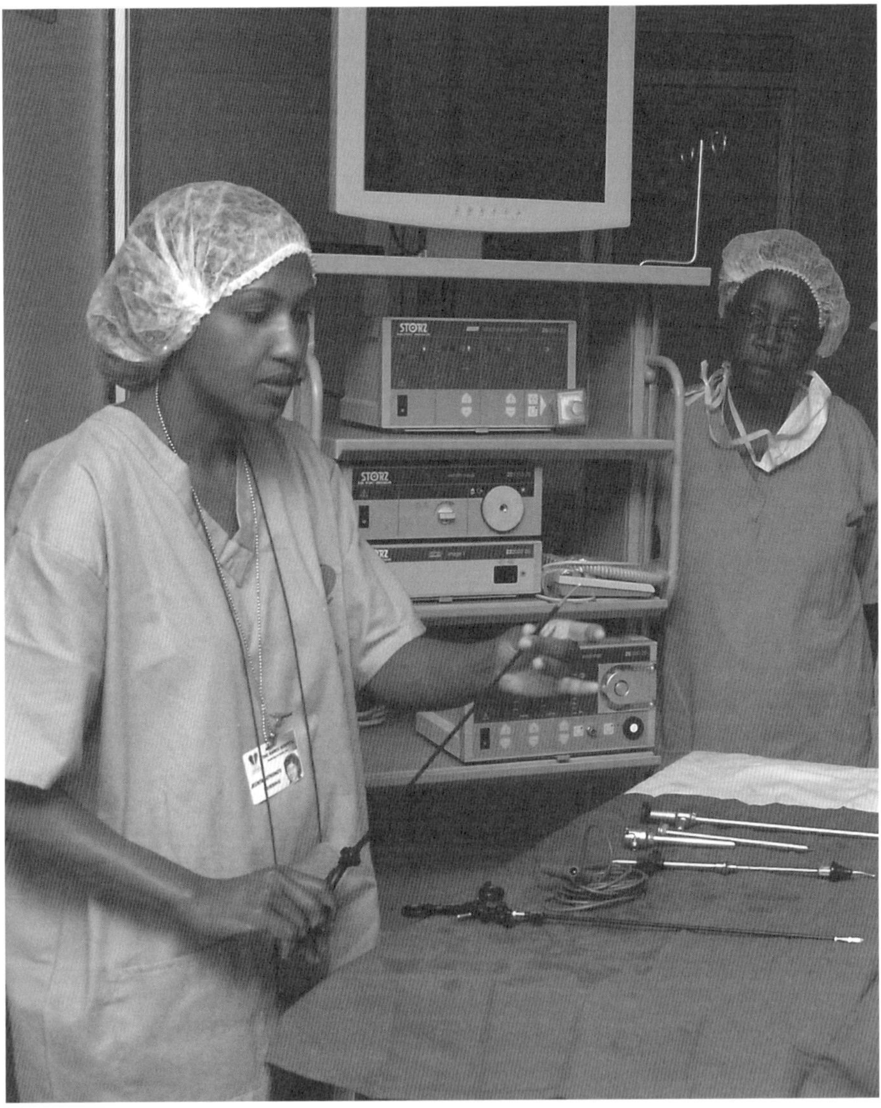
STORZ
STORZ

8 Moving Forwards, Falling Backwards: GATS and the Migration of Skilled Professionals from the Caribbean

Carol Narcisse

Background

The world's peoples have always crossed borders in search of new opportunities to improve their personal educational, skill, economic and/or social capacity. This movement of women and men is now of staggering proportions. According to the International Organization for Migration (n.d.), there are currently an estimated 200 million international migrants, some 3 per cent of the global population; 49.6 per cent of them are women, demonstrating the strong feminisation of migration patterns.

The Caribbean region has been defined by a history of migration, both voluntary and forced. Skilled and unskilled Caribbean people have travelled within the region and to Europe and North America in search of a better life. Thomas-Hope (2005) refers to a Caribbean 'culture' of migration, noting that:

> Opportunities for movement are readily taken by persons in a wide range of skills and education categories, not only workers but tertiary and secondary level students as well. This makes recruitment for migration, for almost any purpose, easy ...

Indeed, she suggests that:

> ... migration potentially extends the opportunities for populations living in limited national spaces. When and where opportunities allow persons to extend their livelihoods into the wider global environment, and since people at all levels are pre-conditioned to associate the achievement of their goals with migration, then such an opportunity is immediately regarded as the desired option. The more the society depends on this option, the more it continues to do so until, as in the Caribbean and across many other developing countries in Africa and Asia, it becomes part of the normal consideration within the careers of individuals and life cycles of households. (ibid.)

Women are the majority of migrants from the Caribbean. For example, as cited by Thomas-Hope (2002), the Caribbean Community Regional Census Office showed in 1994 that in every decade since the 1950s 43–47 per cent of Caribbean migrants to the USA were male, compared to 53–57 per cent who were female. She further notes that:

> In all the major groups of Caribbean nationals in Canada and for each decade of their arrival, females have been larger in number than males. The percentage male and female in the immigrant stock (1981) were for Jamaica, 43.7% male and 56.3% female; Trinidad & Tobago, 47% male, 53% female; Barbados, 44.7% male, 54.4% female; Haiti, 45.6% male, 54.4% female. (ECLAC, 2000 in ibid.)

Changes in trade and economic policy: trade agreements and the movement of labour

Trade liberalisation has applied in the main to goods, with trade in services being less robust. The WTO indicates that ' ...while services currently account for over 60 per cent of global production and employment, they represent no more than 20 per cent of total trade' (n.d.) It emphasises, however, that 'This – seemingly modest – share should not be underestimated ... [as] many services, which have long been considered genuine domestic activities, have increasingly become internationally mobile' (ibid.).

The General Agreement on Trade in Services was brought into force by the WTO in January 1995 as a result of negotiations in the Uruguay Round. Under the GATS, the movement of labour is restricted to the movement of 'natural persons' as service suppliers. 'Natural persons' refers to actual individuals (as opposed to companies or other institutional actors) subject to physical laws and being 'persons of one Member entering the territory of another Member to supply a service (e.g., accountants, doctors or teachers). The Annex on Movement of Natural Persons specifies, however, that Members remain free to operate measures regarding citizenship, residence or access to the employment market on a permanent basis' (Nielson, 2002).

Some regional free trade agreements go further than the GATS. However, in these agreements too there is selectivity as to which groups are accorded labour mobility. A joint WTO-World Bank Symposium in 2002 noted that:

> Some agreements cover the mobility of people in general (i.e. including permanent migration and non-workers); others offer free movement of labour (including entry to the local labour market); others are limited to facilitated movement for certain kinds of trade- or investment-related activities; and others, like the GATS, are confined to temporary movement and only for service suppliers (and explicitly exclude entry to the

> labour market or permanent migration). Additionally, some cover workers at all skill levels, while others are limited to the higher skilled.
> (Nielson, 2002)

Specific provisions include 'full national treatment and market access for service suppliers (ANZCERTA); commitments on visas (NAFTA), including for groups beyond service suppliers (US-Jordan); [and] special market access or facilitated access for certain groups, including beyond service suppliers (CARICOM, NAFTA)' (ibid.).[20]

As the movement of people has increased globally, governments and the international community have responded with migration policies and regulations. By the early 1990s, countries were emphasising migrants' skills and favouring those that met 'specific labour needs, such as those in science and technology, those with skills considered in short supply and those with capital to invest' (Merkin, 2005). In order to do so, they established preferential categories (USA) or points systems (Australia and Canada) (ibid.).

A variety of factors have influenced this trend:

> Significant labour shortfalls in a number of sectors due to skill shortages, population ageing and population decline have fuelled an increase in the intake of migrant workers ... intake that is limited to highly skilled workers ... Although receiving countries have emphasised the need to attract highly skilled workers, population ageing and rising job expectations are also producing labour shortages in such low-skilled fields as agriculture, construction and domestic services. (ibid.)

Targeted recruitment of skilled workers as a development strategy is being utilised mainly by developed countries. Merkin indicates that 'While one third of developed countries seek to increase the immigration of the highly skilled, only 8 per cent of developing countries pursue such a strategy'.

The economic and development costs of migration

According to Degazon-Johnson (2007: 2–3), the trade in skills

> ... offers opportunities to highly skilled persons to exercise their right to free movement in search for career enrichment. The flip side to this may be, at the same time, the depletion of human capital of small countries in particular, human capital which has been created through health and education outlay supported through the revenue of their tax payers. The trade in skills may involve 'the buyers' – universities, schools and hospitals – seeking skills abroad to develop a dynamic professional staff, but it can also involve unscrupulous recruiters who seduce the unwitting to

> undertake positions without providing them with full information about these positions. Migration – either temporary or permanent – has become a major part of the trade in the highly skilled, certainly for the Commonwealth Caribbean.

The Caribbean supplies workers for the skilled and unskilled labour force of North America and the UK and struggles to balance the loss with the gain from remittances – an important source of foreign exchange and for many countries a significant percentage of gross domestic product (GDP). Mishra (2006) indicates that:

> Caribbean countries have lost 10–40 per cent of their labor force due to emigration to OECD member countries. The migration rates are particularly striking for the high skilled. Many countries have lost more than 70 per cent of their labor force with more than 12 years of completed schooling – among the highest emigration rates in the world.

The economic cost to the Caribbean of the level of migration of nurses and teachers is considerable. In a presentation in 2005, Winston Cox, then Deputy Secretary-General of the Commonwealth Secretariat, noted that studies estimate the cost of nurses migrating from CARICOM countries in 1999–2000 to be in the region of US$16.7 million. This, he said, was:

> ... a transfer of resources from lower-income Caribbean countries to higher-income destination countries that is only partially offset by the reverse flow of remittances. ... studies have also shown that due to the ageing population in OECD countries, the demand for health-care professionals, especially nurses, in those countries will rise rapidly over the next 15 years'.

This rise in demand, he noted, would certainly lead to increased recruitment.

However, as Thomas-Hope (2002) posits, the volume of skilled migration does not itself determine the extent of impact of the movement or indeed its role as a 'brain drain'. She suggests that the impact is relative to the wider social and economic environment and compensatory movements and processes. Negative impacts are more likely if: (a) the inflows of people through return migration or new migration is insufficient in quantity or quality; (b) the inflow of other forms of capital (financial or social) do not compensate for the loss of human resources; (c) the national or regional potential for skill replacement is less than the resource losses due to out-migration; and (d) a larger or more specialised skilled labour force is being produced in individual countries or the region than can be absorbed by either (ibid.).

An examination of the situation with respect to the out-migration of nurses and teachers from the Caribbean, on the basis of the criteria that Thomas-Hope sets out, suggests that the impact is indeed a drain that will have negative long-term implications for development in the region unless positive measures and policies are put in place.

Increased recruitment of nurses and teachers

Direct recruitment of professionals from the Caribbean, Africa and Asia has increased in recent years. Citing trends since 2000, Thomas-Hope (2005) notes that there has been 'a new wave of recruitment of skilled persons and students'. This recruitment has been not only through advertisements in the local media but also through in-country recruitment centres, as well as through 'a range of informal operators, most of whom are Caribbean nationals' (ibid.).

The impact on the nursing and teaching professions of the Caribbean – and, by extension, the health and educational services – has been significant. Degazon-Johnson (2007) outlines that 'the Pan-American Health Organization estimated that between 2001–2004, more than a quarter of the 13,046 nursing positions in the Caribbean region were vacant, and whilst 1,199 new nurses graduated during that period 900 nurses left the region'. A smaller-scale but similar pattern of nursing outflows can be seen from small States such as Samoa in the Pacific to Australia and New Zealand, and the case is also true for the out-migration of nurses from several countries in sub-Saharan Africa, e.g., Malawi.

For teachers, Degazon-Johnson (2007: 5) states that: 'Jamaica with a population of fewer than 3 million lost to the UK between 2001–03 nearly 1,000 teachers, more than a country the size of Canada with a population of 30 million. Guyana trains 300 teachers each year and loses that number to migration overseas'.

As Thomas-Hope (2005) points out 'it is the schools and health clinics that serve the poorest sectors of the society that suffer the most'.

Gender issues in the recruitment of nurses and teachers

Migration of nurses and teachers has particular gender dimensions. International recruiters are targeting employees in gender-segregated professions. Women are the greater percentage of workers in the 'caring professions', particularly in the health and education sectors. These sectors are characterised by relatively low pay, difficult working conditions and limited opportunities for advancement. Given the large numbers of female-headed households in Jamaica, women teachers and nurses may feel additional pressure to provide for their families as the sole or primary breadwinner. The need to sustain their households may be a 'push' factor that leads these professionals to seek or accept work abroad (see Box 8.1).

Box 8.1 The case of Jamaican nurses

Jamaica loses roughly 8 per cent of its registered nurses and more than 20 per cent of its specialist nurses annually (*Daily Gleaner*, 2002). Migration provides these women with higher incomes. Additionally, their families who remain at home benefit from remittances, which are then channelled into the economy. However, there are extremely high costs involved in migration. One is that many women must leave their children and make long-term arrangements for them or for elders if they work abroad. These arrangements may be financially taxing for the immigrants, and there are additional emotional and familial repercussions when women are separated from their loved ones. Moreover, since many women may emigrate legally but remain illegally (since labour flows have not been liberalised like capital flows), they not see their children for many years. In addition, a woman's immigrant lifetime earnings may decrease since she will not accrue retirement or social security savings in Jamaica while she is working abroad.

Yet another concern is that recruitment agencies target experienced nurses and specialists (obstetric, paediatric or geriatric nurses, for example) for overseas employment. The University Hospital of the West Indies has in past years had to close wards because of the severe shortage of nursing personnel. In 2001, the Ministry of Health noted that the health sector had been operating at 75 per cent capacity for several years. Since it takes three years to train nurses to replace the ones who have migrated, Jamaica is in a constant state of 'catch up' to try and make-up for the shortfall. The staffing shortage means that there is an inequitable distribution of nurses between urban and rural areas – with rural areas coping with fewer nurses.

The overseas demand is likely to continue. As the US population ages there will be a greater need for nursing staff, but the average age of a working nurse is 43.3 years and she is likely to retire just as her cohorts will require more care. Few college students are entering the profession because of the pay, working conditions and perceived lack of status. Rather than respond to the 'shortage' by increasing wages in the sector, thereby stimulating an increase in supply, US hospitals have actively recruited Jamaican nurses, for whom wages and working conditions in the USA are better than at home.

Box 8.1 (continued)

The Government of Jamaica has grappled with finding an appropriate response, as the loss of public investment is considerable. In October 2001, Minister of Foreign Trade Anthony Hylton announced that it would try to reduce the emigration of teachers and nurses to the USA to prevent the 'brain drain' of the country's brightest professionals. In October 2003, Prime Minister PJ Patterson proposed that Jamaica train teachers and nurses (both nationals and foreigners) specifically for 'export', as the country would benefit from the fees charged. The Government is also reported to have started discussions with the USA about increased US support for tertiary education in Jamaica.

Source: Adapted from Wyss and White, 2004

Women may be more likely than men to use illegal recruitment and migration channels because of their limited access to credit and legal counsel. Some agencies charge fees to the migrant, and women may go into long-term debt (since they have less access to money and networks than men) to pay the charges. Despite the fact that nurses and teachers are highly trained, the receiving government may not accept sending countries' qualifications and credentials as equivalent and may assign the migrant work that is lower paid or has lower status.

Measures taken in response to the migration of skilled labour

Countries in the region have taken steps to develop a programme to manage migration and to put in place appropriate codes of practice for recruitment. The Managed Migration Programme of the Caribbean resulted from a 2001 PAHO/CPC-initiated review of the scope and impact of nurses' migration in the Caribbean, which led to the creation of a steering committee (Salmon *et al.*, 2007). This defined the Managed Migration Programme as '... a regional strategy for retaining an adequate number of competent nursing personnel to deliver health programs and services to the Caribbean nationals' (ibid.).

The report further indicates that:

> ... a Managed Migration Implementation Team was created in 2001, from which grew a partnership of national, regional, bilateral and international partners. The list includes ... PAHO/CPC, Commonwealth Ministers Secretariat for Nursing and Midwifery, UWI, GRASP Inc, the American Nurses Credentialing Center Magnet Program, International

Labour Organization, and individual governments within and outside of the region. (Salmon *et al.*, 2007)

The Programme addresses six areas: terms and conditions of work; recruitment, retention and training; value of nursing; utilisation and deployment; management practices; and policy development (ibid.). This initiative has affected country-specific policy and programmes (see Box 8.2).

Box 8.2 Country-specific initiatives to tackle migration of nurses

St Vincent and the Grenadines: According to the Ministry of Health Planning Unit, the Government of St Vincent and the Grenadines is establishing bilateral agreements to obtain compensation from health-care provider institutions that recruit nurses away from the country. At the time of hiring, the US partners will reimburse the Government with training costs of EC$45,000 (approximately US$17,000) for each Vincentian nurse they employ. The funds will be reinvested by the Government to enhance nurse training.

Jamaica: The Jamaican Nursing Council notes that its nurses seek registration to practice in the USA through an arrangement that allows them to work in Miami two weeks per month (travel costs are paid by the nurses) and in Jamaica for the other two weeks. In this way nurses gain additional skills, earn more money to support their family and assist with their own country's staffing needs.

Antigua and Grenada: Through agreements between the two countries' ministries of health in 2003, Grenada opened up its excess training capacity to nursing students from neighbouring Antigua. Twenty individuals from Antigua will receive nursing training in Grenada at a minimal cost. The Regional Examination for Nurses Registration and the Common Nursing Education Standards in the Caribbean allow the Grenadian trained nurses to return and practice in Antigua.

St Kitts and Nevis: An offshore nursing school, the St Kitts International School of Nursing, has been established with the aim of meeting the needs of the global market for trained professional nurses. It is projected that this will admit an average of 1,500 individuals per year from around the world.

Source: Adapted from Salmon *et al.*, 2007

A Commonwealth Code of Practice for the International Recruitment of Health Workers was adopted in May 2003 and a Commonwealth Teacher Recruitment Protocol in September 2004. A Quality Mark for recruitment agencies was also adopted in 2003. Cox (2005) explains:

> ... neither code is a legally binding document but, by virtue of their moral authority, they provide guidelines for the international recruitment of health workers and teachers in a manner that takes into account the interests and welfare of the professionals, the obligations of the recruiting countries and the potential impact of such recruitment on health and education services in the source countries, which are for the most part developing countries.

Lessons learned

Migration affects the individual migrant, her family, community and nation; it also has numerous impacts on the receiving country. Though migrants have agency, they are also affected by external demand, conditions and forces. Although the liberalisation of trade has been applied more to goods than to services and is slower still in its application to the free movement of labour, targeted recruitment of skilled labour is nonetheless increasing. Among the most targeted groups are teachers and nurses, both of which are highly feminised professions in the Caribbean. With female household headship in the region over 40 per cent, any policies or programmes for the management of migration among occupational groups should take into account family and community impacts and address these through positive measures related to family unification and social protection.

Managed migration of skilled labour can mitigate negative economic and social impacts in source countries and ensure good practice in the receiving countries' observance of appropriate labour standards and protection of human rights. Rather than just reacting to the external pull on their skilled labour force, Caribbean countries can deepen their labour force management to include managed migration strategies. Unemployment among women is more than double that for men in the region. A managed migration programme that identifies opportunities and trends in overseas employment, trains women (and men) for these occupations and ensures good practice in recruitment and conditions of work can go a long way to improve development outcomes at the national and individual levels.

References

Cox, W (2005). 'Opening Remarks' at a Commonwealth meeting on Training and Temporary Movement: Towards a Trade and Development Approach in the Caribbean Region, Sherbourne Conference Centre, Barbados, 30–31 March, http://www.crnm.org/documents/press_releases_2005/caribbean_nurses/address_by_Mr.Cox.pdf

Daily Gleaner (2002). 'US, UK Seeking More Local Nurses', 20 May, cited in Thomas-Hope (2005).

Degazon-Johnson, R (2007). 'The Trade in the Highly Skilled: The Case of the Commonwealth Caribbean', paper presented to the Institute of Commonwealth Studies Seminar on International Competitiveness of Small Vulnerable Economies, London, July.

ECLAC (2000). 'Demographic Bulletin: International Migration in Latin America', Santiago, Chile, XXXIII: 65, cited in Thomas-Hope (2005).

International Organization for Migration (n.d.). 'Global Estimates and Trends', http://www.iom.int/jahia/Jahia/about-migration/facts-and-figures/global-estimates-and-trends

Mirkin, B (2005). 'International Migration Policies: An Overview', presentation at the Caribbean Expert Group Meeting on Migration, Human Rights and Development in the Caribbean, Port of Spain, Trinidad, September.

Mishra, P (2006). 'Emigration and Brain Drain: Evidence from the Caribbean', IMF Working Paper, WP/06/25.

Nielson, J (2002). 'Current Regimes for Temporary Movement of Service Providers: Labour Mobility in Regional Trade Agreements', report of Joint WTO-World Bank Symposium on Movement of Natural Persons (Mode 4) Under the GATS, 11–12 April, www.wto.org/english/tratop_e/serv_e/symp_apr_02_nielson1_e.doc

Salmon, ME, Yan, J, Hewitt, H and Guisinger, V (2007). 'Managed Migration: The Caribbean Approach to Addressing Nursing Services Capacity', *Health Services Research*, 32 (3 Pt 2): 1354–1372, http://www.pubmedcentral.nih.gov/articlerender.fcgi?artid=1955379

Thomas-Hope, E (2002). 'Skilled Labour Migration from Developing Countries: Study on the Caribbean Region', International Migration Papers #50, International Migration Programme, International Labour Office, Geneva.

Thomas-Hope, E (2005). 'Current Trends and Issues in Caribbean Migration' in *Regional and International Migration in the Caribbean and its Impact on Sustainable Development: Compendium on Recent Research on Migration in the Caribbean*, presented at the Caribbean Expert Group Meeting on Migration, Human Rights and Development in the Caribbean, Port of Spain, Trinidad, September.

Wyss, B and White, M (2004). *The Effects of Trade Liberalization on Jamaica's Poor: An Analysis of Agriculture and Services*, Women's Edge Coalition, Washington, DC.

WTO (n.d.). 'The General Agreement on Trade in Services (GATS): Objectives, Coverage and Disciplines', World Trade Organization, http://www.wto.org/english/tratop_e/serv_e/gatsqa_e.htm

9 Digitalising It: Women and Trade in ICT in Developing Countries

Mariama Williams and Carol Narcisse

According to the International Telecommunication Union (ITU), information and communications technologies such as the internet, mobile phones and computers can contribute to enhanced productivity, competitiveness, growth, wealth creation and poverty reduction, and can spur the knowledge-based economy (ITU, 2008). They can have a significant impact on the lives of women and men by transforming the nature and organisation of work in the industrial and service sectors (Hafkin, 2002); they also have implications for agriculture and rural development. For example, BRIDGE reports that in Gujarat, India, women dairy producers use the Dairy Information System Kiosk to maximise productivity and earnings (Gurumurthy, 2004).

With increasing trade and investment liberalisation, ICT will become an essential feature of developing countries' economies. Increasingly, the workforce in many countries is working with some form of ICT, and women are rapidly being absorbed into the outsourced areas of call centres, data processing, tourism, banking, finance and the insurance industry. The use of ICT devices such as PDAs (personal digital assistants) and financial software applications in micro-credit activity is also being explored by development agencies and NGOs to enhance women's economic opportunities.

Changing trade policy in the ICT sector

Many developing countries have fully or partially liberalised their ICT sectors under the WTO or through bilateral or regional trade agreements that go beyond agreements reached at the multilateral level. Internationally, the General Agreement on Trade in Services and the 1996 Ministerial Declaration on Trade in Information Technology Products (ITA) are the key arbiters of the rules that apply to telecommunications and overall ICT regulation and authorisation (see Box 9.1). The GATS schedules contain additional trade commitments by individual member countries concerning specific services, including basic telecommunications services (ITU, 2008).

Box 9.1 Trade in information technology products

The Ministerial Declaration on Trade in Information Technology Products (ITA) was concluded by 29 participants at the Singapore Ministerial Conference in December 1996. According to the WTO, the 'ITA is solely a tariff cutting mechanism'; it does not specifically address non-trade barriers. It offers coverage of three basic areas: (1) all products listed in the Declaration must be covered; (2) all must be reduced to a zero tariff level; and (3) all other duties and charges must be bound at zero. While there are no exceptions to product coverage, it is possible to have an extended implementation period for sensitive items. All commitments are on an MFN basis. The implementation and oversight of the ITA is administered by the Committee of Participants on the Expansion of Trade in Information Technology Products. The Committee periodically reviews product coverage (so-called ITA II) specified in the Attachments to the Declaration.

Though no developing countries were signatories to the original ITA, the following are now signed-up participants: Costa Rica; El Salvador; India; Macau, China; Malaysia; Panama; Philippines; and Thailand. As of February 2008, 107 WTO members had made commitments to open some or all segments of their telecommunications markets to foreign suppliers, and 80 members had committed themselves to the 'Reference Paper', a blueprint for sector reform (WTO, n.d.).

This liberalisation is occurring through many different pathways. In some cases, countries are dismantling their system of state and monopoly control of telecommunications sectors by privatising and selling them off and/or issuing additional licences to encourage more competition; others are simply removing tariff and non-tariff barriers and opening up the sectors to foreign participation. ICT-specific liberalisation, in combination with other aspects of liberalisation such as trade-related intellectual property rights and trade-related investment agreements, has implications for women's and men's employment opportunities, conditions of work and overall access to ICT services. These services range from radio, TV and the internet to electronic banking, online educational services, telemedicine and data processing. In all cases, women's roles, needs and concerns will be significantly affected.

ICT-related trade

ICT is a complex area and is highly nuanced in its impact on women's and men's employment, and in their ownership, control and access to its products and services. Women and men are users, workers, service providers and creators of ICT. For ease of presentation, this chapter adopts the World Bank (2007) framework and distinguishes between three types of trade: ICT-enabled trade, which covers employment-related activities in call centres and data processing for overseas clients; ICT-facilitated trade, which explores the utilisation of websites and other ways of selling products; and ICT trade, which focuses on international phone calls, websites and email. This case study is primarily interested in ICT-enabled trade as it seeks to examine the impact of trade policy on women's employment.

ICT-enabled trade

In the first phase of IT trade, which was labour-intensive electronics assembly line work, women were employed to make IT products for low wages, working long hours in unsafe and unhealthy working conditions. In the more recent phases, women continue to predominate as a source of cheap labour, but now are using IT in their work – for example, using automated technology in call centres and teleworking. However, as an economy progresses towards more knowledge-based activities requiring higher computer literacy and technical skills, there has been a noticeable downturn in the employment of women. Similarly, as more automatic and robotic type processes are involved, women's employment has declined (Hafkin, 2002). There is increasing evidence of this in several Asian countries, with Malaysia a good case in point. In the peak days of electronic assembly line sweatshops, women made up over 90 per cent of the workforce; by 1986, however, they comprised 67 per cent of the workforce in the IT sector.

At the same time, there has been an increase in women's employment in the service industry. Because of their typing skills on the QWERTY keyboard, they make up 90 per cent of data entry workers in the Caribbean, China, India, Philippines, Singapore and Vietnam (Hafkin and Taggert, 2001). Women dominate online export-oriented information processing (medical transcription, airlines, banking and insurance). In banking, for example, they predominate in information processing and computer typing, and as tellers. In India, women make up 70 per cent of the workforce in insurance, printing and publishing. The majority of staff in call centre customer services are women (Hafkin and Taggert, 2001). Medical transcribers in India earn an average of US$1,200 a year, which is significantly less than the US$25,000 that would be earned by their American counterparts.

However, in the high-tech areas of software and computer analysis women are in the minority. A study in Vietnam shows that men tend to dominate the conceptualisation aspects (designing and building) of software, whereas women dominate the testing or executing tasks (commonly explained by their calm and patient ability to spend long hours running the same test). Similarly, in examining the ICT sector in Barbados and Jamaica, Dunn and Dunn (1999) note the wide disparities in wages and working conditions between high- and low-tech industries. Both wages and working conditions are much better in the (male-dominated) software programming companies than in the (female-dominated) data entry companies.

In some developing countries, such as Brazil, India and Malaysia, women make up 20–30 per cent of workers in the professional levels of the software industry (for example software programmers and computer analysts) because of proactive national ICT policies that focus on higher education for women (Hafkin, 2002). This is comparable to the situation in Organisation for Economic Co-operation and Development (OECD) countries such as the UK and USA, where about 25 per cent of computer professionals are women (1998–2004 data cited in Van Welsum and Montagnier, 2007). Hafkin and Taggert (2001) note that African countries such as Togo and the United Republic of Tanzania are also quickly moving up this ladder. In both developing and developed countries women form the majority (90%) of the clerical workforce in the IT sectors.

Just as in the old electronics assembly line sweatshops of the 1970s and 1980s, the new trade-enabled ICT work environment poses particular health and safety hazards for women. Lack of adequate breaks and ergonomic working conditions mean that women suffer from chronic and sometimes debilitating eye strain, back injuries and a multiplicity of repetitive strain injuries. ICT is also associated with the expansion of informal sector activities such as home-based work (old IT) and teleworking (new ICT), both typical subcontracting activities. As in the rest of the informal sector, contracts and benefits are lacking in these sectors in developing countries.

ICT-facilitated trade

ICT-facilitated trade is best exemplified by India, which since 1984 has evolved an elaborate strategy for building a knowledge-based economy across all sectors (agriculture, services and manufacturing). This strategy has enabled Indian firms to penetrate global export markets in a wide range of product sectors and areas. It is grounded in a strong education policy, starting with basic education and going up to tertiary level.

ICT trade

Current data show that women are 38 per cent of all internet users in Latin America, 22 per cent in Asia and just 6 per cent in the Middle East. No regional figures by gender are available for Africa (Hafkin and Taggert, 2001). Women are very involved in domestically oriented ICT-driven profit centres such as phone shops, which require little capital and skills. These have been profitable areas for women in Bangladesh, Ghana and Morocco.

Impacts of changes in trade policy on women

In any examination of the impact of changes in trade policy on women, the distinction between ICT-enabled trade, ICT-facilitated trade and ICT trade is crucial, given their often quite distinct and contradictory effects.

In the case of ICT-enabled trade, the effect of liberalisation is somewhat different than with traditional products. For example, trade policy here is more about export promotion (linked to investment and intellectual property rights protection) than simply about classic tariff or non-tariff barrier reductions. The focus is on welcoming foreign investors and offering inducements to enable them to produce IT and IT-related products in a relatively secure (with regard to profit repatriation, trade facilitation and taxation measures) and conducive environment. It can be argued that openness to trade means more employment for women. This is certainly the case with the export of services via call centres and teleworking. The downside is the impact on women's health and morbidity, which must be taken into account as well as its effect on wages, benefits and opportunities for economic advancement and long-lasting empowerment. Of course, the usual substitution effect may occur if wages in the export sector exceed wages in the domestic competing sector, leading workers to switch into the higher wage sector and affecting the domestic demand for labour. Most developing economies, however, have a labour surplus.

In the area of ICT-facilitated trade, it is generally argued that liberalisation poses both challenges and opportunities for the domestic sector. Challenges arise in terms of global competition for products, which can now be purchased through the internet, etc., but this depends on the nature of cross-border online payment and on bricks and mortar systems (including customs/trade facilitation) for package distribution. Opportunities arise in terms of local firms having direct access to a wider market of international clients through the internet and e-commerce. This can clearly help small and medium-sized firms, including those that are owned by women.

In terms of ICT trade the issue is at least threefold: price effect; domestic policy/social regulation effects; and the impact on government revenues. In the first place, liberalisation is expected to decrease the end user prices of many ICT products and services. On the face of it, this should be beneficial to women. According to Hafkin (2002), high customs duties on mobile telephones and computer equipment, as well as high prices for telephone services, are deterrents to women users. With the reduction of tariffs, prices for ICT products and services should be lower, thus yielding significant benefits to both female and male end users. But there may be an offsetting counter effect. Hafkin (2002: 13) argues that:

> In preparation for competition in the telecoms sector, many countries are rebalancing international and domestic tariffs to eliminate existing subsidies, most frequently on local service. This rebalancing has meant higher rates for local calls in many places, which hit the poor, the majority of whom are women, the hardest. Although it is expected that competition will lower prices in the long run, in the interim many users cannot afford local service. Among the ways to compensate for rebalancing costs are basing tariffs on forward-looking costs and establishing regional (e.g. rural vs. urban) tariffs.

Liberalisation means adjusting domestic laws with regard to telecommunications and other ICT services, including domestic regulations to promote universal access to phone and internet services in rural and poor communities. Proactive governments may include the promotion of women's empowerment and enhancement of opportunities for women's advancement, in terms of employment and business, up the ICT value-added ladder.

As with traditional product liberalisation, there are the usual concerns about the loss of tariffs and the consequential impact on government revenues. The specific concern centres around how this translates into cuts in social sector programmes. In the area of ICT there does not seem to be an acute cause for alarm. This is due to the fact that ICT is a very small proportion of many developing countries' revenue stream. For example, though ICT grew by 32 per cent between 2006 and 2007 in Uganda, it directly employed only about 6,000 persons (Uganda Investment Authority, 2008). For Kenya and the United Republic of Tanzania, ICT accounted for 4.8 per cent and 4.1 per cent of GDP, respectively (World Bank, 2007).

A further complication of ICT liberalisation is, as noted above, the potential leakage of funds abroad. Developing countries may be unable to tax internet transactions and capital is now extremely mobile. Equally important is the fact that ICT represents a high level of profit repatriation from developing countries. Apart from direct transfer in the purchase of ICT-related infrastructural equipment, developing countries must also pay huge amounts to international backbone providers – which supply access to high-speed transmission lines – through settlement rates and payment for bandwidth. The high mobility of capital is forcing developing countries to lower tax regimes in order to attract foreign direct investment, which has eroded their revenue from taxation (Torres, 2001, cited in Ya'u, 2002). Additionally, in terms of trade and commerce, local firms are not able to compete with transnational ones, thus exacerbating capital flight (Ya'u, 2002).

A recent story in *Modern Ghana News* argues that West Africa's ICT industry faces a major threat from liberalisation, as small-scale operators in software development will be forced out of the market (Ghana News Agency, 2009). This has serious implications for the long-term development of indigenous creativity and innovation. Gender also plays a role, as women will be the most vulnerable group among the small players trying to compete against foreign multinationals in the software development area.

Measures taken to help women deal with policy changes

While ICT-enabled trade offers opportunities for export growth and women's socio-economic empowerment in Asia, Africa and the Caribbean, it can also perpetuate women's marginalisation and reinforce gender inequities. Ngone Diop from the African Centre for Gender and Development (ACGD), speaking at the forum on Information Communication Technologies, Trade and Economic Growth at the UN Conference Centre in Addis Ababa, argued that trade and ICT could be a critical pathway to socio-economic growth and development in Africa, but that without a gender perspective, the potential benefits of ICT and trade would not be experienced by women and girls. Rather, gender inequalities and the socio-economic exclusion of women and other vulnerable groups would be perpetuated, hampering Africa's development prospects (Zulu, 2006).

As a result of these concerns, there is a local, regional and national agenda to use ICT to promote the social and economic empowerment of women in developing countries. In terms of employment, there are efforts at all levels to promote better working conditions for women in call centres.

National measures

The most direct attempts to ensure that workers have access to benefits and health care are by unions and professional associations. In India, these include the well-established Union for Information Technology and Enabled Services (UNITES) and the IT Professionals Forum (ITPF). A newer entrant into the struggle to improve the welfare of IT workers is the Centre of Indian Trade Unions (CITU) launched by the West Bengal Information Technology Services Association.

In general, however, most efforts around women workers in the IT sector have centred on enhancing education as the pathway for improving their conditions and opportunities for greater access to and ownership and control of ICTs, whether for personal growth, poverty reduction or career advancement. In this respect, many NGOs are taking action to increase the computer literacy and skills of large segments of the population.

In Benin and Ghana, for example, NGOs have set up community learning centres for building computer and other ICT skills. In Benin, with the assistance of the United States Agency for International Development, Cyber Shonhai NGO has trained many people and focused its outreach on women. A Ghanaian NGO trained over 14,000 people in 2000. However, due to inattention to gender issues (such as timing, location and gendered customary rules of behaviour), about 85 per cent of those trained were young men between the ages of 18 and 40. Elsewhere, NGOs such as CEEWA-Uganda (Council for the Economic Empowerment of Women in Africa) have focused on improving women entrepreneurs' access to ICT (see Box 9.2).

Box 9.2 Benefits from and issues with an ICT project in Uganda

CEEWA-Uganda set up an ICT project in 1997 that targeted women entrepreneurs. Women at four sites were provided with access to various ICTs, including computers, email and internet services, telephones, fax, scanner, printer, photocopiers, radio and television. Women were also given business and agricultural information through a database-driven website. The project developed ICT training materials as well as entrepreneurship training on CD-ROMs tailored to the needs of local women. The materials were in audio-visual forms and were translated into the local language, Luganda.

Some of the women involved testified that the project enabled them to access training and information that improved their standard of living and their businesses. However, some of the women said they experienced abuse from their husbands, especially when they received calls from male clients or when they came home late from the telecentres. Even if women owned their own phones, access was restricted by their spouses, who wanted to control who could call their wives and the times at which this was acceptable. The economic benefits of ICT also disadvantaged women in some instances, as an increase in income meant additional burdens because the men simply left all financial responsibilities to their wives.

Source: Adapted from Litho, 2007

There is also a great deal of effort at national level to ensure women's access to and control of new ICT, such as computers, emails and the internet, as well as to enhance their access to traditional or older technologies, including non-electronic media such as print, radio and television. Furthermore, some national governments, for example India, Mauritius and Uganda, have pioneered the use of ICT in social development, including the delivery of health care (telemedicine). South Africa's Telecommunications Act includes provisions to redress gender imbalance and other areas of disadvantage.

Regional and international measures

The liberalisation of the movement of skilled professionals, including ICT workers, in the Caribbean Single Market and Economy (see Box 9.3) is one example of a regional approach to gender and ICT. In general, as in other regions, males and females in the Caribbean are found in specific types of occupational sub-groups in the ICT sector, with women dominating the low-skill, low-wage occupations such as teleworking and men dominating the high-skill, high-wage occupations such as software programming (Dunn, 2008).

Civil society groups in West Africa are advocating for harmonisation of national policies on ICT and telecommunications within the Economic Community of West African States (ECOWAS) legal framework. In the Asia-Pacific Economic Cooperation (APEC) region, the focus of attention has been on en-gendering ICT-facilitated trade, in particular the interconnections with women's small and medium-sized enterprises.

International measures

Some of the measures taken at the international level include:

- Better and more effective mechanisms to facilitate global money transfers and remittances;
- Promotion of ICTs and women's entrepreneurship through the growth of micro finance;
- The development by the International Telecommunication Union (ITU) of a gender-sensitive framework that promotes gender mainstreaming not only within the ITU itself, but also through its gender task force, which is working to promote greater gender sensitivity and end the gender digital divide;
- USAID's Greater Access to Trade Expansion (GATE) and Academy for Educational Development projects that seek to promote the provision of public access to the internet and other ICTs – particularly for low-income populations and micro, small and medium-sized enterprises.

Box 9.3 Gender and ICT in the Caribbean Common Market

The CARICOM Single Market and Economy (CSME) is an integrated development strategy agreed in 1989 by the Heads of Government of the states comprising CARICOM. In addition to the free movement of goods, the CSME allows for free movement of services and of skilled persons without the need for work permits. The CARICOM Free Movement of Persons Act, now enacted legislation in all CSME countries, initially applies only to certain categories, but calls for eventual free movement of all persons.

Given the gender differentials, gender inequalities and occupational sex segregation in the labour market in the Caribbean, it is important to determine how different groups of women and men will benefit. For example, the first category of skilled persons is university graduates. Until recently, the University of the West Indies was the main institution for university education across the region. Gender analysis of data from UWI Mona shows that there is a 70:30 ratio in favour of female graduates. It can therefore be assumed that the majority of these mobile professionals will be females.

Dunn and Dunn (1999) note that Barbados targeted investment companies involved in the high end of the IT market, while Jamaica focused on attracting those at the low end in response to the realities of their workers' profiles. As a result, most IT companies in Barbados were involved in software engineering and programming, while those in Jamaica were involved in data entry, data processing and call centres. CSME-qualified workers are thus more likely to migrate to Barbados, Jamaica, and Trinidad and Tobago, which are most 'e-ready', to utilise the emerging job opportunities in the ICT sector.

Source: Adapted from Dunn, 2008

Lessons learned

ICT in the three areas briefly touched on in this sector review – ICT-enabled trade, ICT-facilitated trade and ICT trade – present both challenges and opportunities for women's and men's economic and social progress and the empowerment of women as a group. However, restrictive and oppressive gender relations and socio-cultural barriers stand in the way of the successful attainment of these goals, which are the central objectives of development. It is therefore imperative to make gender a key aspect of national ICT policies. Gender needs to be taken into account in assessing the location of ICT facilities, infrastructure, costs and training of workers. Gender constraints and challenges also need to be considered in the formulation of plans to further liberalise ICT in developing countries.

In order to retain and build on the employment gains associated with globalisation and the spread of ICT, women need to move into more technical or higher-level, better-paying jobs. For this, they need access to the educational and training opportunities necessary to equip them for the rapidly changing skill requirements. Policies should encourage girls and women to use ICT early in education and pursue higher studies in ICT and technical careers as scientists, researchers, administrators and educators (Hafkin, 2002).

Greater consideration of local and national social and cultural gender biases needs to be factored into programmes aimed at improving women's computer literacy. The research shows that simply having a curriculum does not ensure that women will benefit unless great care is taken to schedule workshops and training at times appropriate for them. Further, case studies from Benin and Mauritius show that different methods of accessing time at computer terminals need to be creatively established in order to ensure that girls and women have equitable access (Fontaine, 2000; Diga, 2009; Mbambo-Thata *et al.*, 2009; Oumrane, 2009). First come, first serve approaches do not serve women as well as they do men, and boys seem to be better able to access computer time than girls for a variety of cultural and behavioural reasons.

Lessons for governments are many. These range from making sure that gender is at the centre of ICT policies, and that gender issues as well as rural-urban dynamics are taken on board in setting up the infrastructure of ICT and telecommunications, to including a gender perspective when formulating and implementing universal access policy and universal service obligations (USO) with ICT suppliers, both foreign and domestic.

In terms of enhancing the contribution of ICT-centred employment in both the foreign and domestic sectors of the economy, there is a need to go beyond the issues of access and to develop policies, programmes and strategies that encourage more women to pursue careers in high-tech occupations such as software engineering and computer programming (Dunn, 2008). IT companies also need to specifically target and recruit women to these jobs. In order to promote women's role in this area both as workers and businesses owners, governments need to ensure access to free/open source software and providers in their ICT policy and regulation.

At the international level, many NGOs, international agencies and governments are developing outreach to support the projects mentioned above.

References

Diga, K (2009). 'University Women Struggle for Knowledge Access in Africa', http://www.genderit.org/, 9 April.

Dunn, LL (2008). 'Milestone or Minefield? Gender, Technology and Development in the Caribbean Single Market', University of the West Indies, Mona, Jamaica.

Dunn, LL and Dunn, HS (1999). 'Employment, Working Conditions and Labour Relations in Offshore Data Service Enterprises: Case Studies of Barbados and Jamaica', ILO Working Paper 86, Multinational Enterprises Programme, International Labour Organization, Geneva.

Fontaine, M (2000). 'High Tech/Grassroots Education: Community Learning Centres (CLCs) for Skill Building', *TechKnowLogia*, July/August, http://ict.aed.org/infocenter/pdfs/hightech.pdf

Ghana News Agency (2009). 'West Africa's ICT Industry Faces Major Threat Unless', *Modern Ghana News*, 11 April, http://www.modernghana.com/news/210735/1/west-africas-ict-industry-faces-major-threat-unles.html

Gurumurthy, A (2004). 'Gender and ICTs: Overview Report', BRIDGE Cutting Edge Pack series, Institute of Development Studies, UK, http://www.bridge.ids.ac.uk/reports/CEP-ICTs-OR.pdf

Hafkin, N (2002). 'Gender Issues in ICT Policy in Developing Countries: An Overview', UN Division for the Advancement of Women Expert Group Meeting on Information and Communication Technologies and Their Impact on and Use as an Instrument for the Advancement and Empowerment of Women, Seoul, Republic of Korea, 11–14 November.

Hafkin, N and Taggert, N (2001). 'Gender, Information Technology, and Developing Countries: An Analytic Study', Academy for Educational Development for the Office of Women in Development Bureau for Global Programs, Field Support and Research, USAID, June.

ITU (2008). ICT Regulation Toolkit, InfoDev and the International Telecommunication Union, http://www.ictregulationtoolkit.org/en/Index.html

Litho, P (2007). 'Do Women's Access to ICTs Lead to Empowerment? Looking at the CEEWA Project in Uganda', genderIT.org, 13 July, http://www.genderit.org/en/index.shtml?w=a&x=95381

Mbambo-Thata, B, Mlambo, E and Mwatsiya, P (2009). 'When a Gender-blind Access Policy Results in Discrimination: Realities and Perceptions of Female Students at the University of Zimbabwe', in Buskens, I and Webb, A (eds), *African Women and ICTs: Investigating Technology, Gender and Empowerment*, IDRC/Zed Books, Ottawa.

Oumrane, FME (2009). 'ICTs: Women, Free Software, Copyrights ... Forgotten by Mauritania Legislators and Decision Makers', http://www.genderit.org/, 11 April.

Uganda Investment Authority (2008). Uganda ICT Sector Brief www.ugandainvest.com/uia2.php?uhpl=ict&&uhpl1=ICT

Van Welsum, D and Montagnier, P (2007). 'ICTs and Gender: Evidence from OECD and Non-OECD Countries', presentation at an OECD and World Bank seminar,

27 January, http://go.worldbank.org/XO1CVD38D0

World Bank (2007). 'Trade Information and Communication Services: Opportunities for East and Southern Africa – Uganda Case Study', World Bank, Washington, DC, 3 October, http://www.authorstream.com/Presentation/minges-126180-trade-ict-services-uganda-case-study-2007-10-science-technology-ppt-powerpoint/

WTO (n.d.). 'Telecommunication Services', WTO, Geneva, <http://www.wto.org/english/tratop_e/serv_e/telecom_e/telecom_e.htm>.

Ya'u, YZ (2002). 'Globalization, ICTs and the New Imperialism: Perspectives on Africa in the Global Electronic Village', paper for the 10th General Assembly of CODESRIA, 8–12 December, Kampala, Uganda.

Zulu, B (2006). 'Gender, Trade and the Role of ICTs', *iConnect Africa*, 3(1), July, http://www.uneca.org/aisi/iconnectafrica/v3n1.htm#6

Non-Tariff Trade Barriers

10 Packaged to Perfection: The SPS Agreement and Aquaculture in Bangladesh

Marilyn Carr and Sanae Ito

Background

With the reduction of tariff barriers, there is a danger that alternative forms of protection will be utilised, including arbitrary technical barriers to trade, as well as sanitary and phytosanitary measures. The Uruguay Round Agreement on the Application of Sanitary and Phytosanitary Measures (the SPS Agreement), adopted by WTO members in 1995, attempts to address the application of measures associated with the protection of human, animal and plant health in such a way that they are not a disguised restriction on international trade. The Agreement states that the measures should be scientifically based and stresses the importance of risk assessment in determining the appropriate level of protection.

However, there are strong indications that these measures are being applied in ways that affect livelihoods in developing countries – in some cases bringing about a total ban on exports of food products and in others leading to a restructuring of food industries in ways that have a negative impact on the livelihoods of poor farmers in general and women in particular.

International trade in fish and fish products has grown rapidly over the last 20 years. Export values rose from US$15 billion in 1980 to $56 billion in 2000. In the same period, developing countries' share of total exports rose from 40 to 50 per cent, with their net receipts from the fish trade increasing from less than $4 billion to almost $18 billion. Developed countries – primarily Japan, the USA and European countries – absorbed 80 per cent of total world imports.

It is in the economic and national interests of fish exporters from developing countries to ensure that they supply acceptable products to maintain their export earning as well as their commercial reputation (Greenhalgh, 2004). However, the complex requirements for food safety assurance and traceability set by major markets, particularly in Europe and North America, represent a threat to existing exporters and a barrier to new ones. Increasing outbreaks of food-borne illness, alongside consumer concerns over inter-regional disease transmission, have driven the development of more stringent laws and regulatory frameworks. New regulations with regard to quality control, such as the Hazard Analysis Critical Control Point (HACCP), have been adopted by all major importing countries (except Japan) and have been made compulsory for their fish processing industries. In terms of the impacts on developing countries, the regulations based on the HACCP shift the burden of responsibility to the exporting processors or traders by making them fully responsible for the quality of the product in terms of food safety.

The EU has been at the forefront in developing food safety standards and has had a profound influence on the development of the fish trade in developing economies. In particular, it has introduced 'farm to fork' principles that cover not just the main processing functions, but all steps from the primary producer (e.g. fishermen and aquaculture units) to the consumer. These override individual commodity-based directives. The result for exporting countries is that all steps in the chain have to take on board, in a more structured way, the principles of HACCP systems and other quality assurance needs, thus broadening the scope of the competent authority in regulating the industry.

The need to ensure that quality assurance measures are instituted prior to arrival at the processing factory gate poses a major challenge to export industries, particularly for the small-scale and non-industrialised sectors. Of even greater concern is the fact that in order for the 'farm to fork' principle to be seen to be working, a system of traceability of products throughout the chain needs to be instituted. This requires that each person in the chain is able to demonstrate that they know where the product has come from and where it has gone. Where small quantities of product are consolidated into larger batches from, say, traditional fishermen to purchasers at landing points, this presents particular problems as mixing of batches means that particular raw material supplies cannot be traced back to source (Greenhalgh, 2004).

This case study looks at the knock-on effects that these new measures are having on poor producers, particularly women, in the aquaculture industry in Bangladesh.

Women and the poor in shrimp and prawn farming in Bangladesh

In Bangladesh, shrimp and prawns constitute more than 70 per cent of exports of primary products and about 25 per cent of all exports excluding ready-made garments. The industry also employs about one million people up and down the supply chain. A large proportion of those in occupations such as fry catching are women, who are also the majority of workers in processing plants. Of the total volume of exports, 85 per cent are cultured. Half of the exported volume is freshwater prawns (known locally as *golda*) and the other half is brackish-water shrimp (*bagda*). *Golda* farming involves a larger number of small and landless farmers than *bagda* farming.

There are five major layers of activities that link local stakeholders in the export-oriented shrimp industry. At the top are the frozen fish processing and export companies located in the capital, Dhaka. At the next level are agents who buy shrimp from local middlemen (depot owners) and sell them to the companies for a commission. Many of these commission agents are wealthy, city-based businessmen who have easy access to bank loans. At the third layer are depot owners, that is, the storage owners who purchase shrimp from local producers, often through local small traders known as *farias*. Then there are shrimp farmers at the fourth layer who produce shrimp. At the bottom are suppliers of shrimp fry and feed. Fry traders procure them from fry collectors, many of whom are poor women, men and children living near estuaries in the coastal areas.

In addition, both government-owned and private sector nurseries and hatcheries supply post-larval and juvenile shrimp to traders and farmers. Feed traders, apart from selling factory-made fish feed, bring snails from surrounding districts as the local snail population dwindles. They then hire women, men and children from poor households to separate snail meat from the shells and sell it to shrimp farmers as high quality feed (Ito, 2007).

A 2006 USAID study on gender and value chains found that:

- The shrimp value chain is highly sex-segmented, with women and men clustered in different activities;
- Women and girls constitute 40 per cent of all fry catchers and 62 per cent of all processing plant workers, while there are few women higher up the chain;
- Women's absence from several levels of the chain limits their ability to gain economically from the sector;
- Inequality in women's participation is also evident in the lack of security of the jobs in which they work, with a greater proportion in temporary or casual employment;
- In farming, although men are reported to outnumber women, 73 per cent of women's labour time is concentrated in temporary or casual employment, compared with 31 per cent of men's time;
- In processing, where estimates reveal that women outnumber men, 92 per cent of women's labour time is considered temporary or casual.

The shrimp sector is a buyer-driven chain where producers, particularly small producers, have little ability to influence the price at which they sell their product and are frequently locked into contracts that limit the price they receive. At lower ends of the chain, among fry collectors and intermediaries, bargaining is also limited. At higher ends of the chain, among the larger farmers and processors, there is more opportunity for negotiation (USAID, 2006).

The impact of HACCP and 'farm to fork' principles

Issues of technology choice and poverty reduction were brought into focus in 1997, when the EU – the major market – banned all shrimp imports from Bangladesh because the industry failed to comply with the stringent provisions of its HACCP regulations. It is estimated that the industry lost approximately US$15 million in revenue between August and December 1997 and that the adoption of HACCP procedures in terms of inspection and upgrading of plant facilities cost owners US$17.6 million, with plants that could not afford this having to close down (Ito, 2007).

Part of the process of adopting HACCP measures involved making choices between *golda* and *bagda* farming, which have significant differences in production scales and techniques. *Golda* farming is conducted on a much smaller scale than *bagda* farming and involves a far larger number of poor farmers who are engaged in extensive and 'organic' farming without using expensive production inputs. While *bagda* farming probably has more potential for export growth, *golda* farming would have a far greater impact on rural poverty reduction. At the same time that the Government's 2005 Poverty Reduction Strategy Paper (PRSP) talked about an export policy that would increase exports, create job opportunities and alleviate poverty, it was also introducing certification standards in the shrimp industry to ensure quality and traceability at all stages of shrimp hatching, growing, processing, packaging, transporting and shipping of frozen shrimps (Ito, 2007).

To a large extent this involved favouring *bagda* farming, where it is much easier to consolidate the supply chain, but where 'producers' are largely 'wage workers', who are marginalised within the industry. This, together with the much greater negative environmental impact of *bagda* farming, has led many to suggest that a better way to help reduce poverty would be to concentrate on improving food safety standards of *golda* farmers so that they can meet the less stringent conditions of middle-class consumer markets in Bangladesh (Ito, 2007).

The rapid growth of the shrimp farming industry since the mid-1980s has generated optimism for Bangladesh's insertion into the global agrifood trade. At the same time, fish farming – including shrimp farming – has always been strongly associated with poverty reduction. Indeed, fish farming and the diversification of poor people's livelihoods are seen to be intricately related in the national policy discourse. According to the Government of Bangladesh (2005) 'the inland culture fishery provides poor people, and especially women and children, employment and livelihood opportunities in backward and forward linkage activities – fingerling production, fish catching, processing, marketing, etc.'. The potential conflict between the business goal of enhancing the export competitiveness of the shrimp sector and the development goal of supporting poor people's livelihoods has not received much attention so far.

At the inaugural session of the Aquaculture Certification Council's Training Course, held in August 2005, the Minister of Commerce promised 'full government support' for shrimp certification to comply with consumers' demands abroad. He also emphasised that the effort demonstrated his 'commitment for the poor people of the country' (ACC, 2005). The Department of Fisheries is more cautious, as it is directly involved in rural poverty reduction. Its officers at the district and sub-district level work closely with poor farmers, while senior officers are well aware that compliance with complex international standards would cause problems at farm level. Because of this, the Department is working on domestic safety standards and is developing its own quality assurance programme (QAP) in place of the HACCP. It is also working with the Ministry of Commerce to strengthen the Bangladesh Standard Testing Institute (Ito, 2007).

However, the co-ordination required between different government departments to bring this about is weak and, if left to itself, the industry cannot be expected to switch from one type of market to another with different standard requirements. One reason for this state of affairs is that many policy-makers fail to recognise the differences in production scales and techniques necessary for *golda* and *bagda* farming. Some agencies have tried to assist *golda* farmers – out of concern either for the livelihoods of the poor, especially women, or for the environment (see Box 10.1).

Lessons learned and future directions

This case study clearly points to the way in which a non-tariff trade barrier, HACCP, can cost a poor country a great deal of money in order for it to comply with the complex standards involved. There are also implications for the structure of the industry – in this case favouring the larger-scale and environmentally unfriendly *bagda* farming over the small-scale and environmentally sound *golda* farming.

Box 10.1 Measures taken to help prawn farmers in Bangladesh

The Danish International Development Agency (DANIDA) funded the Greater Noakhali Aquaculture Extension Project (GNAEP) to work exclusively with *golda* farmers with the aim of poverty reduction. It explored ways to cultivate the European niche market for its freshwater prawn products. In its early days, the project tried to collaborate with the Shrimp Seal of Quality Programme (SSOQ) set up by the Agro-based Industry and Technology Development Project (a joint project of USAID and the Bangladesh Government), but it decided to go it alone because SSOQ's emphasis on *bagda* farmers conflicted with GNAEP's focus on poverty reduction. Several NGOs have also been active. Nijera Kori and the Society for Environment and Development are especially involved for environmental reasons. CARE International (Bangladesh) implemented a *golda* project funded by the UK Department for International Development (DFID) in the late 1990s in recognition of its potential for growth. And 13 NGOs, led by the Coastal Development Partnership, co-operated with the SSOQ programme in monitoring the social and environmental codes of conduct involved in shrimp farming (Ito, 2007).

This bias, if not addressed, could cause hardship for many small farmers and suppliers in the *golda* supply chain – and especially women and children. While the Department of Fisheries has recognised this problem because of its close working relationship with small farmers, the measures it proposes will be difficult to implement without a stronger government structure and better links between different departments. And while NGOs are implementing some projects of assistance to poor farmers, these are few and far between.

Several measures have been tried or suggested. These include finding European niche markets for organic prawns, improving domestic food safety standards and supplying *golda* cultured by small farmers to middle-class consumer markets in Bangladesh. Alternatively, consolidating the supply chain for *bagda* to promote export growth could create off-farm employment for small farmers in the long run – through, for example, employment as contract farmers or as workers in processing factories – although wages and working conditions in these factories at the moment leaves something to be desired (see Halim, 2004).

References

ACC (Aquaculture Certification Council) (2005). ACC News, October, www.aquaculturecertification.org

Government of Bangladesh (2005). *Bangladesh – Unlocking the Potential: National Strategy for Accelerated Poverty Reduction*, General Economics Division of the Planning Commission, Dhaka.

Greenhalgh, P (2004). 'Policy Research – Implications of Liberalization of Fish Trade for Developing Countries', Trade Issues Background Paper: Sanitary and Phyto-Sanitary (SPS) Measures and Technical Barriers to Trade (TBT), FAO, Rome, July.

Halim, S (2004). 'Marginalization or Empowerment? Women's Involvement in Shrimp Cultivation and Shrimp Processing Plants in Bangladesh', in Hossain, KT, Imam, MH and Habib, SE (eds), *Women, Gender and Discrimination*, University of Rajshahi, Rajshahi, http://www.bangladeshsociology.org/Sadeka%20Paper%20on%20Shrimp%20Culture.pdf

Ito, S (2007). 'Export Competitiveness and Pro-poor Growth in the Shrimp Industry in Bangladesh', *Enterprise Development and Microfinance*, 18 (2 and 3), June/September.

USAID (2006). 'A Pro-Poor Analysis of the Shrimp Sector in Bangladesh', Women in Development (WID), USAID, Washington, DC, http://www.usaid.gov/our_work/cross-cutting_programs/wid/pubs/Bangladesh_Shrimp_Value_Chain_Feb_2006.pdf

11 Sitting on the Docks: The SPS Agreement and the Fish Industry in Uganda

May Sengendo[21]

Background

Uganda is a low-income, trade and aid dependent country in sub-Saharan Africa. Exports (primarily traditional items such as coffee, tea and cotton and non-traditional items such as fish and fish products, electricity, horticultural products and vanilla, plus remittances) are 10 per cent of gross domestic product (GDP) while imports (manufactures, equipment and machinery) are about 20 per cent. It is a predominately agricultural-based economy that is self-sufficient in food and has a relatively small but growing manufacturing sector. In an effort to widen its export basket and ease the burden of its chronic trade deficit, the country has been seeking to shift from traditional exports into dynamic primary and higher valued exports such as horticulture and fish and fish products.

The 1980s saw Uganda taking 'unilateral measures' to reduce tariffs and remove other trade restrictions. It was 'persuaded' by the World Bank and International Monetary Fund (IMF) to take such liberalisation measures and to adopt programmes for further liberalisation as a condition for receiving assistance under structural adjustment programmes. Therefore, trade and market liberalisation were established under these programmes in the 1980s and 1990s. This has been followed by diversification of agricultural crops with the aim of ensuring that producers have a variety of low and high value crops for export.

Uganda has been increasingly involved since 1994 in the Multilateral Trading System (MTS) as a response to the Final Act of the Uruguay Round. The Government is also engaged in a series of legal and institutional reforms not only to implement its commitments under the MTS but also to take advantage of the opportunities created by the system. The most important perceived advantage is the understanding that countries will have access to big markets created by reductions in tariff and non-tariff barriers. However, the country is also required to abide by specific trade rules, as this case study illustrates.

Provision of effective information for improved market access is a major priority in the country's efforts to modernise agriculture and improve its industrial base. This study shows that different market access challenges are faced by female and male producers and exporters in terms of information, technical assistance and capacity building. These are embedded in the social, political and economic aspects of the macroeconomy, which are influenced by the way international trade agreements are implemented.

The fish sector

Uganda has substantial fisheries resources. Fish and fish products are among the youngest national export industries, having emerged in the early 1990s, but have grown to be the largest contributor in the non-traditional export sector, accounting for 12 per cent of the country's exports in 2007/2008. The major markets are the EU, Far East (Japan, Australia and Singapore), Middle East (United Arab Emirates and Israel) and the USA. The main exports to these markets are fillets (processed fish), while most whole fish (smoked, salted) are exported to neighbouring countries such as Burundi, Democratic Republic of the Congo, Kenya, Rwanda and Sudan). Fish by-products (fish maws) are mainly exported to Hong Kong and China. It is estimated that the sector provides direct and indirect employment for over one million people.

The imposition of SPS standards

Between 1997 and 2000, Uganda experienced three bans on fish exports to its most lucrative market, the EU (to which 95 per cent of the fish exported is fresh). The bans were a result of higher SPS standards developed by the EU relative to international standards. Export earnings fell to a low of US$24 million in 1999 as the landed price was reduced to approximately USh700 (US$0.50) per kg. Overall, the bans generated a loss of over US$36.9 million (Sengendo and Tumushabe, 2005) and had widespread effects on the fishing community.

There was reduced economic activity in processing plants, where women were employed to fillet the fish, among agents of exporters and among male fisherfolk who could not sell their catch. Three out of 11 fishing factories were closed and those that remained open operated at 20 per cent capacity. Overall, this resulted in a reduction of the labour force in the sector by 60–70 per cent. According to an FAO report, around 100,000 people involved in various fishing activities – including fisherfolk, fishmongers and transporters of fish – were negatively affected by the ban, with 32,000 unable to find alternative employment, except at less than one-third of their normal earnings. Families and other dependents of these directly employed people were also affected.

In addition, the bans had a spin-off effect on related industries such as packaging, fishnets and transport and on the economy in general. Legislative reform, additional infrastructure development through technical assistance and increased investment in the sector by exporters had to be undertaken to meet EU standards, as well as a number of other changes (see Box 11.1).

Box 11.1 Meeting the SPS requirements in Uganda

Changes in the fish sector undertaken to meet the SPS requirements included the following:

- Introducing insulated fish collection boats/vessels to collect fish from the islands;
- Upgrading the landing sites with cold facilities and appropriate sanitation measures;
- Introducing insulated/refrigerated trucks for the transportation of fish;
- Development of another cold store at the airport (adding US$0.03 per kilo on handling fees to pay for this facility);
- Development of other cold chain facilities;
- Redesigning and construction of processing plants to suit the HACCP system (ceilings, walls, flow of water, workers' rooms, uniforms, stainless steel equipment, etc.);
- Establishment of laboratories at the processing plants, as well as independent ones (US$80 is charged per test and this costs companies up to US$15,000 per year for testing for pesticide residues);
- Development of Hazard Analysis Critical Control Points;
- Training of factory personnel in HACCP, critical management points and good hygiene practices;
- Improvements in record keeping and document control.

These new requirements increased the costs of investment in the sector and led most local exporters to abandon the trade, thus leaving it largely to foreign investors with companies in the importing countries. Where technical assistance was provided in terms of training, the capacity built was minimal as it was limited to just a few people, who then ended up being employed by the foreign companies.

Impact of changes in trade policy on women

Apart from the general employment impact on women as direct employees, the welfare and livelihood of their families and household members were negatively affected by the ban. The changes that were necessary to become EU compliant made it difficult for women and other small-scale business entities to survive. A case study of fisheries on Lake Victoria highlights the following:

- Almost all the small-scale fishmongers and processors were traditionally women.
- They had developed relationships with particular fishermen, from whom they purchased fish.
- They had special markets in which they sold their fish.
- Since factories have taken a larger share of the catch, relationships with fishermen have been severed.
- Fishermen are under contract to supply factory agents.
- The availability of fish for fishmongers is gradually declining; the alternative is factory waste and fish bones.
- Domestic fish consumption has fallen, as fish exports have driven prices up beyond the means of local people, leading to concerns about food security in terms of the availability of fish protein.
- Women are taking greater risks travelling at night to purchase immature fish in order to survive, and poor fisherfolk in general take greater risks fishing at night to dodge soldiers.

(International Gender and Trade Network, 2007)

Sengendo (2005) notes three critical factors that affected women's ability to rebound from the economic contraction generated by the SPS ban on fishing: asymmetry between women and men in access to information on market conditions and requirements (including high search cost for market information that women experienced); differences in utilisation of market information between women and men; and access to technical assistance.

In terms of informational asymmetry, Sengendo (2005) notes that the institutions for generating and disseminating market access information both in the public and private sector are scattered and lack proper co-ordination. Although a wide array of information is available from different providers, the public institutions responsible for disseminating it are both centralised and highly bureaucratic. Many of these institutions, such as the Uganda Export Promotion Board, are located in Kampala and have no up-country offices or outreach programmes. Producers and exporters seeking information encounter considerable delays and increased transaction costs in the process. Moreover, dissemination methods do not take into consideration the different needs of women and men that result from the differences in the tasks they undertake.

In terms of differences in access to and utilisation of market information, it was noted that most market information was obtained through verbal communication during the process of selling fish. However, in discussion groups, women who dealt with fish processing and smoking indicated their desire to receive the information via the radio. As one explained, 'We can even listen to the radio while at home instead of coming over all the time even when we don't need to'. Most of the women had radios in their homes and radio was the medium they were used to. Male fisherfolk also agreed that radios would be the most appropriate channel, followed by verbal communication, although men also said that they did not have time to listen to the radio.

In terms of technical assistance, the study found out that at least 45 per cent of fish providers have never accessed any technical assistance to help them in their fishing activities. In fact, a sizeable number of fisherfolk lacked knowledge of standards and were experiencing rising fish losses. Male fisherfolk felt that these losses should be solved in the traditional way, which was through cultural consideration of the right time to fish. Because of the bans, there had been changes in the space and labour used for fishing. Although labour for fishing in the lake used to be provided by men due to cultural taboos and perceptions, women increasingly participated in the aquaculture activities that were undertaken as an alternative fishing production approach.

Female fisherfolk also requested more market information that would help them in identifying set prices. Both female and male fisherfolk identified two problems with the current fish prices: that they were low and that they fluctuated. These problems were caused mainly by the large amounts of unmarketed output (40.9%) and lack of market information (22.7%). In addition, the women wanted loans, while the men wanted more security and rain jackets.

Measures to help women and men deal with policy changes

The changes in the fisheries sector led to the setting up of community-based institutions such as beach management units that worked as channels for increasing participation of male and female actors who used to be left out of decision-making about sanitation, health and clean environment around the fishing and landing areas. Women also used such initiatives to participate in decision-making on strategies to address the income and labour use that had been lost due to the ban.

In addition, women mobilised institutions in other ways to respond to their needs and those of their families. An example is the Katosi Women's Fishing and Development Association, formed in 1996 by eight women fisherfolk. The Association has grown to more than 50 members and includes six other women's groups established at parish level (Yawe, 2006). Such mobilisation has enabled the Association to form a trust. It has played a role in skills development to support women's participation in the value chain for fish. This required changes in perceptions of women's roles in fishing, a task which the Association has successfully focused on.

The members manage a group fishing business with four motorised boats and have built their capacity through business and enterprise management training. They have responded to technological innovations that support SPS measures by having ice container boats and fishing gear. They have also devised strategies to address cultural limitations to women's participation in fishing by hiring men in cases where fishing has to be done in deep waters.

Women's response to the fish ban also included diversifying their businesses to include cattle rearing, poultry, tailoring and other activities They have continued to work on such diversified businesses even after the lifting of the ban, and the income from the fish business is put into a revolving fund that members can utilise (Yawe, 2006). Members have been empowered in ways that have enabled some of them to occupy leadership positions that they use to advocate for women's concerns and interests to be priorities in the fishing business and other fields of development.

Lessons learned

Uganda must invest in SPS capacity and the associated knowledge infrastructure. Institutional mechanisms for gender-responsive planning and implementation are available in terms of a national gender policy, capacity building for key ministries, including planning and finance, and civil society organisations dealing with the economic empowerment of the poor. However, the practical integration and mainstreaming of gender in trade-related aspects remains a challenge in the work of officers responsible for this, because of perceived problems of combining gender with economics at macro, meso and micro levels. Participation of female and male representatives of the private sector, academia and civil society in the preparation of national positions in the MTS negotiations has been limited, although that was possibly the best place to ensure the integration of gender concerns in the negotiations. In terms of the inclusion of women and men in consultative efforts and co-ordination of trade policy-making, some progress has been made with the formation of the Inter-Institutional Trade Committee (IITC). However, the process of constituting this as a national trade policy co-ordination body is hampered by the same limitations.

Female and male producers and exporters require market access information that can help them make relevant and reliable production and export decisions. While there are similarities in the market access information needs of female and male producers and exporters, differences exist in the ranking of priority needs. Whereas male producers search for and demand information on improved seeds and organic certification that link directly to the requirements of the international market, female producers consider information on production skills as their immediate and priority concern. This difference can be attributed to male producers' exposure, as they are usually the ones involved in training and information dissemination on new issues in trade.

Local intermediary centres acquire information from international sources. They then pass it to their clientele, who are the appointed focal points, projects and private organisations. The focal points are mainly public institutions appointed by the WTO, UNCTAD and IITC. They include the government ministry in charge of trade, the business community, academia, the National Bureau of Standards, and the ministry in charge of agriculture. These institutions acquire, store and disseminate information to private and public institutions, and researchers. The Ministry of Agriculture, Animal Industry and Fisheries provides information on fish products. There are also some stand-alone projects that support private sector organisations and operators.[22] While these also target producers and exporters, some face constraints due to the cost of dissemination to rural areas.

While public bodies indicate that they attempt to supply information on a wide range of categories, the level to which they can supply most information types – particularly market information and regulations – is limited. In general, there is a need to build and strengthen partnerships between public and private sector information providers. This would encourage efficiency in information generation, repackaging and dissemination to producers and exporters. In addition, in order to ensure co-ordinated and coherent interventions to address the various limitations on the market access information chain, Uganda needs to move rapidly to put in place a national export policy which should articulate in concrete terms the gaps in current market access information.

Furthermore, due to the political economy of the MTS, the Government needs to build strong alliances with civil society advocacy organisations. The IITC is therefore a welcome idea, although there is still much which needs to be done. It is through such alliances that collective action can be brought to bear on WTO member states to implement the in-built agenda on agriculture and services and make technical assistance to developing countries a priority.

While at first the EU-imposed standards were considered in a negative way by actors in the fish value chain, the technological innovations that were undertaken to respond to the situation helped to improve Uganda's fisheries sector (Kiggundu, 2006). The sector has continued to utilise and benefit from these technological improvements.

References

International Gender and Trade Network (2007). 'Raising African Women's Voice in Trade, Globalisation and NEPAD: A Case Study of Lake Victoria Fisheries in Uganda', PowerPoint presentation, http://web.igtn.org/home/index.php?option=com_docman&task=doc_download&Itemid=6&gid=489

Kiggundu, R (2006). 'Innovation Systems and Development: The Journey of a Beleaguered Nile Perch Fishery in Uganda', PhD thesis, United Nations University and Maastricht University, Netherlands.

Sengendo, M (2005). 'Hidden Power: Gender Relations in Export-Oriented Tasks and Access to Resources for Uganda's Horticulture Sector', PhD thesis, Cape Town University, South Africa.

Sengendo, M and Tumushabe, G (2005). 'Market Access Information Provision and Needs for Female and Male Exporters in Uganda's Horticulture and Fisheries Sectors', Gender and Economic Reform (GERA), Ghana.

Yawe, A (2006). 'Unleashing the Potential of Women Entrepreneurs in Export Growth: The Case of Women Fishing and Development Associations in Uganda', CEEWA, Uganda, http://www.intracen.org/wedf/ef2006/Gender-Issues/Paper_Yawe.pdf

12 Lessons Learned from Part One

Mariama Williams

There is a positive relationship in developing countries between women's involvement in the economy, their contribution to the competitive dynamics of trade, and the growth and development of these countries. However, as the cases studies in this section show, it is unclear that the same positive relationship holds between trade performance and women's overall economic and social empowerment. In general it would seem that trade intensification is quite beneficial to women. It creates employment that can improve their situation. However, increased trade and women's employment on their own do not vitiate the persistence of gender inequalities and gender gaps with regard to access to and control over tangible and intangible resources. As noted by Litho (2007), in many African countries 'on the contrary, women's social position in society has not changed much. Women's economic position may have improved slightly, but they remain culturally constrained.' These inequalities and gaps tend to work to the disadvantage of women as a group relative to men as a group. Their existence and persistence also help explain why negative shifts in trade patterns and policies and overall trade liberalisation-led reform tend to affect women more than men.

While trade liberalisation does not create structural gender inequalities, the trade reform that it engenders can affect – for better or worse – conditions in the labour market, relative prices for products, and resources and government revenues. Thus it can lead to increased or decreased employment and livelihoods, higher or lower prices for inputs, and investments or cuts in government social expenditures. All of this may affect women more than men.

The case studies also illustrate in different country contexts and across different sectors that while in one period trade expansion can lead to benefits, in another period, as a result of changes in trade policy, there can be a contraction of economic activity that suddenly reverses most of the previous gains. In many cases, this reversal leaves women and men worse off than they were before the onset of trade expansion. It is therefore important to review and reflect on these examples to pinpoint what lessons can be drawn. Can they provide guidance to policy-makers and development practitioners? Is there a set of universal mitigating and compensatory actions that could lessen the negative impacts of changes in trade policy regimes or mechanisms and processes on women's employment and entrepreneurship and on their informal and household sector activities? What are the mechanisms and measures that will enhance the positive benefits of trade intensification on women's overall economic and social empowerment?

A number of broad overarching principles or guidelines can be drawn from the case studies that emanate from the challenges and contradictions around gender, trade and development. There are also a number of interventions that can be undertaken, relevant to the four broad groupings around which the studies are clustered.

Principles and guidelines

Promoting women's empowerment

Women's empowerment must be a key pillar of any trade and development strategy. Each of the case studies shows that trade expansion on its own does not generate sustained improvement in women's overall situation. At best, there are marginal improvements in their economic and social status. Proactive policies and programmes are needed at national and local levels that seek to address issues of structural inequality between women and men. Given the shifting nature of international trade patterns, there are ups and downs in employment gains. One sector grows, employing women and men, then peaks and declines. Women lose income, poverty increases and the overall situation worsens for women and their families.

Both the Kenyan and the St Lucian case studies graphically illustrate the fragility of trade dependence. In both cases women seemed to achieve a high level of functioning and ability to command resources when trade was booming. But as trade declined in the sugar and banana sectors respectively, women's livelihoods became increasingly precarious. Some women were left in much the same situation as they had been before. Others, who had given up their food subsistence economy for the cash crop opportunity, were now in a food deficit situation. To avoid such situations, women need to be empowered through access to education, services, land and credit.

Investing in women

Maximising sustained gains from trade expansion and trade reform necessitates investing in women and girls. This means devoting money and resources to the factors that affect their capabilities, access to resources and security in all areas and aspects of their lives and lifecycles. Investing in women means spending on health, education and essential services that are critical for social reproduction and household production.

Focusing on poverty eradication

Trade strategies must evolve from a better understanding of poverty dynamics in the economy and how trade and poverty are interrelated. For African countries such as Kenya and Uganda and small island nations such as Jamaica and St Lucia, this is extremely important in order to ensure sustainable development in the agriculture and natural resource sectors. Attempts to increase trade must go beyond the search for market access – i.e. provisions for the access of goods and services across national borders on a non-discriminatory basis – to focus attention on the factors critical for raising productivity and revitalising agriculture, which remains the backbone of all the economies reviewed in these case studies. These factors are all intimately linked to poverty and gender gaps and biases. Poverty is linked to people's nutritional and health status, both of which are important for ensuring a stable and reliable workforce and raising productivity. If there is not an adequate level of social development in terms of basic infrastructure and access to health care and education for women and men, then adverse changes in trade at best reinforce or at worst exacerbate poverty.

Infusing trade policy with a gender-sensitive social mandate

The design, negotiation and ultimate implementation of trade policies and agreements have serious implications for all areas of women's and men's daily lives. These may differ depending on the economic background of the country, the nature and sequencing of the changes in trade and economic policy measures, and the nature and scope of the pre-existing social and cultural situation and location of women and men in the economy.

Trade reform must be more broadly viewed to take into consideration social, gender, human development and other concerns. Effective trade reform must be developed as a process that goes well beyond narrow economic concerns with changes in tariff levels and bindings. To be holistic, trade reform should be grounded in a comprehensive view of and a concern with how its mechanisms and modalities affect the pattern of resource allocation and other policy parameters (fiscal and social) and shape the behaviours and values that influence the opportunities and constraints of different groups in the economy. Given the contrary and often contradictory impacts of liberalisation-induced trade reform, very careful attention must be paid to how trade policy measures are reformed and fine-tuned.

Promoting environmentally friendly trade

While promoting trade and seeking foreign exchange, governments must be mindful also of the need to promote the conservation and protection of natural resources. Five of the case studies show, to different degrees, that export-led growth and/or trade liberalisation tend to have a negative effect on the environment and questionable implications for the long-term sustainability of natural resources. Deteriorating air and water quality has implications for the health of women and men, as well as particular implications for women's time burden and overall welfare. This compromises women's role in food and agricultural management, as well as potentially affecting productivity in domestic and export production. There is an important lesson to be learned about the need to situate trade policy within the context of environmental sustainability and natural resources management. This points to the fact that governments must be cautious about the further liberalisation of trade in natural resources such as forest products, fish, oil, gas and minerals. They must also not be narrowly focused on market access to the detriment of the very environment that is necessary for the life and livelihoods of their citizens.

While trade liberalisation is not the only causal factors in marine degradation, with environmental and climatic factors also playing a role, shrimp farming for export from Bangladesh is implicated in the destruction of mangrove, increased salinity of inland waters and soil acidification. Shrimp yield is declining and indigenous fish species are being lost. All of these issues significantly affect food security. In Lesotho, the key environmental issue has been the pollution of drinking water by the production of textiles. In Kenya, sugar production has affected soil fertility.

Specific interventions around trade liberalisation

With the exception of the Lesotho and St Lucia studies, which focused on non-reciprocal agreements, all the case studies in this section reinforce the point that market access concessions, which are grounded in reciprocity and embedded in the 'single undertaking' framework, may constrain the flexibility of governments to undertake domestic adjustments that cater to the particular needs of different sectors of the economy. It is therefore important that such negotiations are grounded in, and are extremely responsive to, a gender equality-based, development-centred approach.

A majority of the case studies point to the following as critical ingredients for trade policy negotiations mandates:

- Food security;
- The ability to offer protection to a specific sector identified as critical to poverty reduction;

- The protection of health services and access to other services that are critical for social reproduction and women's overall empowerment.

With this backdrop, specific lessons can be drawn from the four areas of import liberalisation, preference gain and loss, service liberalisation and non-tariff trade barriers.

Import liberalisation

In the area of tariff liberalisation, food security and the rural livelihoods of poor women and men farmers do not appear to have been critical criteria in determining commitments. This is clearly the case in Kenya, where the severe contraction in the sugar sector caused dramatic upheavals in the lives of women, men, girls and boys. As the crisis worsened, not only did it increase the debt of families and the overall burden of women, it forced children to go to work in the fields in an attempt to garner some kind of marginal income to help families survive. Due to pre-existing high levels of poverty, small cane-farmers, especially women, were unable to access money to upgrade their operations and become more competitive. More importantly, there was no underlying social safety net or basic infrastructure for women and men to fall back on. So when sugar was no longer providing an adequate living, poverty rose rapidly, causing increased food insecurity, child labour, prostitution and other coping mechanisms.

It is also clear that governments need to act quickly to take measures to protect against rising imports that jeopardise livelihoods in the domestic economy. As noted in the case study of Kenya, WTO agreements provide a specific safeguard for agriculture and three safeguards – anti-dumping, countervailing and emergency safeguards – under the GATT. However, it is difficult for developing countries to take advantage of these for procedural and financial reasons.

In the current Doha Round of WTO negotiations, countries such as Jamaica and Kenya are working hard to secure special safeguard mechanisms that can be use to thwart import surges and price declines in agricultural imports. In the context of WTO Non-Agricultural Market Access (NAMA), the group of developing countries known as NAMA-11[23] are also trying to ensure that any resulting agreement on the liberalisation of industrial tariffs does not result in de-industrialisation.

Preference gain and loss

Loss of quota protection, as experienced by India, Kenya and Lesotho under the phase-out of the Multifibre Arrangement, and loss of preference, experienced by St Lucia with the reform of the relationship between the EU and the ACP countries, can lead to high employment losses and increased poverty. More often than not, these aspects of trade liberalisation lead to 'an infusion of cheap imports that compete with domestically produced' items (Williams, 2003). The effects in Kenya, for example, included lay-offs, casualisation of labour contracts and lower wages.

One lesson from this is that governments need to develop social protection strategies that will prevent women, men and families from slipping into poverty when they are affected in this way by trade policies. Education and capacity building are also important. Where countries have focused on a single export crop, governments need to diversify into other areas – for example, in the case of the Caribbean, tourism, information technology and agro-processing (Ahmed, 2001).

Service liberalisation

The main lesson from the case studies on the impact of service liberalisation is that governments must seek, at all times, to ensure the fulfilment of their public health and social mandates. In the case of the migration of nurses and teachers, multiple challenges and contradictions are involved in pursuing liberalisation of the movement of natural persons. On the one hand, it invariably involves loss of human capital that is often developed with taxpayers' funds and is concomitant with declining health services. From the sending country's vantage point, this both imperils citizens and puts the government at risk of violating its commitment to ensure human rights in terms of health and education. On the other hand, the same government may benefit in the form of a return flow of international remittances. By allowing citizens to seek better conditions of work overseas, a government is also ensuring their enjoyment of human rights.

Ultimately, for countries in the Caribbean, Africa and Asia which are experiencing increasing flows of professionals abroad, the solution lies in remedying the underlying causes of emigration. These include institutional lack of capacity in terms of professional development, working conditions and remuneration at home. So governments must pay attention to policies that encourage professionals to stay put.

A similar situation exists in the case of ICT, in the sense that it too concerns domestic regulations for service providers. The responsibility for ensuring decent conditions of work and access to affordable services lies with government. The same set of institutional constraints applies to capacity building and must be overcome by proactive policies and the re-alignment of national resources.

In terms of future service liberalisation, governments of developing countries in Africa, Asia and the Pacific should seek to ensure that women workers across all spheres are well protected in terms of wage compensation and benefits when they move as temporary workers to host countries. Thus gender needs to be a catalytic factor in the discussion of Mode IV of the GATS.

Particular attention is also needed to ensure that micro, small and medium-sized enterprises have adequate access to business type visas to facilitate their presence at trade shows, exhibitions and similar cross-border marketing events. In the area of ICT, governments must seek to ensure that service providers are committed to the transfer of technology and joint venture programmes that enhance knowledge and access to ICT so that more women can be actively involved in this cross-border trade. Even if there is currently no local capacity in this area, governments should ensure that they do not make commitments that preclude such options in the future.

Non-tariff trade barriers

The issue of trade-related health and safety regulations and their gendered impact is particularly contentious. Countries have the obligation and the right to protect the health and safety of their citizens. At the same time, unilateral applications of sanitary and phytosanitary measures and technical barriers to trade (TBT) are asymmetric in terms of standard setting and implementation between developing and developed countries. They are also woefully lacking in transparency, may result in trade diversion and have been tainted with protectionism. SPS and TBT requirements are administratively difficult and cost prohibitive for poor developing countries.

As both the Bangladesh and Uganda cases illustrate, a ban based on health and safety requirements can have a costly impact on the workers and economy on which it is imposed. The two case studies indicate that women and men face specific and different challenges in rebounding from lost employment. It is also a big challenge for small and large business entities to secure the necessary financial and technical resources for upgrading their existing facilities, introducing safety requirements and performing risk assessments.

The lessons to be learned are manifold, but two key lessons stand out. First, governments need to develop compensatory trade adjustment funds at national level to assist women and other small-scale providers in cases where there are SPS challenges. Second, there is a need for social safety nets such as unemployment compensation and temporary work schemes to mitigate the most negative impacts of such events.

Aid for trade and trade-related capacity building

Developing countries' governments should also advocate at an international level for a SPS/TBT trade-related health and safety regulations trust fund that would provide ongoing technical assistance funds for the upgrading of food and related export sector activities. Such a fund could be a specialised fund within the domain of aid for trade (AfT) or trade-related capacity building (TRCB) mechanisms and processes that had already been established. Within the scope of the ban, there should be an emergency window for cases where it affects vulnerable populations such as women and those who are food insecure. Developed country members imposing the ban should put up additional reserves to meet the disbursement needs of the emergency window during the operational period of the ban.

Given the effects of the loss of quota protection or preference, it would seem that both AfT and TRCB are two specific areas of intervention in the trade policy environment that link synergistically with trade and women's empowerment. Many of the key considerations of market access that are problematic for small and medium-sized enterprises and smallholders in the agricultural sector – such as physical infrastructure and access to ICTs – have their own distinct gender dimensions that need to be specifically targeted and addressed within the context of AfT and TRCB planning.

Domestically, market access involves considerations that may apply in terms of:

- Demand conditions and the need to continually improve productivity to meet international competition;
- Physical infrastructure – roads, ports, airports and railways;
- Human (or soft) policy to deal with distortion, regulation, incentives and protection;
- Costs of information, transportation and communication;
- The global supply chain.

Women and poor minority businesses operating in the export and import sectors have a greater need to access many of the softer elements of market access and entry, such as incentives, tricks of the trade with regulations and assistance with the costs of information and communications, as well as dealing with global supply chains and product development. Programmes geared to providing export training, building and maintaining trading networks and assisting with capital upgrading, technical standards and regulations for specific export markets, if tailored with adequate gender sensitivity, can prove highly beneficial to women.

AfT is a contentious topic, but it is relevant to the discussion of women's economic empowerment and gender and trade because of its wide scope, which ranges from the issues of trade policy and regulation, trade development and trade-related infrastructure to trade related adjustment. Gender equality should be a central concern in all aspects of AfT, including 'trade-related adjustment' and 'other trade-related needs', but especially in those programmes and projects aimed at building the 'supply side capacity' and the 'human resource availability of developing countries' (AfT Task Force, 2006).

References

AfT Task Force (2006). 'Report', World Trade Organization, Geneva.
Ahmed, B (2001). 'The Impact of Globalization on the Caribbean Sugar and Banana Industries', The Society for Caribbean Studies Annual Conference Papers, vol. 2.
Litho, P (2007). 'Do Women's Access to ICTs Lead to Empowerment? Looking at the CEEWA ICT project', http://www.genderit.org/en/index.shtml?w=a&x=95381
Williams, M (2003). *Gender Mainstreaming in the Multilateral Trading Sector: A Handbook for Policy Makers and Other Stakeholders*, Commonwealth Secretariat, London.

PART TWO

Linking Women With Export Markets

13 Introduction to Part Two

Marilyn Carr

As was seen in the previous set of case studies, much of the literature on gender and trade has focused on the negative impact of trade policies on women as producers and workers, and on women as consumers, homemakers and care-givers. For example, many traditional non-farm enterprises operated by women, such as basket-making and the processing of cooking oils, are disappearing as a result of import competition; and women's ability to grow food is decreasing as farmers devote more land to commercial export crops and as women's labour shifts from food production into unpaid labour on family farms producing crops for export. Women's work on plantations and in factories producing for export is becoming increasingly less secure as globalisation fuels the 'race to the bottom' in which intense competition drives down wages even lower than they already are; and women's time poverty is increased as health services are privatised and women take on added responsibilities in caring for the sick and elderly (Carr and Chen, 2004).

However, trade liberalisation in general, as well as specific changes in trade policy, also offer new economic opportunities for women if they are enabled to take advantage of these. Thus, while it is important to assess the likely impact of changes in trade policies from a gender perspective and to advocate for such policies to be more gender sensitive, it is also necessary to give attention to national economic and social policies and legislation that aim at overcoming the constraints women face in benefiting from increased economic globalisation (Carr, 2008a). As one researcher puts it:

> It is important to remember that what happens in trade is likely to be much less important for reducing poverty than the other national policy and economic conditions that influence how opportunities from trade are transmitted to different groups within the economy. On the other hand, the indirect effects of trade can allow a government which is committed to reducing poverty and increasing opportunities for women to do so, even if there is no direct link through production. (Page, 2004)

The challenges faced by women in becoming involved in productive activities include more restricted access than men to land, credit, improved technologies, skills and business training, and market and price information. These are at once caused and compounded by their reduced mobility and greater time poverty as a result of socio-cultural factors and family responsibilities. And research shows that the constraints faced by women wishing to reach export markets are twice as severe as those faced by women supplying domestic markets (Tandon, 2003). This is because quality standards are so much more stringent in the case of export markets, there are stricter conditions in terms of time and quantities of supply, and the logistics of exporting are so complex.

A number of different policy and programme initiatives have been initiated by governments, NGOs, international agencies and the private sector with the aim of assisting women to adjust to and take advantage of global economic changes. Economic policy initiatives include: financial policies such as guaranteed loan schemes and provision of microfinance and meso-level finance for women; education and training policies that widen women's access to the knowledge and skills important for integration into a globalised economy; and gender policies, including changes in women's rights to the land, which can provide collateral and also a base for economic activities. Other policies that can help women include those that improve national infrastructure for ensuring standards for particular products that are acceptable in importing countries, and national export promotion strategies for particular economic sectors. Often, however, these policies fail to benefit women because they are gender-blind and ignore women's particular needs, even if they relate to sectors in which women predominate.

Various direct initiatives have been implemented by NGOs, international agencies and the private sector. In some cases, women have been assisted to organise into trade associations, producer/marketing co-operatives and community-owned businesses so that they can more effectively bargain with middlemen and gain greater control over the marketing chain. They have also been provided with greater access to improved production/processing technologies and training that will enable them to add value locally and produce high quality goods that meet international standards. In other cases, individual (social) entrepreneurs have set up socially responsible export businesses that either provide markets for individual women farmers and producers through buying raw materials or processed inputs from them, or provide them with (factory) jobs in processing and manufacturing for export.

The important point in all this is to find ways in which informal women workers can maintain their livelihoods at the same time as retaining their sense of security. Both of these aspects are necessary. Throughout the developing world, women's enterprise activities are of key importance in providing the food and income that enable their families to exist. Official statistics estimate this income at up to half of each country's national income. It is earned almost exclusively within the large and growing informal economy, where women are over-represented (ILO, 2002). In Africa, for example, official statistics indicate that the share of the informal economy in the non-agricultural workforce is over 70 per cent, and that 84 per cent of women non-agricultural workers are informally employed, compared with 63 per cent of men. Moreover, many jobs in large export-oriented factories provide income but no security and therefore no long-term prospects of empowerment.

Research indicates that what is needed is to find ways of helping women to:

- Upgrade quality and/or reduce prices so as to compete with imports;
- Upgrade quality and organise in such a way as to supply large volumes of products that are acceptable in export markets; and/or
- Diversify into products that can find regional and global markets – either directly or through a socially responsible business or intermediary.

(Carr, 2008b)

This section contains ten case studies that provide a wide range of examples of how governments, NGOs, international agencies and the private sector have been working – either alone, or more often together – in order to link rural poor women with export markets. The case studies come from diverse Commonwealth countries – Cameroon, Fiji Islands, Ghana, India, Jamaica, Mozambique, Swaziland and Uganda – and most of the authors either own or are intimately involved in the enterprises being described.

Three of the case studies relate to traditional primary commodity exports: cocoa in Ghana, coffee in Jamaica and cashews in India and Mozambique. In all cases, special efforts have been made to link with export markets in ways that emphasise the livelihoods of poor farmers and rural communities, and especially women, and have introduced innovative ideas in the process. In Ghana, cocoa farmers are linked with the fair trade market in the UK and USA and are shareholders in their own chocolate companies in these countries. In Jamaica, ways are being found for small women farmers to overcome constraints in exporting organic coffee to niche markets and organise in ways that allow them to also get Fairtrade certification. And in India and Mozambique, alternatives to large-scale cashew nut processing factories are being promoted that offer decentralised, rural-based employment opportunities.

Four of the case studies relate to exports based on natural products that are aimed at niche markets: beauty products made from marula oil in Swaziland; natural body-products from virgin coconut oil in Fiji Islands; dried flowers in India; and honey and other bee-products in Uganda. In all cases, although the products use traditional resources that have been used by local communities for generations, they involve new and/or more sophisticated types of products for which there are growing markets in Europe, Japan and the USA. In Swaziland, a local community organisation has linked with an international NGO to process marula nut oil supplied by thousands of women to a factory in which they are shareholders and that exports high quality beauty products to commercial buyers and fair trade organisations. In Fiji Islands, a woman entrepreneur and her family run a successful natural body product export business that provides incomes for rural communities that supply the central factory with raw materials and semi-processed and processed goods in a way that keeps alive local skills and traditions. In India, a local entrepreneur runs a dried flower export business that sources raw materials from a complex network of rural women and men farmers and provides work for 2,000 poor women in a central processing factory. And in Uganda, women's co-operatives, community-owned businesses and private companies are all helping women to increase the quality and quantity of bee-products to replace imported goods and then increase exports.

Three of the case studies relate to manufactured exports: shoes in India, embroidered goods in India and ready-made garments in Cameroon. In the Indian examples, innovative ways have been found to provide high quality goods and enable rural women to link with global markets without being exploited in large-scale export factories or as home workers earning less than US$1 per day. In the case of shoes, hundreds of women and men artisans have been assisted to form their own collaborative organisation and to undertake their own international marketing. In the case of embroidered goods, thousands of women who are members of India's largest women's trade union have been helped to reach export markets through a complex network including a trade facilitation centre that is owned by its members. In both cases, the goods being exported are based on women's traditional skills for which there is a limited domestic market. In the example from Cameroon, the women involved in exporting ready-made garments are fairly well educated, and although they provide some work for other women, the project is obviously different from the other nine case studies in terms of its outreach to the poorest women in the informal economy. It is included, however, because it is one of the few examples of how ICT has helped women to break into export markets.

Although there are only ten case studies in this section, they include many different types of organising structures, from small women's groups to community-owned businesses and commercial businesses owned and operated by social entrepreneurs. They target all types of markets: fair trade, organic and niche, and mainstream retail and chain stores. At the same time, all of them to a greater or lesser extent seek to establish and run a profitable and expanding export business, while also taking into consideration the livelihoods, skills and traditions of poor and mainly rural women. Most also have a concern for the environment and their carbon footprint.

References

Carr, M (2008a). 'Spreading the Gains of Globalisation: Linking Women with Global Markets' in *Small Change or Real Change?, Commonwealth Perspectives on Financing Gender Equality*, Commonwealth Secretariat, London.

Carr, M (2008b). *Gender and Non-Timber Forest Products: Promoting Food Security and Economic Empowerment*, International Fund for International Development, Rome.

Carr, M and Chen, M (2004). 'Globalization, Social Exclusion and Gender', *International Labour Review*, 143(1/2).

ILO (2002). *Women and Men in the Informal Economy: A Statistical Picture*, ILO, Geneva.

Page, S (2004). 'The Trade Policy Context', in Carr, M (ed.) *Chains of Fortune: Linking Women Producers and Workers with Global Markets*, Commonwealth Secretariat, London.

Tandon, N (2003). 'Micro and Small Enterprise and ICT: A Gender Analysis', unpublished paper prepared for the World Bank, Washington, DC.

Traditional Primary Products

14 Raising the Bar on Chocolate: Cocoa Farmers in Ghana Shape the Future

Pauline Tiffen

Background

In 1993 the Government of Ghana initiated the partial liberalisation of its most significant economic export, cocoa beans. Having resisted World Bank pressure to liberalise fully, the Cocoa Marketing Board retained its monopoly on exports through the Cocoa Marketing Company. It thus sustained its farm-to-port quality control system of every sack and its authority to determine the terms of trade from farmer to free on board (fob).[24] This was an attempt to keep Ghana's premium status as the second largest cocoa supplier in the world and as a reliable exporter. In contrast to the situation in neighbouring Côte d'Ivoire, the largest supplier, it also left a dependable export channel for farmers in place.

In common with other liberalisations of the period, however, farmers – particularly the considerable number of women cocoa farmers in Ghana – were considered not as 'protagonists' in the exercise but as subjects. This assumption is epitomised by the terminology of the liberalisation itself, which granted trade licences to 'buying companies', ignoring the fact that what farmers want is to 'sell', not 'buy' cocoa.

In 1993, just over 2,000 farmers in 22 villages were therefore assisted by Twin, a UK NGO, and the Netherlands development organisation SNV to establish a co-operatively owned company to 'buy' its own cocoa and then 'sell' it to the Cocoa Marketing Company. From those modest beginnings, Kuapa Kokoo has evolved to become a complex, multifaceted institution working in five of the six growing regions of Ghana, with an active membership of more than 45,000 farmers in more than 1,300 villages or Kuapa Kokoo societies.[25]

There is a visible and positive trend in women's involvement at all levels of the organisation. Between 1998 and 2006 female representation increased at society executive level from 29 to 32 per cent, at area level from 29 to 45 per cent and on the National Executive Council from 15 to 60 per cent. This exceeded the target set in 2001 for 30 per cent female participation at all levels of decision-making (Ronchi, 2002). In addition, Kuapa Kokoo farmers have a direct and meaningful stake in the Divine chocolate brand marketed in the UK, Ireland and the USA and in several other countries. In this period, their equity stake in the UK company rose from 33 to 45 per cent.

At the heart of the growth of the Kuapa Kokoo project has been its transparency and its democratic process. It has seen the orderly arrival and departure of a number of leaders and, as noted above, a growing number of elected women. This structure distinguishes Kuapa Kokoo from its competitors, both at home in a now highly competitive cocoa trading environment (where a number of the major cocoa multinationals also operate), and overseas in the performance and impact of the two chocolate companies in which Kuapa Kokoo has a significant equity stake: The Day Chocolate Company (renamed Divine in 2006) in the UK and Divine Chocolate Inc., set up in 2007 in the USA.

Conditions in the cocoa industry and chocolate market

The cocoa industry in Ghana

Within Ghana the logic of partial liberalisation has proceeded, with more buying companies competing, including several transnational corporations. Tightening global supply due to climatic changes and more unpredictable harvests, together with stable demand, have led to rising prices for cocoa beans from below the fair trade 'minimum' level of US$1,600, reaching the highest level for 30 years in 2009. A continued global shortfall has persisted for four consecutive years, adding to incentives for buying companies and sharpening competitive practices at village level.

Independent research shows that Kuapa Kokoo has played an important role in shaping the expectations of all farmers familiar with their model, to the extent that there are now few licensed buying companies in Ghana who do not at least pay lip-service to social benefits. This usually means giving out small, discretionary rewards – salt, soap, pens, notebooks – and minor bonuses to cocoa agents or collectors at the point of purchase. However, only Kuapa Kokoo stresses local management and ownership of weighing scales – a vital tool and one of the main ways for buyers to cheat farmers in the villages.

The cocoa business in Ghana is fundamentally a volume business: the fixed operational costs are hard to control since the systems that all traders must follow are set out by the Cocoa Marketing Board. By achieving scale – around 35,000 tonnes annually – Kuapa Kokoo has the means to compete with the larger companies, but faces constant challenges from competitors. More significantly, the entry of international players has changed the dynamics in the local cocoa buying industry because they have:

- Access to externally sourced, lower cost trade finance; and
- An ability to hedge, i.e. to manage the risk of fluctuating prices through to the final purchaser, enabling cash rewards to feature in purchasing practices to ensure that supply and volumes are achieved.

Local buying companies do not have these advantages. Since the cost of finance available to local companies, including Kuapa Kokoo, is extremely high (16–24%), this quickly erodes operating profitability and margins. The credit crunch is now rendering local cocoa trade finance yet more costly and less available.

According to interviews in 2008, the Cocoa Marketing Board continues to find Kuapa Kokoo a model that gives significant financial and other returns to farmers. It particularly noted that Kuapa Kokoo was the only buying company that accounted to farmers by reporting in public each year to its membership. Kuapa Kokoo's segregated export channel – essential for their small but growing proportion of fair trade cocoa sales – remains the same as when it launched its trading in 1993. Around 8 per cent of its cocoa ends up in Fairtrade certified products. However, pressure is growing for more 'traceability', organic beans and semi-processed products (in one of the several cocoa processing facilities now built in Ghana with foreign direct investment). Concessions are being made, especially to transnationals and their end clients, which is putting the future of this professional, third party mechanism in question. The cocoa trading world is a small one, with just a few intensely competing players. Being forced to enter this world directly could prove a significant new barrier to Kuapa Kokoo accessing conventional cocoa export markets in its own right. It could directly inhibit the entry of many new women's or farmers' groups in Ghana; indeed, most of the new farmer-centred initiatives there are sponsored by transnational cocoa and chocolate corporations.

The international chocolate market

The international chocolate market has undergone a transformation in the last decade. In common with many other product sectors, the market has been 'broken up', not in terms of ownership of the brands and products – which, if anything has undergone yet further concentration – but in terms of product segmentation. Previously, single origin cocoas (i.e. chocolate bars that proclaim the actual provenance of the beans) were virtually unheard of. Now there is a proliferation of single origin bars, providing important opportunities for cocoa farmers across the tropics. Similarly, the distribution of niche products – unusual flavours, messages and ingredients – as well as certified organic chocolate, has been growing, leading to the take-over of a number of emerging niche brands such as Green & Black's and Dagoba by the major chocolate companies (Cadbury and Hershey, respectively).

In addition, the community of cocoa processors – those who turn beans into cocoa butter, liquor and cocoa powder – has contracted even further, with firms like Barry Callebaut now responsible for most of the world's processed cocoa after an aggressive expansion and investment in all continents. This narrowing of the channels to markets inhibits grassroots initiatives from getting off the ground (and into the marketplace) without the direct collaboration – and therefore control – of the major cocoa/chocolate firms.

Within this context, this case study looks at the experience of the Kuapa Kokoo-Divine relationship and trading model in terms of its impact on Ghana's cocoa farmers, especially women, and on the international chocolate market as a whole.

Kuapa Kokoo and Divine Chocolate: cocoa farmers influencing their own lives and international consumer markets

History and purpose

Divine Chocolate was founded in 1998 by Kuapa Kokoo, Twin Trading UK, The Body Shop International plc and other direct supporters of fair trade, such as Christian Aid and Comic Relief. Divine is a unique kind of chocolate branding and marketing company, co-owned by Kuapa Kokoo whose members have a 45 per cent equity share in the company. The relationship between its various entities is shown in Figure 14.1.

Divine set out to improve the livelihoods of smallholder cocoa producers in West Africa by establishing their own dynamic brand in the UK chocolate market, thus putting them higher up the value chain. The way Divine sought to do this was to:

- Take a quality and affordable range of fair trade chocolate bars into the mainstream chocolate market;
- Raise awareness of fair trade issues among UK retailers and consumers of all age groups; and
- Be highly visible and vocal in the chocolate sector and thereby act as a catalyst for change.

Figure 14.1 Divine and Kuapa Kokoo: relationships and scope

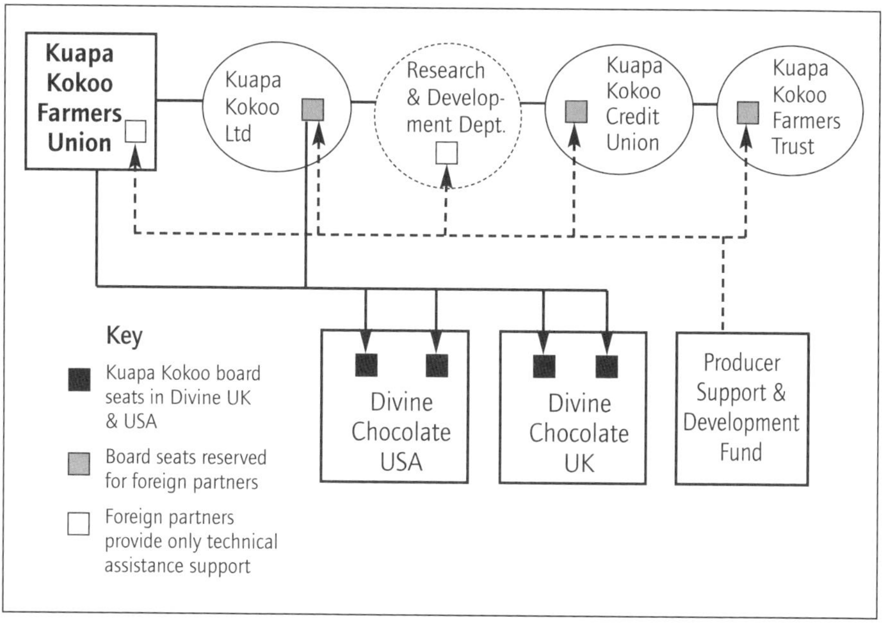

Source: Divine Chocolate Ltd

Achievements in the international market

Building on its provenance and farmers' direct ownership, Divine has achieved all these aims in a little over ten years. It offers a range of more than 30 high quality products distributed in all major UK supermarkets and many other outlets. It has been commended for its role in prompting a major sea-change in the chocolate market generally. The proudly displayed *adinkra*[26] symbols on Divine products emphasise the brand's authenticity.

Growth in sales and presence in the UK market, and more recently in the USA, have undoubtedly added to the credibility of the 'strategic project' of bringing cocoa farmers to the fore of their high value, glamorous industry, transforming them from the ignominious role of 'tree minders'. In 2005/06, Divine's total UK sales were almost £9 million and for 2006/07 £10.7 million. This represented a 100 per cent increase on the first year's sales for 1998/99 of £103,000.

Figure 14.2 Divine sales turnover, 1998–2007

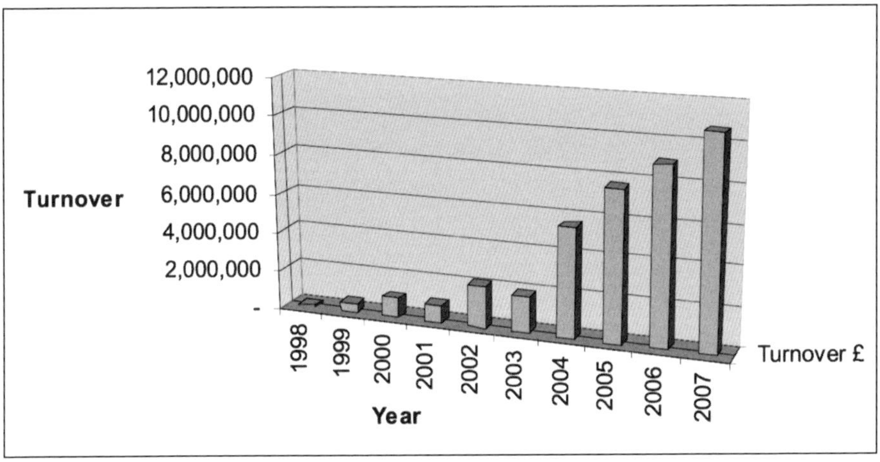

Source: Divine Chocolate Ltd

As Fairtrade certified products have found space in mainstream retail outlets, cafés, restaurants, cinemas and offices, a number of large companies have opted to 'go fair trade', at least to an extent, in order not to 'miss out' on this growing market and to indicate their company's social credentials. Opting to apply Fairtrade certification to a whole range of own label or branded products has become one of the major drivers of growth in fair trade markets worldwide. One commentator from a chocolate competitor acknowledged: 'I would go as far to say that Divine are the architects of retailer own label fair trade chocolate' (cited in Twin, 2008).

Chocolate is a highly processed product. While cocoa beans have a high market value, they are bought and sold as a commodity. This is the situation for all farmers in the world except those at Kuapa Kokoo. The most significant aspect of brand ownership of a chocolate company by cocoa farmers is their stake in the brand equity of the end product – and thereby their right to earn financial returns from the intangible value generated by brands in the final marketplace.

Commercially, the impact has been radical. Nobody expected a small newcomer to the mature £4 billion chocolate market, with such a different structure and vision, to succeed. When the Co-op Food Group in the UK switched its whole own label chocolate range to fair trade in 2002, in partnership with Divine and Kuapa Kokoo, the (then) head commented:

> It was the strength of the Divine Fairtrade branding and the Fairtrade provenance. I don't think there was anybody else doing Fairtrade chocolate in the way and with the credibility Divine did it and the links back to

> the producers because from our point of view, the links back to the producers are key. (David Croft, cited in Twin, 2008)

Subsequently, there have been full transitions to fair trade by retailers of their own label ranges of coffee, tea and bananas at Sainsbury's and Marks & Spencer, massively expanding farmers' opportunities, consumer accessibility and Fairtrade's profile in the marketplace.

With chocolate, however, apart from a few tiny niche players, there was no movement for about five years. Then, within the last 18 months, something shifted. In March 2009 Cadbury announced it would convert its iconic Cadbury Dairy Milk brand to Fairtrade certified status by the end of 2009.[27] Selling 300 million bars a year in the UK and Ireland, Cadbury will start to source its cocoa from Fairtrade farmers in Ghana, potentially tripling the amount of fairly traded cocoa coming into the international market from that country. It is the biggest brand of its kind to make the move. Even companies like Marks & Spencer, which have done full own label conversions in other product areas, have not done so for chocolate. Large companies like Nestlé have apparently stopped at the launch of one single new Fairtrade coffee product, 'Partners' Blend', out of a potential 8,000 existing products that could have been converted.

Mars, the largest end user of cocoa in the world, has eschewed the fair trade approach, but in April 2009 made a commitment to transform all of the US$10 billion worth of cocoa it sources annually to 'sustainably sourced' by 2020 (Wiggens, 2009). Among its cited motives is a desire to 'secure our long-term sourcing' and the expectations of consumers and employees of Mars 'to do the right thing'. It may be tempting to chocolate activists the world over to ask these employees what 'the right thing' might be when compared to the model of farmer-ownership, in-market participation, women's empowerment and consumer education espoused by Divine.

In this sense then, with a 'generation' of conscious chocolate consumers now active in the market place, the international impact is continuing.

Impact on cocoa farmers in Ghana

In 2007 Divine paid its first dividend, i.e. share of profits, to its shareholders, including Kuapa Kokoo farmers as co-owners of the brand, and it has followed on with further dividend payments in 2008–2009. In the global economy today, fully one-third of the major corporations' balance sheets are accounted for by intangible, rather than tangible, assets. That is, their brands, symbols, logos, designs and patents versus their factories, buildings and machinery. This revenue stream for Kuapa Kokoo's farmers is a great source of distinction and pride. It adds to two other important revenue streams:

1. *Divine's fund for producers' support and development.* To date this amounts to more than £700,000. These funds are provided directly by the consumers of Divine with every bar purchased, and they are applied to women's projects, organisational development, farmer education and co-operative training. This income stream is built into the model, i.e. it is not discretionary aid, periodic project investment or PR-motivated social project work. It is a recognition that to mature, cope and grow, all organisations need to continually learn, change and experiment.
2. *The fair trade social premium.* Divine has contributed more than US$1 million in Fairtrade social premium payments to Kuapa Kokoo over the last ten years. This has been spent largely on reaching the same poverty targets as are aimed at by the Millennium Development Goals: clean water, education, women's income generation and health care.

Kuapa Kokoo records suggest that the total value of additional bonus payments made to members over the last 12 years is in excess of £1.7 million. This Divine fair trade package compares very favourably to other recently introduced cocoa certification systems. The fundamental differences with these other systems, which aim to offer reassurance on farm management practices, are that they:

1. Do not directly address price and the terms of trade between very unequal partners in any systematic manner;
2. Leave the conventional trading relationship unchanged and unaudited;
3. Leave premiums (higher prices for cocoa beans) as a discretionary item; and
4. Do not support organisational development through self-managed social premiums or any focus on participatory or democratic organisations.

Knock-on effects throughout the value chain

Divine's efforts at wrapping a quite different 'package' up in a bar of chocolate, selling more chocolate year by year, communicating effectively about ideals and connectivity, reaching young people in a fun and unprecedented manner through schools and educational linkages between Ghana and the UK all make its partnership with Kuapa Kokoo unique in the global chocolate industry. It is still a benchmark of what the major players – few though there are – could be aiming for.

Perhaps the most important contribution to the evolving chocolate industry has been Divine and Kuapa Kokoo's emphasis on the formal nature of their relationship. As shown in Figure 14.1, there is representation at the heart of the Kuapa Kokoo-Divine structure, cemented and provided for in the election of leaders, direct representation on each others' boards and decision-making bodies and ownership of shares.

Supply chain best practice certainly now widely promotes the notion of 'linkages' to producers of raw materials. Many producers have started to learn about the routes their product takes to market and the various players with whom they may need to connect in order to be able to influence their market destiny. Furthermore, many socially responsible companies lay public claim to 'partnerships' with their developing country suppliers. However, their definition of partnership usually lacks structure, has few if any defined mutual rights and obligations, and certainly has no legal force. 'Partnership' is becoming a new catchword for aid-financed development projects.

In the context of the major chocolate corporations' valid concerns about the future supply of their important raw material, it is not difficult to see the proliferation of new investments by chocolate companies in a sceptical light. The figures bandied around are very high: 'tens of millions of dollars' (Mars), '£1.5 million' (Cadbury) (Wiggens, 2009). New cocoa industry bodies formed in the wake of child slavery scandals[28] have struggled to engage with cocoa farmers at all. NGOs, governments and the private sector still dominate these forums, with strong cocoa farmer organisations few and far between. Local governments in cocoa-producing areas also face a dilemma: the power of the chocolate companies is clearly daunting, the language is constructive (the discourse is all about sustainability), but nothing much is changing in the underlying top-down structure of the relationships between corporates and farmers in West Africa. Efforts to develop a sustainable cocoa partnership in Ghana have followed this traditional style, despite the intervention of Fairtrade certifiers.

Kuapa Kokoo representatives have been active and vocal in explaining their lives and their challenges and learning about the overseas societies in which chocolate is sold, how branding companies are run and what makes great chocolate. All this has a direct impact on the status of cocoa farming in Ghana, the farmers' attention to quality, the confidence of farmer leaders, and especially the visibility of women in the organisation and overseas.

Lessons learned

There are important lessons to be learned from the experiences of Kuapa Kokoo and Divine. Among these are:

1. Competing in a global business and changing business environment requires

guts, tenacity and allies; these are more easily found when they can be mobilised around an inspiring vision and prospect for change (not to mention delicious products!).

2. Kuapa Kokoo has learned, in a harshly competitive local environment, that permanent education and local marketing is important to sustain its members' support, raise farmers' consciousness of their industry and continuously improve services and operations. Promoting its story, values and vision is a local and not just an international priority.

3. Branding, brand equity and producers' stories and images are increasingly important to the large companies promoting products made from traditional raw materials sourced in the developing world. Divine has forced the issue of farmer-ownership onto the agenda in ways that few of the larger, more dominant brand owners have yet tackled. For farmers to negotiate and leverage value from their intellectual property – i.e. their systems, their names and their values – from large international companies for their own benefit requires courage, information, helpful tools (such as prior consent agreements) and moral, and sometimes legal, support.

4. Women's rights need to be proactively defended and mutual respect fostered. Kuapa Kokoo has since its outset practised a quota system for representation, a practice that has seen women gain confidence and visibility over time. Women outnumber men in many Kuapa Kokoo bodies, notably the National Executive Council.

There are also lessons for governments concerning policy and reputation. First, export policy and marketing structures directly affect low-income producers and their access to markets. They can make or break the fortunes of local companies, especially when these are pitted against the resources and interests of transnationals. Second, a country's reputation is important and derives from many sources: the performance of its 'best ambassador companies'; its attitudes, which are duly enshrined in policy, towards complex issues such as child labour, fair competition, and access to finance and financial services; and its defence of women's roles and rights.

For international agencies promoting transparency and equity in supply chains, the Kuapa Kokoo and Divine story also offers some revealing lessons. Certification systems matter a great deal in the retail environment; they inform and shape consumer expectations and action. As certification in the chocolate industry is expanding, reflection and great care needs to be taken in order:

- To ensure cocoa producers are not taken advantage of in a new generation of top-down supply chain arrangements;

- For women's and low-income producers' advocates not to lose a vision of empowerment as part and parcel of the 'deal' in the face of commercial expediency, familiar brands and what can only be called the allure of 'large numbers';
- To communicate the core values of different brands and certification marks to consumers honestly and fully, including, where necessary, calling all players to account through civil society action or even legal mechanisms (e.g. the Advertising Standards Authority that monitors the veracity of claims).

In this way farmers can progress from their role as raw material producers, and consumers can continue to play an informed and vital role in driving forward change in business practice among major companies through the continued discriminating application of their purchasing power.

References

BBC (2009). 'Cadbury Dairy Milk Goes Fairtrade', *BBC News*, 4 March, http://news.bbc.co.uk/2/hi/business/7923385.stm

Cooper, B (2009). 'The Just-food Interview – Sophi Tranchell, Divine Chocolate', 5 March, http://www.just-food.com

Economist, The (2007). 'Thinking out of the Box: How African Cocoa Growers Are Moving Upstream into Chocolate', *The Economist*, 4 April.

Ronchi, L (2002). 'Monitoring Impact of Fairtrade Initiatives: a Case Study of Kuapa Kokoo and The Day Chocolate Company', Twin Trading, London.

Tiffen, P *et al.* (2004). 'From Tree Minders to Global Players: Cocoa Farmers in Ghana' in Carr M (ed.), *Chains of Fortune: Linking Women Producers and Workers with Global Markets*, Commonwealth Secretariat, London.

Twin (2008). 'Divine's Impact on the UK Chocolate Market and Kuapa Kokoo Farmers in Ghana, 1997–2007', Report for the Department for International Development, London, February.

Wiggens, J (2009). 'Mars Goes Sweet on Ethically Sourced Cocoa', *Financial Times*, 9 April.

Websites:

Divine Chocolate: http://www.divinechocolate.com

Kuapa Kokoo: http://kuapakokoo.com/kuapa/

15 Cultivating Organic Coffee: Challenges for Small Farmers in Jamaica

Dorienne Rowan-Campbell

Overview

Jamaica Blue Mountain Coffee is one of the country's premier exports. It is also one of the most expensive coffees in the world, often selling for US$35–40 per pound. It can thus provide an income for small farmers, as well as employment opportunities for agricultural labourers. However, many challenges are involved in supplying the domestic and – especially – export markets. This case study looks at experiences of exporting organic Blue Mountain Coffee from the perspective of a small-scale woman farmer who owns and operates the six-acre Rowan's Royale Organic Farm.

Challenges at various levels

Production and marketing challenges

It takes three years for a coffee tree to bear fruit, and marketing the product is difficult for a small farmer growing a commodity controlled by a marketing and regulatory board.

The first hurdle is the Coffee Industry Board (CIB). The CIB's principal role is to promote, regulate, monitor and guide the development of the coffee industry in Jamaica and to assure the coffee's quality and integrity. It controls trademark registration licensing and monitors coffee dealers, processors, workers and nurseries. As the certification body for Jamaica Blue Mountain Coffee, it defines quality standards and growing areas and recommends specific plant varieties. It also provides advisory services.

Among the strategies for quality control is the requirement that any producer applying for a licence to process a brand must be able to supply 10,000 boxes annually. A box contains approximately 10 gallons of ripe coffee cherries.[29] As average yields are about 80 boxes per acre, the requirement is clearly addressed to the large commercial farmer who has over 100 acres. It is also clear that while there is undoubtedly a commitment to quality, that particular regulation is directed to the question of quantity. Historically, the CIB bought ripe cherries from small farmers and processed them at its own factories. The production system is now more decentralised, but small farmers are still expected to sell the cherries on to the licensees who have taken over that function of the CIB. It is thus illegal for small farmers to process and sell their crop.

Being an organic farmer has provided a bargaining chip to challenge the system. Organic integrity must be maintained. The cherries cannot simply be sold on or processed by any factory and retain their organic certification. Rowan's Royale is certified organic for both farm production and off-farm processing. Since 2004 it has been awaiting a judgement from the CIB as to its legal status: its right to the brand, Rowan's Royale, and the right to market.[30] While the business can trade in a small way, selling to a group of customers locally who are all repeat buyers, this is a small market and there is a need to expand outreach.

There are a number of benefits involved in organic, as compared to conventional, production. For example, hurricanes are a frequent occurrence in the region and organic coffee trees, although still traumatised by extreme weather, are resuscitated more quickly than conventional trees. In addition, research undertaken for a presentation to a regional Caribbean organic meeting in 2004 showed that the low cost of inputs in organic farming balanced the increased labour required for weeding or pruning (Rowan-Campbell, 2004). As the costs of fertiliser have sky-rocketed, it is likely that conventional farming will call for much higher inputs. The yield was fairly equal for organic coffee and conventional coffee, although in the longer term the high level of chemical inputs on the conventional farms will damage the soil and thus their production capacity.

However, there are also costs involved in organic farming. One of the major ones is certification. For a small farm, international certification costs about JA$43,000 per annum.[31] The costs used to be even higher but, with the growing need for inspection, certification bodies from Germany and the UK have situated inspectors in the region. This has cut down on the heavy travel costs which formerly had to be borne by the farmers.

In 2007, the possibility of farmers working together as community growers' groups and thus obtaining organic certification was dealt a blow. These groups are considered as an entity, with the books given an overall check and a number of representative farms thoroughly inspected. The USA has decided that this is an unsafe practice and recommended that each farm in a community growers group should be inspected once a year as with single farms. This is being regarded in the region as a non-tariff trade barrier as, if maintained, it will put international certification of such commodities as coffee and cocoa out of the reach of most small farmers and block their access to northern markets for their organic products. Fortunately, the EU has not followed suit.

Export challenges

It is possible to legally export up to 10lbs of coffee after obtaining a certificate from the Jamaica Trade and Investment Company (JAMPRO); this must accompany every export shipment. Unfortunately, all courier services out of the island pass through the USA. An exporter must, therefore, register with the US Food and Drug Administration (FDA) and file a Prior Notice of Imported Foods so that the FDA is in possession of the details of the shipment before the package arrives. This stricture is part of US bio-terrorism precautions. Compliance with these regulations does not make exporting from Jamaica to Canada, Europe or the rest of the Caribbean any simpler. The US Customs Department has the authority to detain packages for long periods of time; coffee often arrives at its final destination with a third of the packages slashed and useless. There is no redress and no insurance is available. The exporter simply has to accept the losses. It is small comfort to learn that 'the FDA and US Customs have different computer systems, so sometimes information takes a while to coordinate'.[32]

Costs of export shipments eat into actual and projected profits from sales. JAMPRO must be paid a registration fee, the courier companies charge about US$75 per 10lbs, with the cost changing according to the US dollar-Jamaican dollar exchange rate. For export to the EU, the organic certifying agency must provide a certificate indicating the organic status, and there is a charge for each certificate issued.

Demand challenges

There is great demand for Jamaica Blue Mountain Coffee and willingness to pay a high price. However, there are a number of hidden issues that face a small producer. At the reaping stage, large companies try to seduce growers by offering as much as JA$3,500 per box. Sometimes, after delivery the grower is told that the quality of the beans was not as good as expected and the price per box is reduced. It is difficult to refute this claim as the beans have long since disappeared into the general collection mix. If a small farmer keeps their coffee and does not sell on to other producers and processors, the challenge comes at a later stage and in three forms: the demand for clean green beans; the need for Fairtrade certification; and the need to supply large quantities.

First, most importers or dealers and outlets are interested in clean green beans, not processed and packaged coffee. Coffee is an extremely labour-intensive crop that goes through 13 stages from reaping to cup. It is washed, floated to take off any berries that are less than perfect, pulped, fermented, washed again and set out to dry in the sun. Thorough drying may take as long as three weeks, depending on the weather. The coffee is then stored until needed. When it is time for roasting, the parchment – the thin brittle membrane protecting the seed – is removed, which is traditionally done in a large mortar with a huge pestle. The 'green' coffee beans are then sized and sorted. The remaining stages are those of roasting, sorting and doing a final quality check before packaging. A demand for clean green beans means that all the labour is placed on the producer, while the roaster and packager claim the spoils. For organic green beans, foreign companies offer on average only U$33 per kg. Roasted beans sell at $77 per kg.

The economic gains are thus clearly in the value-added element and any farmer, but particularly a small farmer, needs to maximise production to the stage of premium value. This is what the CIB, to date, does not allow small farmers to do. Relative to the level of labour that goes into producing clean green beans, it is much more attractive financially to package the end product. Many unlicensed producers are thus doing just that. This makes the quality control function of the CIB even more difficult and compromises the strong name of the brand.

The second export challenge is the Fairtrade label. More and more coffee consumers are requiring that the coffee they buy bear this label. The basic certification processes and trade regulations of the label can indeed contribute to more sustainable livelihoods and farming practices.[33] However, there are blind spots. A small farm with only a few people working it does not qualify as a commercial enterprise that can obtain this label. If there are no other farmers around who practice organic production, a small farm cannot qualify as a farmer group or co-operative. Many distributors who would like to source organic Jamaica Blue Mountain Coffee say that their customers want a Fairtrade label. That is, therefore, another market opportunity denied.

The third export challenge is that large enterprises such as Trader Joe's, who sample the coffee and are interested in carrying it, simply want much more of the product than a small farmer can supply. The other route is to establish links with small businesses – small wholefood and organic markets – that take some coffee. Although this type or partnership makes a good match for size, commitment to organic principles and fair trading practices, such partners tend to operate at the margin and often go out of business.

Interventions to help farmers

In order to help small women (and men) farmers to overcome the hurdles faced in exporting coffee, several interventions have been proposed and/or implemented at farm, national and regional level.

Farm level

Given the difficulties in breaking into the coffee market effectively, many small coffee farmers, including Rowan's Royale, have realised that they cannot survive on monoculture and have explored alternatives. Coffee requires soil with a very high *pH* level. Asparagus requires a similar growing medium and is a good complement to coffee. It too is a long-term crop and can be reaped in the same season. It realises high prices on local markets – particularly hotels, which normally have to import from countries as far away as Peru. In addition to asparagus, farms such as Rowan's Royale have also started producing some exotic salad leaf greens and items unusual in the island, such as purple Russian kale, multi-coloured Swiss chard and variegated beets. There are local foods as well. Sweet potato is used as a cover crop that can be reaped as desired. Bananas and plantains are used to offer more shade to young coffee trees. Pineapples beside the leaf lettuces and asparagus are used as a barrier against insects, while lemons, mulberries, rose-apples and tangy yellow raspberries abound and are processed into marmalades and other products.

National level

One area of necessity for organic agriculture is an infrastructure that supports the particular needs of the production process. While the Jamaica Organic Agriculture Movement (JOAM), formally established in 2000, has driven organic production activities in the island, engineering the correct architecture to support this has been slow. JOAM has provided farmer training courses through the International Organic Inspectors Association (IOIA) for inspector certification and has established JOAM organic standards and a local certification body. Despite this track record, the Ministry of Agriculture's organic agriculture policy is still in draft form. The Jamaica Bureau of Standards is in discussion with JOAM about adopting the JOAM standards as national standards.

Small farmers need a strong mesh of business networks with other small farmers. This understanding encouraged a number of women small farmers to decide on a mutual support policy. Each will buy and use the other's products – packaged salad greens, honey, coffee, asparagus, cheeses – and the group is looking to expand to farmers that produce organic chickens, eggs and meats. Some of the group are sharing transportation costs when organic manures are sourced.

Regional level

A series of three workshops on ICT tools and services for women organic farmers in the Caribbean and a subsequent facilitators' training has begun a process of networking among women farmers committed to organic growing.[34] At first the network exchanged and shared information and checked on members after hurricanes and floods. Now a group is beginning to look at inter-Caribbean marketing of organic products, developing alternative marketing arrangements, trading and barter, and examining potential shipping arrangements. The network is also developing the capacity to capture and share traditional farming lore and to document women's and small farmers' 'ways of knowing' and ways of growing.

If the Jamaica Bureau of Standards adopts the JOAM standards, it will be easier to reach a common standard for the Caribbean region using Jamaica as the model because national bureaus of standards are working towards harmonisation under the CARICOM Single Market and Economy (CSME).

Lessons learned and future directions

- Organic agriculture 'not only enables ecosystems to better adjust to the effects of climate change but also offers a major potential to reduce the emissions of agricultural greenhouse gases' (FAO, 2008: 6). Further, CO_2 emissions per hectare of organic agriculture systems are 48 to 68 per cent lower than in conventional systems (ibid.: 3). Agriculture policies should recognise the range of environmental goods and services organic agriculture provides in improving soil, air and water quality, realising energy savings, and increasing and sustaining biodiversity as well as ecological services with natural pest control and conservation, and begin to recompense these in tangible ways through tax benefits, incentives and other support.

- The majority of JOAM members are small farmers and many of their needs are overlooked by existing agriculture policies, which tend to accommodate large farmers. For example, a farmer may get duty concessions on a pick-up for transportation, but these cost over JA$2 million and few small farmers can afford this. Rather, they need a small car to take produce to market or to get to the farm, but these do not attract any assistance. Large equipment such as tractors are deemed to be agricultural and are zero-rated for value added tax. However, a weed-whacker that is not of industrial size is deemed to be a household item and attracts 16.5 per cent tax. Organic farming practice may require a weed-whacker more than a tractor, and incentives should be put in place to assist in the purchase of such equipment.

- Although Jamaica is a party to the Convention on the Elimination of All Forms of Discrimination against Women (CEDAW), women still get asked by many funding agencies if their husband or other significant male can co-sign with them for a loan. It is therefore still difficult for women to access agricultural loans. It is even more difficult if land is being used as collateral. Women own less land than men and often work land on family farms without dedicated ownership rights. Action is needed to bring about equitable access to land.
- Small farmers, women farmers and organic farmers want a system of Fairtrade certification that is more inclusive. Fairtrade has to be more than a halo and 'feel-good' label for northern buyers; it should challenge the world to produce more equitably and sustainably and lead large and small producers and buyers globally to commit to fair trade practices.
- Many drinks, vegetables and coffee packs have labels that identify them as 100 per cent organic; however, there is little existing legal muscle to protect the consumer against the labelling of products that purport to be organic but have no certification to back up these claims. The whole concept of organic production is not well understood. For many people it means 'grown without fertilisers'. Supermarkets have thus been accepting produce as organic without understanding the rigorous process required to attach such a label. There is a need for national awareness programmes and training for wholesalers and produce buyers for supermarkets and hotels, as well as the general public.
- Further organising/networking is needed to enable small women farmers to deal with the challenges faced in producing and marketing coffee – and particularly in securing access to organic and fair trade markets.

References

FAO (2008). 'Organic Agriculture, Environment and Food Security', Natural Resources Management and Environment Department, FAO, Rome.

Rowan-Campbell, D (2004). 'Case Study: Rowans Royale Coffee', Paper for Regional Workshop on Sustainable Organic Agriculture, Guyana, 6–10 September.

16 Corporate Responsibility and the Cashew Nut Industry: Examples from India and Mozambique

Adapted by Nazneen Kanji and Marilyn Carr[35]

Background

One of the most valuable processed nuts on global commodity markets, the cashew nut is also an important cash crop for farmers and has the potential to generate employment through processing and to provide export revenue for developing countries. The world's largest producers are Brazil, India and Vietnam, with many countries in Africa producing smaller quantities.

In the 1970s, Mozambique was the largest producer of cashew nuts, but many factors – including war and drought, inconsistent state policies and aging trees – resulted in a decline in production (Kanji *et al.*, 2002). In the 1990s, the privatisation of large processing factories, followed by rapid trade liberalisation, finally brought the processing sector to its knees. Efforts are being made to revive both production and in-country processing, but most of the crop is exported in raw form to India, which has a processing capacity far exceeding its local production. In India, the 1990s witnessed greater import liberalisation for raw nuts, a relaxation of licensing regulations for processors and an increase in cashew kernel exports (Eapen *et al.*, 2004).

With competition between producers and the entry of Vietnam into the world market, international prices have fallen for both raw and processed nuts. At the same time, quality requirements are increasingly being applied by buyers of kernels in the USA and EU.

Wages and working conditions in cashew nut processing plants

Both the location of value addition and the buyer-driven nature of the cashew nut supply chain have had negative implications for the wages and working conditions of workers in India and Mozambique, where cashew nut processing has provided an important source of wage employment for women. The state of Kerala has the largest processing capacity in India, where an estimated 400,000 women work in the industry. In Mozambique, some 10,000 workers were employed in the industry in the early 1990s, but this subsequently dropped to about 2,000 (Lindberg, 2001; Eapen *et al.*, 2004).

In Kerala, with increased competition in the international market and moves towards complete liberalisation, outsourcing of cashew nut processing on a commission basis (sometimes called *commission varappu*) has increased. Most public sector factories have closed, and employers in private factories have 'seasonalised' and 'informalised' workers. Ownership of the processing sector is dominated by a few Keralan families (later generations of the men who were termed 'cashew kings' some 50 years ago), though foreign companies employ both local and foreign commission agents. Most workers do not earn the minimum wage; this is more likely to be earned in government-run factories than in outsourced work. In all factories men are likely to earn higher, more secure monthly salaries as oven operators and supervisors than women, who tend to be paid piecework rates in the shelling and peeling sections. Workers have faced an overall reduction in working days per year, which is a key concern expressed by women workers. In addition, Keralan processing companies have extended their operations to the neighbouring state of Tamil Nadu, where even lower wages are paid (Eapen *et al.*, 2004).

Conditions in the factories are poor, and regulations concerning ventilation and protective clothing are ignored (ibid.). The cashew nut shell contains a caustic liquid that burns the hands, and the coconut oil that (women) workers use in the shelling section to cover their hands provides limited protection. Women also complain of back and reproductive health problems from sitting or squatting in the peeling sections and standing for long periods in the cutting sections.

In Mozambique, a study of ex-workers in Angoche, a coastal district in Nampula province, shows that workers' livelihoods have been badly affected by factory closures and that women, more than men, have found it difficult to find alternative sources of income (Vijhuizen *et al.*, 2003a). This is linked to the restrictions women face in their mobility. Several newer, smaller-scale factories offer piece rates, and most workers do not earn the minimum wage. However, because there are few employment opportunities, jobs in the factories are coveted – when a new factory opened in Namige, in the same province, 1,000 people turned up to apply for 70 jobs (ibid.).

In the south of Mozambique, workers in one factory started work at 4am and were often there until late afternoon in order to complete their tasks (Vijhuizen *et al.*, 2003b). In general, as in India, women tended to earn less than men and work longer hours, which is linked to the piece rates set for the sections of the factory where women predominate, mainly peeling. Men dominate in better-paid positions within the factory, including supervision and management. The implications of long hours for women are severe, given that they are still primarily responsible for growing food, doing domestic work and looking after children. In addition, in both Mozambique and India, most factories provide no maternity benefits or childcare facilities. In contrast, the large factories in Mozambique that are now closed used to provide more stable employment throughout the year, as well as benefits that included crèches, food and childcare.

Better practices in processing factories

Although there has been a general deterioration in wages and working conditions in cashew nut processing in a liberalised and competitive environment, this case study looks at two cases where better practices have been adopted in the hope of improving conditions and benefits for workers. These are Miranda Caju in Nampula Province (Mozambique) and processing clusters in Panruti in Tamil Nadu (India) (Vijhuizen *et al.*, 2003a; Kanji *et al.*, 2004).

Miranda Caju in Nampula province, Mozambique

This factory, located in the north of Mozambique, started to operate in April 2002. It was set up by a private entrepreneur with a one-year low interest (18%) bank loan that was guaranteed by the government cashew nut institute, INCAJU. The factory was designed with the help of TechnoServe, a US-based NGO that aims to support entrepreneurial women and men in poor rural areas. Cashews are processed using the steaming method and semi-mechanical cutting machines. All the equipment, including ovens, has been manufactured locally. The owner reconstructed a ruined building and employed 70 workers, and the factory began by processing 120 tons of raw cashews with the intention of building up to its capacity of 1,000 tons per year. The kernels produced are graded and vacuum packed for export. The Netherlands development organisation SNV assisted the owner to contact a Dutch buyer who operates from Rotterdam and exports to various parts of the world.

Workers receive a free meal at work and their contracts entitle them to health assistance, paid annual holidays and severance pay in case of work-related illnesses or accidents. A trade union has been started and a crèche constructed – that is, a clean, sheltered area where mothers can arrange for someone to look after their babies (though without food or trained child-carers, as had been provided in the old government-owned factories). The owner of the Namige factory subsequently set up a second factory, and two more similar factories have been established by other entrepreneurs in the province.

Unlike in India, where women dominate the workforce in the cashew nut industry – operating cutting machines as well as peeling and grading the cashews – in this factory, only men are employed in the cutting section, while women predominate in the peeling section, which is perceived to require dexterity and patience. Management explains this division in terms of women's own preferences, but the view was also expressed that women cannot handle the cutting machines as well as men. There were mixed views from the women we interviewed: some did not want to burn their hands as it would affect their farming work, while others were willing to take any kind of work.

SNV, with support from TechnoServe, further supported the Namige factory by developing an initiative to set up small-scale processing units (known as 'satellites') around the factory. One Mozambican NGO provided a training component for production and processing and another provided a microfinance component. The owner of the factory bought the produce from the satellites. In the first year of the programme (2002–2003), three units were set up, each with the capacity to process 24 tons of raw cashews. The units bought the raw nuts, steamed, cracked, dried and peeled them, and packed them for transport to the factory. In the factory, the cashews were sorted, graded and packed for export. The Dutch buyer was able to absorb high volumes of processed nuts for export to various parts of the world. The owner thus built up the factory towards maximum capacity while also outsourcing the initial, labour-intensive stages of processing to the satellites.

To minimise the risks of management failure and to test technical and economic viability, the first three satellites were run by individuals who had an entrepreneurial background and experience in marketing cashews (two men and one woman). The idea was that if these units proved viable, less experienced individuals, interest groups, associations or family groups would be given the opportunity to run future satellites. A total of 21 units was foreseen for the first three years of the programme, each employing about 12 people.

The Namige initiative provides an interesting example of a 'partnership' approach between government, NGOs, communities and the private sector. Better wages and working conditions were provided for workers than in other factories. Because of the involvement of SNV and the positive relationships that were built up, the owner of the factory made an effort to have at least one satellite run by a woman and started the process of importing castor oil to protect the workers' hands, as it provides better protection than the local oil. It was also thought that better protection might mean more women would want to work in the cutting section where wages are higher.

Although the initiative had the potential to increase the quantity of processed nuts, generate employment for local people, minimise the number of intermediaries between producer and exporter, and add value locally, it has not been an all-out success. As early as 2004, the Namige factory owner and TechnoServe had reservations about the financial sustainability of the satellite units because quality and productivity were low (the appearance of the nuts, the proportion of 'whole' nuts produced), costs were high and prices of kernels on the international market remained low.

According to Hanlon and Smart (2008), although Miranda Caju and other new private factories have been hugely successful – moving the industry from virtual collapse in 2001–2002, with four tiny factories and a handful of workers, to 18 factories and 6,000 workers in 2006 – the first experiment with 13 'satellite' units failed because the units lost money. The project had taken for granted that the owners would also be the managers. However, even very small units employing fewer than ten people also hired a manager, which not only meant an extra, unnecessary salary but also led to unacceptable production standards. Another problem was the difficulty of guaranteeing EU standards in these tiny units.

The experiment was tried again in 2006, but the prospects for the tiny 'satellite' units at that time did not look good, and many who had believed that 'small is beautiful' changed their tune in this particular case. For example, Technoserve, which originally promoted the idea of small processing units, has now shifted its policy, arguing for units above 2,500 tonnes per year (Hanlon and Smart, 2008).

Processing clusters in Panruti, Tamil Nadu, India

As mentioned above, many processing factories in India have moved from Kerala (which has the largest processing capacity) to neighbouring Tamil Nadu, where even lower wages are paid to women (and men) workers.

In Panruti, Tamil Nadu, clusters of small-scale cashew nut processors have evolved that are similar to the Namige satellites, though with some minor differences. In particular, they carry out more of the stages of primary processing and are more independent. Local nut production is not sufficient to feed the existing processing units, and export houses are the main conduits through which the external procurement of raw cashews (including from Mozambique) takes place. While the export houses procure raw cashew nuts from the domestic and international markets, most do not have their own processing facilities. Instead, they use hundreds of small processing units, most of which are owned by cashew farmers whose harvest alone does not suffice for the facilities they own and manage.

These small processors own the premises, the equipment (however little they may have), the raw material and the final produce. Employing wage labour to supplement family labour, they are part of a network of small processors linked to a few export houses, each of which has about 40–50 processors. The export house scouts for the raw cashews on their behalf, both in the domestic and the international market, and provides them with information on the price and quality of the nuts. If this is acceptable, then the export house procures the raw nuts and sells smaller quantities to the individual processors. The processing units process the raw nuts on their own, and sort and sell them to the same exporter or to another one.

The small processors also procure raw cashews from the domestic market through their own agents. Three or four small processors pool resources to organise lorry loads of raw nuts that are imported from other states. These processed nuts are also sold to export houses.

Processing cashews generates valuable employment for local people. Combining cashew nut growing with processing can generate employment for almost the entire year. Only women work in shelling (unlike in Mozambique), and they also predominate in the peeling section. In 2003, daily wages varied between Rs50–70, which was lower than the wages in the factories in the region, but the women benefit from the fact that the work is close to their homes. Labour is scarce, especially in the harvest season, and the clusters attract workers from other villages where processing has not been taken up in a big way. An initial appraisal of the institutional arrangements in Panruti seems to indicate benefits for women, particularly in terms of the location of the work.

Lessons learned and future directions

In the 'better practice' examples, the Namige model illustrates the important role of working with government and the private sector. The Panruti clusters, on the other hand, demonstrate the strength that comes from strong grassroots associations or entrepreneurial organisations. However, even in these cases, which are exceptions, there are still gender inequalities in the benefits derived from employment. Also, as was seen above, the Namige factory satellites have not really lived up to expectations.

Choices obviously need to be made. Companies can choose to take advantage of socially constructed gender inequalities or they can choose to invest more in their workforce, women and men, thereby contributing to sustainable development. However, on what basis will they make these choices? How can business incentives be aligned with positive outcomes for sustainable development? And what are the lessons for the various actors involved.

Lessons for workers' organisations and NGOs

Unions are weak or non-existent in the cashew nut processing sectors in both India and Mozambique. Given the need for cash and employment opportunities, workers and unions find themselves in relatively weak positions. Action to promote workers' rights is complex and should not restrict the livelihood opportunities of poor workers or raise labour costs so that their few choices are further reduced. In the Namige case, the union had only just been set up when the research was carried out. The employer wanted the union to mediate between management and workers, to explain to workers the constraints he faced as a result of international prices and to assure them that profits from increased productivity would be shared with them. Unions have often failed to represent the interests of women workers adequately and the development of strong and representative workers' organisations are an important counterweight to more powerful interests.

The Namige case illustrates the potentially important role of support from NGOs working with government and business. Women's groups in Kerala have provided support such as health care for women involved in the cashew nut industry, though the research did not identify any such action for the women in the Panruti clusters.

Lessons for governments

Governments have an essential role in protecting workers' rights and interests, particularly where unions and other civil society organisations are weak. Tripartite discussions between employers, government and workers' representatives at the national level should inform minimum wage agreements and minimum working conditions so that they are adequately contextualised. In the Namige case, the employer has suggested that there should be a minimum wage set between the minimum wage for industrial work and that for agricultural labour. Researchers in both India and Mozambique have suggested that the government should monitor compliance with minimum wages or set up multi-stakeholder groups, including NGOs, to carry out this work.

Lessons for companies and entrepreneurs

Companies often take advantage of gender inequalities, where women are assumed to be 'secondary earners', more willing to accept lower wages for their work or perceived to be less skilled at some tasks than others, while men are still in the higher paid, more secure positions. Companies should seek to provide equal opportunities for women and men in training programmes and employment, and promotion opportunities, and their efforts should be monitored. Entrepreneurs with smaller units should give consideration to the location of employment and/or provide childcare facilities to enable women with children to work.

Future directions

Cashew nuts are considered a luxury food product and there are a host of quality requirements that are increasingly applied by the USA and Europe. There are indications that hygiene, safety and improvements in working conditions will become more important elements in certification. However, the investment needed to upgrade conditions for certification is often costly, particularly for small businesses. It is usually workers in larger companies, particularly those dealing with branded products, who benefit from the higher labour standards associated with certification or codes of conduct.

The corporate responsibility agenda often focuses on 'win-win' situations, where improved social or environmental performance leads to business benefits. Such incentives for higher standards come through several points of leverage, including consumer demand, civil society pressure, public sector enforcement and conditions imposed by investors or buyers. But the case of cashew nuts illustrates the danger of a 'race to the bottom', when companies operating in liberalising sectors have few, if any, of these incentives.

While women workers in this sector face declining wages, deteriorating working conditions and discrimination, the two 'better practices' featured in this case study show what is possible. However, these improvements depend on the awareness and goodwill of a particular employer/exporter and the work of a particular set of organisations working in that provincial location.

Cashew nut processors at the national level feel that greater profits are retained by business (salter-roaster companies and large retailers) in the North end of the chain. The key challenge remains to identify points of leverage along the entire supply chain in sectors where there is little consumer or buyer pressure for higher labour standards. Until this happens, cases of 'better practice' may well remain the exception.

References

Eapen, M *et al.* (2004). 'Liberalisation, Gender and Livelihoods: The Cashew Nut Case', IIED Working Paper 3. India Phase 1: Revisiting the Cashew Industry, International Institute for Environment and Development (IIED), http://www.iied.org/pubs/display.php?o=14510IIED&n=4&l=19&k=cashew>.

Hanlon, J and Smart, T (2008). *Do Bicycles Equal Development in Mozambique?*, James Currey, Oxford.

Kanji, N (2004). 'Corporate Responsibility and Women's Employment: The Cashew Nut Case', CRED Perspective, 02, http://www.iied.org/pubs/display.php?o=16005IIED&n=2&l=19&k=cashew

Kanji, N, Vijhuizen, C and Young, S (2002). 'Cashing in on Cashews: Policies, Production and Gender in Mozambique', paper presented at the 8th International Interdisciplinary Congress on Women, Kampala, July.

Kanji, N, Vijhuizen, C, Braga, C and Artur, L (2004). 'Cashing in on Cashew Nuts: Women Producers and Factory Workers in Mozambique', in Carr, M (ed.), *Chains of Fortune: Linking Women Producers and Workers with Global Markets*, Commonwealth Secretariat, London.

Lindberg A (2001). *Experience and Identity: A Historical Account of Class, Caste and Gender among Cashew Workers in Kerala*, Lund University, Lund, Sweden.

Vijhuizen, C, Braga, C, Artur, L and Kanji, N (2003a). 'Liberalisation, Gender and Livelihoods: The Cashew Nut Case', IIED Working Paper 1 – Mozambique Phase 1: the North, International Institute for Environment and Development, http://www.iied.org/pubs/display.php?o=14508IIED&n=6&l=19&k=cashew

Vijhuizen, C, Artur, L, Kanji, N and Braga, C (2003b). 'Liberalisation, Gender and Livelihoods: The Cashew Nut Case', IIED Working Paper 2 – Mozambique Phase 2: the South, International Institute for Environment and Development, http://www.iied.org/pubs/display.php?o=14509IIED&n=5&l=19&k=cashew

New Export Markets

17 Swazi Secrets: Indigenous Products in the Global Marketplace

Nontokozo Nemarundwe, Maideyi Kutambura, Lucy Welford and Itai Chibaya

Background

The global natural products industry, including key subsectors of foods and beverages, cosmetics, herbal medicines and pharmaceuticals, is valued at more than US$65 billion per annum; it is booming, with an annual growth rate of over 15 per cent (Key Note, 2005). In southern Africa, the natural products trade is currently estimated at about US$12 million per annum, but in the long term, if markets are developed, it is estimated that natural products have the potential to generate up to $3 billion (Welford and Le Breton, 2008). PhytoTrade Africa, the trade association of the natural products industry in southern Africa, develops markets for large volumes of sustainably harvested products from several indigenous plant species that grow throughout the region.[36] Such opportunities have enabled those in small-scale rural communities, especially women, to tap into these markets as an equitable livelihood alternative to meet some of their basic needs, including household food requirements, paying school fees and making family investments such as purchasing livestock. These are resources necessary for the reproduction of physical and social life

This case study focuses on the marula tree, which is of great importance to rural communities throughout southern Africa, as every part of it has several domestic uses (Welford *et al.*, 2008). The fruits are used in traditional medicine to treat diarrhoea, diabetes, fever and malaria; the leaves are used to make relish; and the hard wood makes excellent mortars for pounding corn, as well as kitchen utensils (Palmer and Pitman, 1988; Wehmeyer, 1967). The kernels are crushed to extract a stable oil that is rich in unsaturated fatty acids and used by women to moisturise their skin; anecdotal evidence also suggests application during pregnancy to prevent stretch marks (Welford *et al.*, 2008). In addition, the oil is believed to prevent colds and flu and to soothe colic in babies, among other medicinal uses (Botelle, 2001). The kernels are also cracked for nuts that are consumed as a snack or used to flavour relish.

In countries such as Swaziland, where agricultural production is extremely unreliable, natural products such as marula offer an opportunity for supplementing household incomes and improving rural livelihoods, especially for poor women and their families. There are growing local markets for improved commercial products such as soap, shampoo and body lotion, especially in the hotel industry. And marula oil is becoming more popular in the UK and other countries of the North for use in cosmetics. Efforts are being made by Phytotrade Africa to improve the export trade of marula, focusing on regulatory approval and supply chain development. This draws on successes with other natural products such as baobab fruit, which was approved in June 2008 as a novel food in the EU (Phytotrade Africa, 2008).

Unfortunately, women face many constraints in establishing and running commercial enterprises based on traditional natural resources and in accessing local 'niche/high value' and export markets. Culture-based gender bias, compounded with poverty, hinders African women's access to markets at the personal, community and international levels (World Bank, 2007). Factors that contribute to women's limited access to export markets include conflict between women's traditional roles and their work and business demands, social insecurity, lack of education and business experience, religious barriers, limited space in markets and lack of capital (ibid.).

There have been various attempts by individuals, communities and organisations to help women overcome these constraints and to enhance their ability to participate in natural resource utilisation, trade and conservation across the southern African region (Murphy, 2009). Common to all these activities are organisational structures that support women's activities to enhance rural livelihoods. In Swaziland, organisations such as Gone Rural, a grassroots social enterprise, have helped rural women generate much-needed income by selling products ranging from tableware and floor mats to gifts, accessories and clay pots, as well as promoting the sustainable use of Swaziland's little known natural resource: *lutindzi* grass (Shriber and Peters, 2008).

Swazi Indigenous Products (SIP) has been building the trade in marula products on the history and experience of women organising their entrepreneurial activities. Training for those involved in the marula trade was provided to groups of women, rather than to individuals, building on existing forms of social organisation.

Linking women with export markets: the experience of Swazi Indigenous Products (SIP)

History and rationale

SIP was established in 2004 with external funding and the support of the Swazi Government as a not-for-profit company to empower rural women through the development and commercialisation of marula kernels. SIP immediately became a member of PhytoTrade Africa, recognising that this could provide opportunities for linking the marula producers to global food and cosmetics markets. SIP exports bulk marula oil to Europe, as well as producing a range of marula oil natural skincare products for Swaziland and export markets under the Swazi Secrets brand, with the tagline 'Capturing centuries of African wisdom'.[37] In 2008, bulk oil sales were in excess of E1 million,[38] while sales under the Swazi Secrets brand topped E500,000.

A major goal of SIP is to be 100 per cent owned by its rural suppliers. The suppliers can become shareholders in SIP through the voluntary payment of an E6 joining fee in the beginning, as well E4 in membership fees each trading year. Members receive a membership card that entitles them to a higher price for their kernels. SIP now has 2,600 suppliers, of whom over half are members and 90 per cent are women.

The aims of SIP include:

- Fully commercialising quality products and by-products from the marula fruit;
- Adding value to indigenous and natural resources;
- Identifying prospects of transforming marula into a life-enhancing food and providing an alternative source of nutrition;
- Offering an alternative source of income to those rural communities where poverty and unemployment are most serious;
- Ensuring the hygienic production and preservation of marula fruits;
- Creating employment opportunities in the natural products industry, particularly for women.

Development of the company

At the primary producer level, SIP undertook the following activities to enhance productivity:

- Resource mapping to discover the potential volumes of marula available in the rural areas participating in its trade;
- Training of the primary producers in sustainable harvesting techniques and organic principles;
- Raising awareness among the primary producers on the requirements for organic certification;

- Training community level monitors on their roles and responsibilities in monitoring the collection, cracking and storage of both conventional and organic marula kernels.

Oil presses used at the SIP factory were locally designed and manufactured. Following training, staff members are more aware of the principles of organic certification, the importance of adherence and the resultant improved incomes from the organic oils. To support factory level production, 465 organic suppliers were registered by the start of the 2009 season. Moreover, 1,400 kg of organic kernels were purchased during the first year of organic certification (although the target was 3 metric tonnes of organic kernels for 2007). This means the primary producers have increased their incomes as organic kernels have a higher price than conventional kernels.

The organic production of marula requires specific handling and storage methods to ensure that there is no contamination of the kernels. To ensure adherence to these principles by the suppliers, the following measures were put in place:

- Provision of clear, detailed collection and handling rules to the primary producers both verbally and in writing;
- Selection of an organic spokesperson in each area to ensure that harvesters and processors of marula follow rules for organic production and monitor the handling and storage of kernels;
- Mobilisation of peer control, paired with emphasising the suppliers' stake in the success of the organic project and the prevailing honesty of rural women;
- Internal inspections done through home visits, either by SIP staff or by organic spokespersons;
- Having separate queues for organic and conventional kernels at procurement and using different packaging materials for the different types of kernels.

Market opportunities have been created within the country through the hotel industry, which purchases marula products such as body lotions, soap, shampoo and shower gels from SIP. This facilitates increased purchases of kernels from the primary producers.

Examining the product value chain, rural suppliers receive E114 for the kernels needed to produce one litre of oil. This is then sold in bulk at E174 or used in Swazi Secrets products where its resale value rises to E460. Organically certified suppliers receive E128 for the same weight of kernels and the litre of oil produced is sold in bulk for E261. Total 2008 kernel purchases were E651,000, paid directly in cash to the rural suppliers.

The commercial partnership approach adopted by PhytoTrade Africa facilitates the linkage of producers to global natural product markets for bulk oils. The organisation is in the process of developing direct links between SIP and Body Shop International plc. Previously, bulk oils were only sold directly to PhytoTrade Africa's French commercial partner. In addition, SIP has developed a network of clients in 14 countries across four continents. These have often been cultivated through the local hotel industry, as some foreign guests who used marula products in a hotel developed trading links with SIP after returning to their own countries. Three returning guests (from Canada, Germany and the UK) have been sufficiently impressed to start their own companies and websites, selling exclusively Swazi Secrets products.[39]

The Government has contributed towards market access for marula products by making the trading environment more conducive. It has provided SIP with a rent-free factory for the last four years. The Swazi Queen Mother is the patron of SIP and assists the organisation to obtain government support when the need arises.

Outcomes for women and their families

Key informant interviews undertaken by PhytoTrade Africa with primary producers in 2007 show that women receive both economic and non-economic benefits. Prior to active involvement in marula kernel harvesting, most key informants indicated that they used to make reed mats, engage in agricultural production and sell small livestock. These sources of income had some constraints. For instance, in order to produce mats women had to cross the Mozambican border to collect reeds. This meant spending several days camping at the reed site, leaving their children alone at home or being cared for by relatives.

The commercialisation of marula kernels, especially targeting the cosmetics industry, has opened up new economic opportunities for women, as the kernels were previously a waste product after the home brewing of marula beer. Income realised by the primary producers from marula kernels is used to:

- Buy basic foodstuffs such as maize meal (particularly in a drought years such as the 2006/2007 agricultural season), cooking oil, sugar, salt and flour for baking cakes for sale;
- Pay school fees;
- Buy soap and other groceries;

- Buy clothes, especially for children;
- Make investments such as purchasing livestock and starting up small businesses.

Non-income benefits realised by the participating women include:

- Enhanced organic marula kernels production through training in various activities;
- Confidence building among the primary producers, especially through empowerment by being shareholders of SIP;
- Exposure to the existing and potential opportunities for marketing marula kernels and related products;
- Interaction with outsiders who visit their community to learn from their activities related to marula, which also exposes them to new ideas and gives them the opportunity to share their story with outsiders;
- Economic independence of women, especially married women who previously depended on their husbands to access money for even basic foodstuffs such as salt, sugar and cooking oil.

The story of Khelina in Box 17.1 illustrates how trade in marula products has contributed towards improving the welfare of families involved in the trade.

Effects on the community

There has been improved resource use and conservation management on the 'incentive-based conservation' principle. The women producers acknowledge that they became more aware of the need to conserve the marula tree after realising its economic importance in meeting their basic needs. Non-destructive harvesting and protection of species from grazing improves conservation. Men who use marula trees to carve mortars and pestles are encouraged to cut the trees that do not bear fruit (though the men may be cutting the male fruit trees, which could have negative implications for the fruit production of the female trees in the long term). Conservation of the species is also a way of investing in natural capital assets, thus avoiding any future costs that would otherwise have resulted in attempts to restore degraded woodlands.

The rise in the value of marula has also resulted in a renewed interest in organic farming, sustainable use and community stewardship for marula trees in support of customary and local regulations. Community residents have initiated a secondary market that coincides with marula procurement days to take advantage of the additional income flows.

Box 17.1 The story of an organic marula kernel producer

Khelina Hluphekile Magagula is 49 years old and lives in the Hlane area. She is divorced and has seven children, three of whom live with her, together with two grandchildren whom she looks after. Khelina started working with SIP in 2005 as a supplier of conventional kernels. Following the training that she received from SIP, she now supplies organic kernels. She is very happy about this as it gives her more income, which she says 'takes care of us and helps us in many ways'. It is used to buy maize meal, laundry soap, sugar and salt and pay school fees for her grandchildren. Khelina also uses the money to buy flour for use in baking buns for sale, especially during the off marula season. In addition, she buys airtime for the mobile phone that she got from a son who works in South Africa.

In 2005, Khelina sold her kernels for E23 per kilogram; in 2006 she sold them for E24/kg and in 2007, because her kernels were organically certified, she sold them for E27/kg. Members of SIP who are selling conventional kernels are paid E25/kg, while non-members receive E24/kg for their conventional kernels. Khelina is an SIP member. She normally sells 20kg of kernels per month, but on the day of the interview she had sold 25kg of organic kernels. In 2006 she received approximately E900.00 from selling kernels.

Another source of income is brewing beer from the marula trees. However, this does not give her significant income as many other women also brew marula beer, resulting in poor sales. Brewing is also costly, as she has to buy sugar for it, whereas no inputs are needed for cracking kernels except her labour and time.

Source: Key informant interview in Hlane area, April 2007

While there has been an increase in the number of women involved in kernel production, this has not affected the number of trees available, as women collect only the fruit that has fallen on the ground. Traditional leaders have also put in place rules and regulations that govern the use of the trees. For instance, to ensure that the trees continue to bear fruit, women in the village at a given time brew marula beer that is then taken to the relevant traditional leader in the area as a form of thanksgiving to the ancestral spirits.

Lessons learned and future directions

Experiences from PhytoTrade Africa show that meaningful benefits realised are an incentive to biodiversity conservation. For instance, rather than clear land that has marula trees for agricultural production, which was contributing to deforestation in the past, the area is conserved so that people can have access to marula products. In the process, the biodiversity of the area is also conserved. Increasing the awareness of producers about the value of the species through market opportunities at the global level has been very instrumental in promoting conservation.

There has been improved access to incomes that are used to meet household needs and other forms of investment such as purchase of livestock. At the same time, the project has not impacted negatively on traditional/local practices, e.g. brewing of marula beer from fruits, which are still practised. Commercialising marula products has also contributed towards collective engagement in sustainable use and conservation activities by the local communities. There is better co-ordination and linkages between producers of natural products and the global markets. Lessons learned that are relevant to various stakeholders are summarised below.

Lessons for local organisations

Experiences from Swaziland show that there is a need for transparency if communities are to be actively involved in natural products commercialisation at the global level. Similarly, empowerment of the primary producers is key. In the case of SIP, this is facilitated through ownership of shares in the company by groups of rural women who are producers of marula kernels. Training and capacity building are important in building women's confidence and self-esteem to enable them to engage in trading activities. There is also a need to ensure that fair prices are paid to primary producers for their products. Lobbying and advocacy at national, regional and international levels contribute to ensuring that fair prices are paid to primary producers. Last but not least, the importance of creating strategic partnerships with a wide range of organisations and clients (e.g. in the European and Canadian markets) cannot be overestimated. Such partnerships contribute towards the realisation of significant incomes by rural women producers.

Lessons for governments and international players

Governments need to create an environment that is conducive to trade in natural products. For example, there should be export regulations in place, as well as supportive legislation. Trade policies supportive to the trade in natural products would contribute towards success in global markets.

There is also a need to develop the whole market chain – from primary producers' level to global markets. This will ensure that local producers are able to meet the volumes and quality standards required. Producers must be paid fair prices for their products if their livelihoods are to be enhanced.

Future directions

SIP's future development strategy is firmly targeted on expanding sales of its higher value-added products – the Swazi Secrets brand – in order to achieve profitability free of donor funding and thus enable payment of a community dividend from profits. Bulk oil sales contribute to increased purchases of raw materials from primary producers, compared to finished products, enabling the company to continue expanding its supply chain to new rural areas.

References

Botelle, A (2001). 'A History of Marula Use in North-Central Namibia', Eudafano Women's Co-operative Ltd, the Centre for Research Information Action in Africa (CRIAA) and the Southern African Development Company (SADC), Windhoek, Namibia.

Key Note (2005). 'Natural Products – Market Report', Key Note Publications Ltd, Hampton, Middlesex.

Murphy, E (2009). 'Marula Oil and the Fight Against Poverty in Rural Swaziland', http://www.scotiafairtrade.com/blog/marula-oil-and-the-fight-against-poverty-in-rural-swaziland/

Palmer, E and Pitman N (1988). 'Sclerocarya birrea', in *Trees of Southern Africa*, 2nd revised edition, Struik Publishers, Cape Town, South Africa.

PhytoTrade Africa (2008). 'Europe's Door Open for "Superfruit" Baobab', *PhytoNews Update*, December, http://campaign-archive.com/?u=ab22c075d077664dc03b7d6d1&id=bfb6eff28a

Shriber, N and Peters, L (2008). 'Gone Rural Grassroots Business Initiative', World Bank, Washington, DC.

Wehmeyer, AS (1967). 'Edible Wild Fruits of the Transvaal', Food Industries South Africa, 19: 49–53.

Welford, L and Le Breton, G (2008). 'Bridging the Gap: PhytoTrade Africa's Experience of the Certification of Natural Products', Forests, Trees and Livelihoods, 18: 66–79.

Welford, L, Abad Jara, M and Gerike, N (2008). 'Tree of Life: The Use of Marula Oil in Southern Africa', *HerbalGram*, 79: 32–41.

World Bank (2007). *Private Sector Development and Gender*, The World Bank, Washington, DC.

18 A Beautiful Business: The Case of Pure Fiji

Compiled by Marilyn Carr from information supplied by Pure Fiji[40]

Overview

One of the fastest growing markets in Europe, Japan and the USA is that for beauty and health goods based on natural products, mainly non-timber forest products (NTFPs), many of which are found in developing countries. It is estimated that there are approximately 150 NTFPs of major significance in international trade and that this market is growing dramatically each year (Carr, 2008). While there are some exports without value added, there is an increasing trend towards local processing of a range of more sophisticated goods, and it is important that the rural communities – and particularly the women – to whom these resources belong are able to benefit from this trend.

However, although new economic opportunities exist in this sector, it is not easy for women to take advantage of them. For example, if NTFPs are not processed locally, they yield low returns. If rural communities do not have access to fair markets and market information, they can be cheated out of fair prices. And if expansion of the NTFP sector has no concern for the environment, then it can result in overexploitation and loss of access to the natural resource base (Carr, 2008).

This case study looks at a natural body care product business in Fiji Islands that has attempted to address these problems and ensure that there is concern for the local environment and the livelihoods of rural women and communities, while at the same time establishing a profitable, rapidly expanding company with an international reputation for environmentally friendly botanical products that contribute to the country's export earnings.

Pure Fiji: women exporting natural body care products

Origins and purpose

Pure Fiji is a natural bath and body products manufacturer that caters to the exclusive spa and salon industry and exports beauty products to niche markets in Australia, Europe and the USA. Founded in 1995 by Gaetane Austin and her daughter Andree, Pure Fiji began research, development and production of its uniquely Fijian products around the family kitchen table.

Co-founders and directors, the mother and daughter team were inspired by the beautiful traditions and handicrafts of the island culture they had lived in for their entire lives. They realised its traditions and crafts were being pushed into oblivion with the advance of modern and Western lifestyles and that something had to be done to preserve these traditional skills and make them financially viable for communities. They also realised that these crafts could have massive appeal in international markets, if only they could be quality controlled and creatively marketed.

So it was that Pure Fiji was set up with the following tenets:

- Passion;
- Environmental sustainability – dedication to environmental and socially sound practices;
- Cultural and social sustainability – helping communities maintain their way of life and traditional skills by giving these skills new meaning and making them valuable and useful in the modern world;
- Aid through empowerment – identifying a need in local communities, then educating these communities to use their unique skills in a marketable way (also called proactive product development);
- Aid through education – with island communities beginning to feel the pull of the Western world, it is only through education that the future generation can gain the tools needed to protect and maintain their communities and heritage in a changing social environment.

Development of the company

This pioneering instinct and powerful faith in their vision has served Pure Fiji well. Products are based on the traditions of the Pacific Islands, with raw materials and handicrafts supplied by more than 600 craftswomen and men in rural communities and assembled into the finished product with passion and care at a custom-built state-of-the-art factory in Suva. Many of Pure Fiji's products are still handcrafted and packaged by the 60 staff on site – many of whom sat around the kitchen table alongside Gaetane and Andree in the early days. The latter have been joined in the business by another family member, Alexander, while the youngest daughter, Sophia, manages distribution in Australia. Andree brings to the business the skills she acquired from years working in the hotel business in the USA.

Incorporated in the new factory premises is Pure Fiji's spa, which uses only their products. This supports local community initiatives to provide materials, thus avoiding the importation of goods. It is also a highly effective marketing tool, as satisfied customers are likely to enquire as to the source of the high quality products.

Locally, the company sells its products through the more upmarket stores and tourist hotels. The factory also sets up a outlet every Saturday to meet the needs of local customers who cannot get the products they want from local distributors. Products are often in short supply in many Suva outlets due to high demand (Frodey and Nada, 2008).

Internationally, the company markets through the internet, in-flight magazines and trade fairs in the USA and other countries; it has also started to use exclusive retail outlets in the USA and in the spas and boutiques of prestigious hotels such as the Ritz Carlton group. It puts a lot of emphasis on international distributors, who are in the best position to estimate demand, and invites them to come to Fiji Islands so that they can better understand and sell Pure Fiji products. Emphasis has been put on luxury goods items targeted at upmarket consumers, and requests from large discounters such as Walmart to carry the product line have so far been resisted (Frodey and Nada, 2008).

A table-full of awards on display at the Pure Fiji factory says everything about the company's pioneering initiatives. Pure Fiji was the first natural bath and beauty manufacturer to realise the numerous benefits of cold-pressed coconut oil. It was also the instigator of the first international standard cosmetic manufacturing laboratory in Fiji Islands. It was the first all-women's company to win Fiji Islands' prestigious Exporter of the Year, Excellence in Tourism, Chamber of Commerce and Business Woman of the Year awards, and the first to be nominated as one of the ten most influential people and businesses in the South Pacific. Last but not least – the accolade that the Austins are most proud of – Pure Fiji is the first company to successfully package island traditions for an international marketplace, while simultaneously supporting local communities. Thus, it has achieved the 'win-win' situation of meeting business objectives and building up export markets, and at the same time creating livelihoods for rural communities based on traditional crafts and skills.

Using local products and skills

Body care products

The foundation of Pure Fiji's range of body products is virgin coconut oil, extracted from nuts only hours after harvesting through a process called direct micro expulsion. This revolutionary extraction process does not require any heat, complicated machinery or chemicals, allowing for truly pure, crystal clear, sweet smelling and long-lasting coconut oil to be produced. Pure Fiji is thus able to base all its products on the purest virgin nut oils, which are cold-pressed to retain all their inherent benefits.

Added to this are other nut extracts such as *dilo*, *skeci* and *macadamia*. *Dilo*, also known as 'beauty leaf', has a unique capacity to help heal and nourish the skin – something the islanders have traditionally used as a general panacea for body and hair. These are also cold pressed to retain their benefits.

The women in rural communities who collect these nuts on isolated remote islands now benefit from a new source of income that has an immediate impact on their standard of living. The access to oils (much of which is pressed at source) has also revived their use in the villages by traditional healers, who are returning to using them in healing those suffering from a whole range of skin and other ailments.

Hand-made paper

Pepa Ni Viti, Pure Fiji's handmade paper project, was initiated by the company to provide an income to villagers in isolated areas. Paper is made from cellulose found in plant fibre that is literally beaten to a pulp and dispersed in water. This fibre is sourced in different forms from bark, grass and leaves of local plants and trees. Particular attention is given to the use of the outer bark of the mulberry tree, which is normally discarded. This is an abundant and fast-growing tree that has been harvested sustainably throughout the islands over generations. The paper-making project is almost entirely run by the women of these rural communities, empowering them in ways they have never experienced before. The husbands and sons help to gather materials and prepare pulp, and with other operations.

As well as training in paper-making, the women received some basic business training and they took it upon themselves to organise working in shifts so that one group could work while another looked after the children and engaged in their village commitments. Paper-making has become the major income earner for the communities, with Pure Fiji using the paper for packing soap and in the production of stationary items. With the extra income, the women can afford school fees. Other ways in which the income has been used include improving local primary schools, setting up a village store and building additional classrooms for a secondary school.

Basket weaving

Another venture involves a group of women who live outside Suva in an urban settlement. These women are using their traditional skills to weave baskets that are used to package Pure Fiji products. The major claim to fame of this project is that their baskets were used at the launch of Pure Fiji at the

Emmy Awards beauty event. This basket is lovingly referred to as the 'Emmy basket' and enabled the purchase of a water tank and payment of school fees for the children.

New local initiatives

Pure Fiji is now branching out into candle-making, which is providing new economic opportunities for women in rural communities. Fiji Islands' fledgling beekeeping community continues to be developed through Pure Fiji's creation of a new line of beauty products. The pure honey and beeswax are used in cosmetic products and scented candles. Previously, beeswax in Fiji Islands was often discarded for lack of a market.

The community and the environment

In true South Pacific spirit, Pure Fiji has always believed success can only be achieved if it is shared. With the knowledge and experience acquired through growing up in an island culture, they knew that for all to benefit from the success of their business, they had to reach out to the wider community by providing inspiration and a hand up, not a hand-out. The Fijian people are the custodians of the islands' unique resources and they too must have the opportunity to actively participate in a mutually beneficial manner.

Many of the communities that Pure Fiji works with to source raw materials could not afford to educate their children past primary school level, even with the additional income earned from supplying the company. Rural communities are often just too isolated and a secondary education means having to pay not only for travel, school fees, uniforms and books, but also for boarding. To help with this, Pure Fiji has set up student scholarships that are awarded to 20 of the most promising children to fund their secondary education and help pay their university fees. Children are selected in consultation with school headmasters and village Chiefs. For many communities, these children will be the first to receive such a high level of education. To date, three have graduated from tertiary studies, two as qualified teachers and the third studying Environmental Sciences at the University of the South Pacific.

Pure Fiji is aware of its carbon footprint and the need to utilise Fiji Islands' environmental resources appropriately and sustainably. It makes every effort to minimise and, where appropriate, enhance the local ecosystem. As previously noted, the coconut oil extraction process uses no chemicals; in addition, the oil is used to power cars and generators in rural communities, and a tree planting programme is in place. In fact, over 2,000 mangrove seeds have been planted this year alone, as well as 100 *dilo* trees to protect the islands' fragile coastlines.

Lessons learned and future directions

Major lessons learned from the Pure Fiji experience include that:

- Environmental conservation can only be achieved through full involvement of the rural communities who own the natural products that are used in the business;
- Passion and quality can only be maintained through continued family involvement, long-term employment of staff and full involvement of communities;
- It is necessary to have diverse markets. For example, if for any reason the local market is weak, exports will be the source of funds. Conversely, if exports fall, for example because of the global recession, new markets and development are sought locally.

Pure Fiji's plans for the future include:

- Further diversification of product range;
- Further expansion of international marketing;
- Streamlining of production and processing;
- Sourcing of more local components;
- Investigating the use of traditional plants that after laboratory analysis could be developed for use in products.

Pure Fiji firmly believes in the use of Fiji Islands' plentiful sustainable resources to establish and manufacture a unique cosmetic and beauty care range of products.

References

Carr, M (2008). *Gender and Non-Timber Forest Products*, International Fund for Agricultural Development, Rome.

Frodey, C and Nada, Y (2008). 'Pure Fiji Export Limited: A Skin Care Company in Harmony with Nature and Culture', *Journal of Business Case Studies*, 4(2), February.

19 Trade is Blooming: The Case of Ramesh Flowers in India

Amit Lodha

Overview

India has exported dried flowers and plants for the last 40 years, and today it is one of the leading countries in the field, with exports valued at about Rs100 crores[41] per annum. India exports about 500 varieties of dried flowers to 20 countries, and they are highly in demand in the UK and USA. Dried flowers are the most promising sector of the floriculture industry because they are more easily transported and exported than fresh cut flowers, which are perishable and need special cold chain technology and rapid air transportation to reach distant markets in good condition (Indiamart, n.d.). While dried flowers are still a small part of the total floriculture industry, they have already established a significant presence in the world market and are poised for greater growth as demand for natural products increases.

This case study is about one firm – Ramesh Flowers[42] – that started as a small cottage industry in 1982 and has grown into a globally recognised enterprise that provides employment and income to thousands of rural and urban poor women in the collection and processing of dried flowers for export.

Flower power: Ramesh Flowers

History and purpose

Ramesh Flowers Private Limited is a first generation enterprise started in the 1980s by Mahendra Raj Singhwi with an investment of only US$1,200. At the time, although the Government was strongly promoting small rural and agro-industries, policies and support programmes were largely focused on *khadi* (hand-spun and hand-woven cloth) and handicrafts; the dried flower industry was largely ignored and had no special support from governmental or other agencies. However, some of Mr Singhwi's family members were in the dry flowers export business and he saw an opportunity and jumped at it.

While business motives were obviously of importance, Ramesh Flowers also had other objectives, including social and environmental ones. These included creating income for rural poor people in the collection of wild plants that would otherwise be wasted, creating jobs for urban poor women in processing the plants and conserving the environment through sourcing mainly wild plants that could be easily replaced, rather than cultivating flowers and plants on farmland, which is the case with fresh flowers for export.

Structure and development

Eighty per cent of the plants collected by a huge network of women and men farmers all over India are agricultural waste. After the cotton harvest, the pod generally goes to waste, but it is a raw material for Ramesh Flowers. The central factory deals only with the main suppliers who deliver the goods to the Ramesh warehouse and are paid directly. For example, there is one main supplier located in Calcutta who covers the local belt of Bihar, Orissa and Assam. There are similar main suppliers in other areas, including Madhya Pradesh and Kerala. Below the main suppliers there are many sub-suppliers – individual agents through whom the materials are collected. The agents pay the farmers/gatherers.

As the raw materials are waste botanicals, quality is a challenge. However, there are still parameters by which materials can be judged and that are used by Ramesh Flowers before they pay their suppliers. The price of each botanical depends on its nature. Some are costly and others are very cheap.

Export markets were initially set up in the days before the internet. Ramesh Flowers used telex and would write to the consulates of various countries to get contact details of possible customers. Step-by-step, these contacts were used to source more customers, and eyes and ears were always open to follow market developments. Ramesh Flowers eventually launched a website, but no major customers have been secured through this means.

Initially, wholesalers and importers were used to supply the export market, but in 2000 goods began to be shipped directly to retailers as well. There is also a US warehouse that helps with sales and logistics in that country. Consignments are shipped to many renowned retail chain stores around the world including Walmart, IKEA, ASDA, Bhs, Kmart, Jo Anns and Aldi. Thus, Ramesh Flowers has very definitely targeted mainstream export markets, rather than aiming at fair trade or niche markets in the North. The company won the President's Award for Outstanding Export Performance for 1995–96. It also won the Agricultural and Processed Food Product Export Development Authority (APEDA) Export Award for Outstanding Export Performance from 1994 to 2001/2002 and from 2003 to 2007.

Although no government support was received in the early years, from 2005 onwards Ramesh Flowers received a freight subsidy from APEDA, as well as an incentive of 5 per cent on the export value (fob). From a small start, Ramesh Flowers now has a turnover of US$17.5 million and gives work to thousands of poor rural women and men in collecting plants, as well as in its factory (see below). It remains a family business, with five family members involved.

Impact at the factory level

The factory where dried flowers are processed and packaged is located near the port of Tuticorin. The facilities are vast and employ almost 2,000 workers, 95 per cent of whom are women. There is an administrative staff of 150 people, all men.

Women work for nine hours a day and even though the dried flower industry is not covered under the Minimum Wages Act, they are paid at the national floor level of Rs80 per day and on a monthly basis. This is much better than is given by other dried flower industries operating in the region and compares favourably with alternative forms of employment such as in fish processing and salt mining. Working conditions are also better than in other industries open to poorer women.

Women workers receive regular on-the-job training. They are all covered under accident insurance (up to Rs50,000). They are entitled to 84 days maternity leave paid by employee state insurance and benefit from an Employee Provident Fund as per the statutory requirements. In addition, workers are given a marriage gift of Rs3,000. There is a higher education scheme and a free notebook scheme for workers' children, as well as crèches in the factory. Workers are also given subsidised travel to and from work.

In the same way as the process of sourcing of raw materials is environmentally sound, the factory itself is ecologically sustainable. For example, solar heating is used to boil water for dyeing and a greenhouse is used to provide solar heat for drying plants.

Lessons learned and future directions

Clearly this has been a very successful enterprise that has experienced a huge rate of growth over a 20-year period and built up sustainable mainstream export markets with little or no assistance from government, NGOs or international development agencies. It has, however, benefited from ideas and support from its commercial buyers.

Undoubtedly, it has helped thousands of poor rural women and men through enabling them to turn agricultural waste into a source of income. It has provided good wages and working conditions for nearly 2,000 poor urban women in its factory. Some of the programmes put in place in support of children's education will obviously contribute to a better standard of living for the next generation.

At the environmental level, focusing on wild plants that can easily be replaced, and on agricultural waste such as cotton pods, provides a sustainable source of supply and prevents diversion of land from food crops to non-food export crops. The use of solar energy in the factory is also environmentally commendable.

The management notes several keys to its success. These include:

- A skilled workforce, undoubtedly helped by on-the-job training opportunities (it is also believed that the largely female workforce brings qualities of patience, waste consciousness, involvement and creativity);
- Vast facilities that benefit from being located near to a port, thus reducing transport costs;
- A huge inventory of raw materials and climatic conditions that are favourable to production for most of the year, thus helping with a regular supply of goods to external buyers;
- Recognition by the Government of India, which has honoured Ramesh Flowers with awards, and also by a worldwide network of well-known chain stores.

To this one might add that there was obviously a great deal of vision and co-ordination skills on the part of management. Combined with a sense of social and environmental concern, this led to a 'win-win' situation. It is also interesting to note that as the dried flower industry did not benefit from government support programmes for small industry, it was much less affected than others when these programmes were suspended when the economy was liberalised.

In spite of the economic recession and huge pressure on prices, Ramesh Flowers has a good inflow of orders and new market opportunities continue to arise. There is, however, a major challenge as regards labour availability because other industries in the region – fishing, spinning mills, etc. – are competing for women workers.

Reference

Indiamart (n.d.). 'Dry Flower Industry', http://www.dry-flowers.net/dry-flower-industry.html

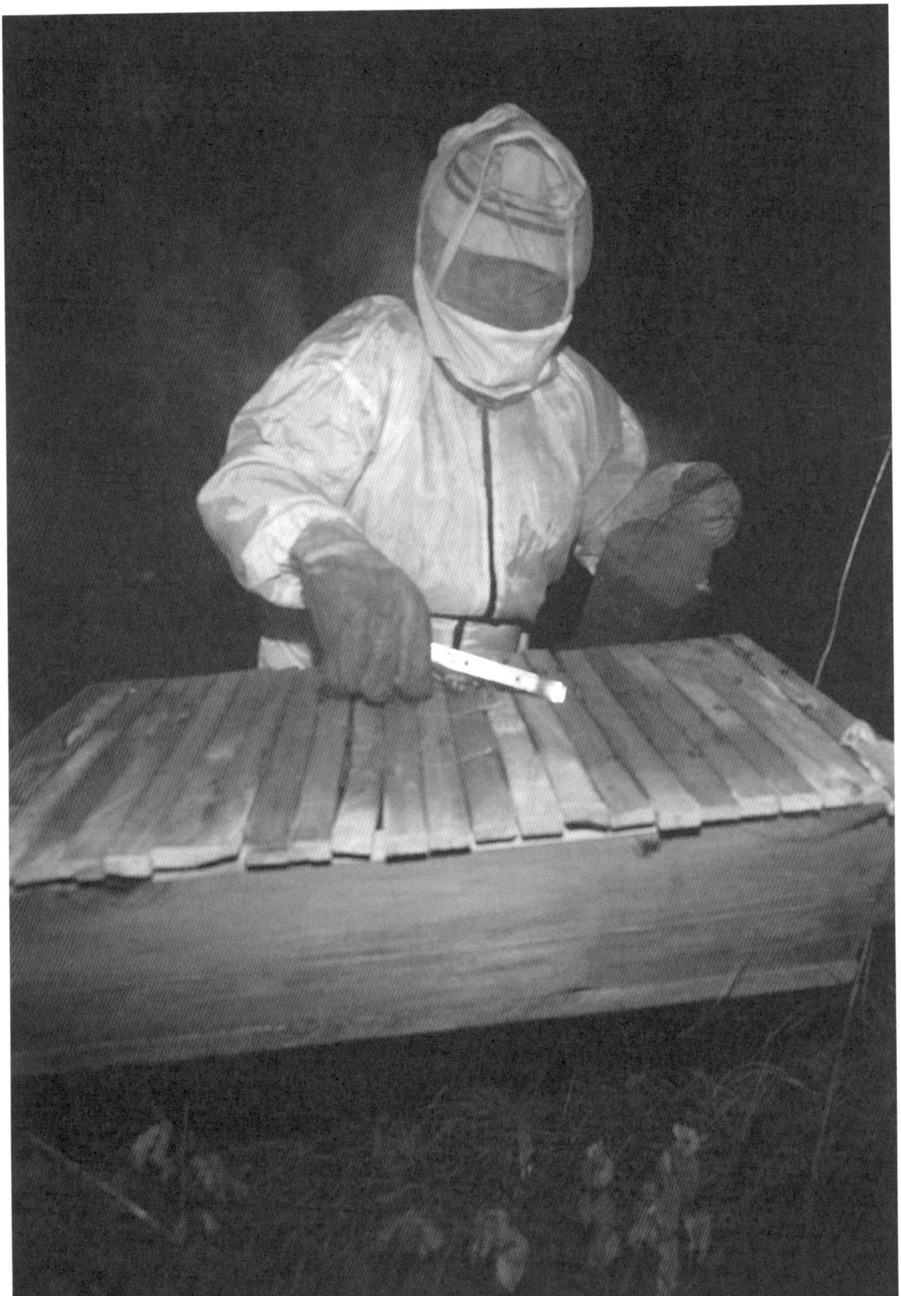

20 Making Money from Honey: Linking Rural Ugandan Women with Export Markets

Rachel Nadelman, Sarah Silliman and Marilyn Carr[43]

Background

This chapter is based on research in Uganda undertaken by a team of researchers from the New School University, New York, during the summer of 2005 (Nadelman *et al.*, 2005; Carr *et al.*, 2007). At that time, the Uganda Export Promotion Board (UEPB) was about to implement a strategy that aimed to increase honey production from the 2004 level of 3,000 metric tons to 13,000 metric tons by 2008 and to simultaneously improve quality with a view to breaking into rapidly expanding export markets. The country has progressed since 2005, increasing production to 5,000 metric tons, but has fallen far short of its goal (Kasozi and Kato, 2009). Fully realising this goal, while only a small step towards achieving Uganda's annual production potential of over 500,000 metric tons of honey, will still require attracting an additional 200,000 farmers into beekeeping. This target will be difficult to achieve without the full involvement of women.

At the time of the research, there were several approaches available to the Government in support of increasing women's beekeeping practices and improving the quality and production of bee products. Of the several potential approaches covered in the research study, two are highlighted here:

1. *Providing support to strengthen women's beekeeping co-operatives by linking with agricultural support services, training and savings and credit programmes.* There were already several of these small-scale production enterprises, although their number was still limited. However, many of them showed evidence of an ability to produce significant supplies of good quality honey, as well to innovate with new processes and products. There was also evidence that these women-owned community-based organisations (CBOs) could link with global markets. Once established, they seemed to have the potential to give members a great deal of control over their own enterprises, thus contributing towards the UEPB's production and export goals, while increasing women's empowerment and ability to control their livelihoods and build assets.

2. *Assisting with the expansion and replication of successful commercial companies that source honey from small-scale farmers (including women) and turn it into high quality product in a central, highly mechanised factory.* There was only one such company operating effectively at the time of the research and this was showing good promise of breaking into export markets. Several measures to address specific training and other needs of women were incorporated into the company's operations. However, while it provided income for rural women, this model seems unlikely to provide women farmers with any control over their participation in the production chain.

A variety of approaches were found between these two ends of the spectrum, including socially owned businesses in which members have shares and that employ staff and cover their own administrative costs from profits. Although they are similar to community-based organisations (CBOs) in that they are member-owned, they are much more formal and share some of the characteristics of private sector companies.

This case study looks at the experiences of a women's co-operative, the Kitgum Women Beekeepers Association, and a commercial company, Bee Natural Products, with a view to examining the potential for up-scaling each as part of an attempt to achieve the dual goals of reaching the Ugandan Government's export promotion goals, and reducing poverty among women producers and building women's empowerment.

Women in beekeeping

First, however, it is useful to review some basic issues involving women in beekeeping in general and in Uganda in particular.

While wild beehives have been harvested by men in Africa for centuries as a means of supplementing food supplies and income, changes in the industry have far-ranging implications for women's economic empowerment. First, there is a sizeable and growing market in North America, Europe and Japan for honey and other bee products, along with many other non-timber forest products. In many cases, there are also large and untapped domestic and regional markets for such products.

Second, many new production and processing technologies have been developed that can significantly increase output of honey and other bee products and improve quality to meet international standards. In addition to enabling African countries to respond to increased demand in export markets, these technological changes also offer the possibility for farmers to contribute to household income on a more significant basis through beekeeping enterprises. For example, research in Bolivia and Mexico shows that NTFPs can represent either a 'safety net' activity in times of crisis or a gap-filling activity that can be carried out on a more regular basis and contribute 7–95 per cent of household income (Marshall *et al.*, 2006).

Third, the introduction of new technologies has been accompanied by efforts on behalf of governments, development agencies and NGOs to increase the involvement of women in the industry to improve growth and reduce rural poverty. Since the early 1970s, thousands of improved or non-traditional beehives and associated processing technologies have been introduced to women's groups in Africa and elsewhere in the South with mixed results. More recently, however, there has been a switch in approach with both governments and NGOs seeking to integrate women equally with men into mainstream plans and programmes for expanding the output and export of apiculture products in response to growing domestic, regional and international demand.

Women and beekeeping in Uganda

There are a number of factors that make Uganda particularly interesting for an exploration of the potential of beekeeping for women farmers and their ability to link with export markets. They include the following:

- Gender-sensitive policies and strategies for the reduction of poverty in rural areas – such as Uganda's Poverty Eradication Action Plan (PEAP)[44] – have as their central goal raising the incomes of rural producers. As part of this they aim to modernise agriculture, where the majority of the poor (especially women) are concentrated, and to promote equal access to land and other assets (Ministry of Finance, Planning and Economic Development, 2000).

- There is a favourable trade environment for the export of honey and other bee products, including the African Growth and Opportunity Act, which allows free import of products from Uganda into the USA; the award of a licence to export honey to the EU; and an ambitious apiculture export strategy for 2005–2009 developed by the UEPB and the Uganda National Apiculture Development Organization (TUNADO).

- There is increased government investment in agricultural support services, including National Agricultural Advisory Services (NAADS) launched in 2002.[45] Funded by public and private sources, NAADS supports increased agricultural productivity and profitability through a demand-driven, farmer-led agriculture service delivery system targeted at subsistence farmers.

- Women are under-represented in apiculture compared to other agricultural sectors (20 per cent compared with 70 per cent), thus representing a huge potential for expansion.

Opportunities and constraints for Ugandan women beekeepers

Although the overall environment for increasing women's involvement in beekeeping seems promising, in practice women face several constraints – especially when it comes to entering export markets.

Beekeeping has traditionally been an independent or family activity in Uganda and is monopolised by men. The structure of the industry has been changing, however, as a result of the availability of new technology and also a new focus on organising both women and men in beekeeping groups or associations. In 2005, the numbers of organised beekeepers involved in these enterprises varied from 3,900 (private companies) to several hundred in the case of associations and/or CBOs, and 20–30 in individual groups. Although more women farmers are becoming involved as a result of these changes, they still represent a low proportion (less than 20 per cent on average) of the members of groups and associations.

Socio-cultural factors play a major role in this low participation of women. These relate specifically to apiculture, as well as to women's involvement in enterprise activities more generally. One reason beekeeping has historically been seen as a man's activity is because retrieving wild nests for harvesting involves climbing trees, an activity taboo for women. Although new models such as Top Bar and Langstroth hives enable both colonisation and harvesting to be done at ground level, thus in theory making beekeeping much more accessible to women producers, the cost of equipment and hives (and women's more limited access than men to credit and to training in new techniques) still hamper women's full participation in beekeeping.

Women's time poverty is a further constraint. It restricts their ability to attend meetings which can provide initial information about beekeeping and to travel away from home to attend training courses. Additionally, the best time for harvesting is normally in the evenings when the bees are less active, and this is when women are particularly busy with family commitments.

Even if women overcome the constraints of starting a beekeeping enterprise, once they are involved they find that it provides only a supplemental source of income. This income can be critical – for example, helping cover school fees or providing stability during emergency periods – but does not provide enough to sustain overall livelihoods. In a country where the average income per annum is around US$250, average incomes from beekeeping recorded in the case studies vary from around $2–80 per farmer or household.

In order for women to move beekeeping from a supplemental to a primary income source, they would have to increase the quality and quantity of honey production and diversify their products. However, there are several obstacles to achieving this, including lack of credit, technology, training and information.

In addition, women are often confined to the less skilled activities along the bee product value chain (see Figure 20.1), such as clearing ground for the hives, providing water and primary level honey processing (using traditional methods). Women's activities are primarily focused on Step 1 (obtaining inputs), Step 2 (apiary management) and Step 4, Stage 1 (product processing), all areas where there are no direct returns or financial rewards; this results in lower returns for women than for men.

Figure 20.1 The bee product value chain

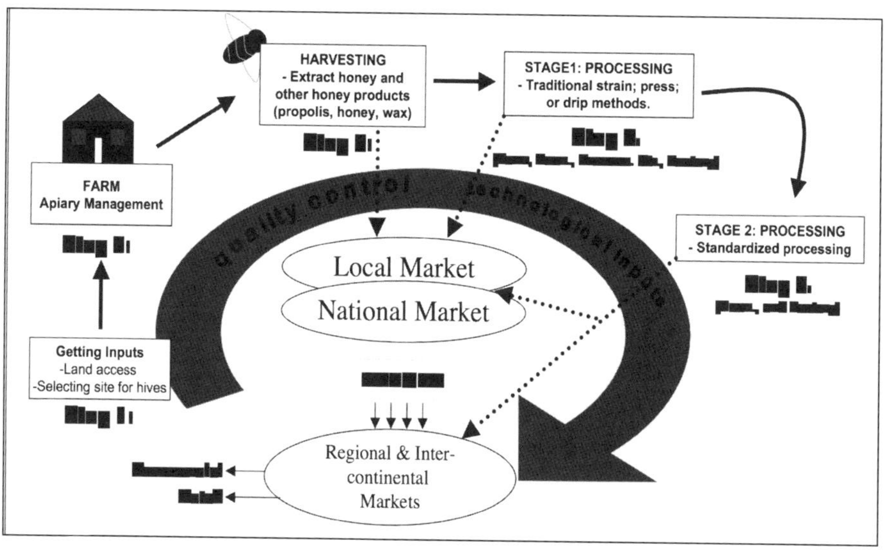

Source: Nadelman *et al.*, 2005

Organising structures and interventions

Organisation of some type is essential for individual farmers to move beyond traditional beekeeping – and vital for moving from local production to production for export.

Membership in self-help groups, producer associations or community co-operatives can enable women beekeepers to access key assets to improve their production, including obtaining loans for hives and shared processing technologies; bulk purchase of inputs; training and information to ensure product quality; bridging information gaps; linkages with consumers; and identification of new market niches (Shreckenberg *et al.*, 2006). Alternatively, women can become contract farmers/beekeepers for the private commercial sector and earn at least some income from the sale of their honey to a central source.

As shown by the following examples, the Kitgum Women Beekeepers Association (KWBA) and Bee Natural Products (BNP) Ltd, the ways in which women are integrated into the bee product supply chain varies considerably. In particular, there are notable differences in women's ability to influence the balance of power and returns within the supply chain – both between themselves and male beekeepers, and between themselves and buyers and retailers.

Experiences linking women with export markets

Kitgum Women Beekeepers Association

KWBA has involved women in the entire value chain, diversifying products and coping with internal tension from gender issues and external tension from ongoing conflict that has plagued the region for 20 years.[46] In addition, its leader has taken the first steps towards linking with export markets by leveraging funds to attend international trade fairs and specialist meetings.

Margaret Ogaba established the KWBA in 1995 in the belief that women working together would have a better chance of success in beekeeping than women working alone. The Association has been able to provide a supplementary income to many women who face challenges related to HIV and AIDS, as well as increased burdens and isolation resulting from the conflict. KWBA has grown into a well-known organisation and has been strategic by tapping into membership connections to access government-supported training and support programmes such as NAADS, which has funded it to extend its membership and to provide training to other groups and associations in Kitgum. In 2005, KWBA recruited and trained 150 beekeepers under the NAADS programme with the goal of reaching and training between 500 and 600 beekeepers.

KWBA has also received support from other domestic and international sources, such as advanced hives from the UEPB, equipment and supplies from the British High Commission and harvest and quality-control training from German donors. It has also leveraged funds to support growth, both from the Government, through 'gender-mainstreaming policies', and from NGOs, which have supported the integration of women in sector strategies. The exposure and the ideas accrued at trade fairs and specialist meetings have enabled KWBA to diversify and be at the cutting edge of the beekeeping industry. The experience has also been put to wider use throughout Uganda. For example, Ms Ogaba has worked with the Ministry of Agriculture on a 12-week informative radio programme to disseminate information on beekeeping.

Challenges for KWBA

KWBA has faced many internal and external challenges. Internally, it has struggled with gender dynamics, including conflicts between members and their husbands who have tried to restrict women's participation. Ms Ogaba has tackled this problem by drawing on her experiences during training in Denmark, where all family members are invited to join enterprises to prevent feelings of exclusion and resentment. With husbands invited to join their wives in KWBA, family tensions have been reduced and productivity has increased.

Externally, the conflict continually threatens production. Just a few years ago, KWBA was producing three tons of honey a year, but by 2005 this had fallen because it was no longer safe for members to reach their hives. Women who had moved to refugee camps were having particular difficulty in travelling, and their hives were subject to theft by rebels throughout the year. The group handled the loss by developing honey-added and value-added products such as groundnut-honey spread, furniture polish and beeswax candles. This solution has allowed KWBA to stay in business and expand production in ways that will provide sustainable incomes even while the conflict continues.

To make up for lost production, KWBA has turned to purchasing honey from local farmers for processing and sale. Still, at times they cannot purchase as much as they could process because they lack available cash to pay the farmers and, although they are trying to build a loan programme with the local village bank, usually they cannot access loans to cover purchases until they sell the final product.

Although the Association has several well-educated members, many have minimal education and are hampered by illiteracy. While beekeeping itself does not require reading skills, training and technical information tends to be available only in written form, while important business activities like accounting and record-keeping are beyond the capabilities of members. This barrier prevents these women from improving their practice and moving into more lucrative beekeeping activities.

Bee Natural Products

BNP is a private company that provides farmers in the West Nile region with training, a guaranteed market, harvesting services, loan programmes for hives, 'farm-gate' purchasing and immediate payment. Yet the high quality standards that qualify BNP for export and its advanced processing systems mean that the majority of women (and men) remain at the bottom of the value chain with little ability for advancement or greater income generation beyond selling raw materials.

BNP was founded in 2002 as a private company with a vision of building a sustainable industry that would have 'social and economic benefits for poor rural communities'.[47] Located in Uganda's West Nile region, BNP brings a viable industry and economic opportunities to an impoverished area, while also taking advantage of the region's natural habitat that is favourable for the production of honey and other bee products. Designed to compete with international honey production, the Arua-based factory has a full annual capacity of 600 metric tons, utilises cutting-edge processing technology and evaluates all production according to internationally determined health and quality standards.

BNP has changed the landscape of beekeeping in Uganda. Initially, BNP procured honey from a group of 126 traditional beekeepers, but by 2005 it was buying honey from over 4,000 farmers (25 per cent women) and operating in five West Nile districts. The number of active beekeepers has continued to increase annually, with an estimated 6,300 in operation in 2007. BNP is credited with having fostered the conditions for this significant annual growth and is thought to contract with a majority of these beekeepers. While most contracted bee farmers only provide BNP with raw bee products, there are some opportunities for advancement by becoming assistant and lead farmers who harvest for and train other beekeepers. As of 2005, eight women had been hired as lead farmers in three of the districts, which increased both their earning ability and their status within the community. Besides farming activities, BNP offers employment in the Arua factory, where it employs 45 workers. Women comprise 60 per cent of the factory staff, but most work seasonally, sorting and packing the honey and very few are in full-time managerial positions.

BNP is unique among bee product buyers because it facilities the production and sale process for all farmers registered with the company. This includes loan programmes to acquire hives, training opportunities, harvesting services, provision of hygienic storage equipment, bee product purchase at the 'farm-gate' and investment in developing lower-cost beekeeping inputs such as locally artisan-made protective gear kits. All registered farmers can purchase hives and beekeeping equipment through loans from BNP (repayable over four years either from profits or directly with honey). This means that small producers can afford to access advanced hives. Although farmers are not expected to repay loans until their hives are colonised, farmers must sell exclusively to BNP until their debt is repaid.

All harvests, whether by farmers or field officers, must utilise BNP buckets to ensure the hygiene of the products. BNP field officers travel directly to producers' apiaries and exchange money for honey at the producer's doorstep, so that they receive payment immediately. BNP pays USh1,000 per kilo for Grade A honey and USh800 per kilo for Grade B honey.[48] This is lower than the rate of USh1,500–2,000 per kilo that buyers in other regions offer. BNP justifies its lower pricing by explaining that contracted farmers save the expenses associated with buying and cleaning buckets and transporting honey that are necessary with other vendors. Even given the benefits, BNP's lower payments have caused some farmers to surreptitiously sell some of their honey to other buyers or to abandon their relationship with BNP altogether.

NAADS contracted BNP to provide training and other beekeeping support, recognising that the company could stimulate honey production in the region not only for newcomers to the industry, but also for farmers whose hives had been dormant because of insufficient training and/or limited access to markets. This public-private partnership has enabled BNP to develop a decentralised training and technical support system which allows it to reach more farmers and to develop a supplier network of high quality honey. Lead farmers are central to BNP's training programme and as the NAADS-BNP partnership expands, so do leadership opportunities for farmers.

BNP tries to include training activities that address women's particular circumstances and encourage their participation. Training confronts issues such as the lingering stigma of women's involvement in a traditionally male activity by helping women overcome their reluctance to wear trousers as part of protective harvesting suits. As in many rural areas of Uganda, women in the West Nile regions wear only skirts and have been taught to feel immodest if they are seen in trousers. BNP addressed this issue by providing harvest gear that includes very large baggy trousers that look like a skirt, adapting the harvesting trousers so that a skirt can be worn over them, and encouraging women to try on trousers during demos and training sessions so they can begin to feel comfortable with the 'costume'.

BNP's aim in 2005 was to reach its production capacity of 600 metric tons per annum, for which there is a large domestic market and also export opportunities. Yet by 2008 it had reached only 100 metric tons, 17 per cent of capacity. Even operating below its potential, however, BNP is recognised as the national leader in the honey and beeswax value chains. The 2005 opening of the European market to Ugandan exports can be attributed to the significant expansion of West Nile's apiculture industry, which BNP has fostered. By 2007 the region supplied 70 per cent of Uganda's bee product exports (Wiegratz, 2007).

Before 2002, Uganda, like other African countries, could not penetrate the European market due to stringent entry conditions. However, after certification for export to Europe was gained in 2005, market opportunities are wide open for bee products. The country is looking to the West Nile region to, among other things, overcome the challenges in meeting export demand. Locally produced honey is now fast outcompeting imported honey and demand conditions in export markets are extremely favourable.

Challenges for BNP

Sourcing sufficient high quality honey from farmers remains a challenge. Farmers' regional production remains far below the factory's production capacity or the consistent level needed for successful export.

BNP also has limited capacity to support producers in scaling up their production. Although lead farmers initially harvest for others with the intention of training them on the job, several factors, including lack of protective clothing, have resulted in long delays in hand-over. This not only gives officers and lead farmers less time for training and the other activities necessary to expand BNP's production abilities, but also prevents producers from learning a key skill that could enable them to scale up their own businesses later. If producers use the resources and training provided by BNP to develop their skills and increase their production, they are likely to move from simply supplying raw materials for a private company to operating and managing their own small enterprises.

Challenges for women farmers who sell to BNP

- While BNP's loan, training and purchasing systems make it far easier for farmers to sell unrefined honey, the majority are locked into the role of raw materials producer with very limited means to move into more lucrative beekeeping activities, such as selling processed honey.
- Assistant and lead farming positions provide advancement opportunities for individual women, but positions are limited and many women beekeepers explain that it is difficult to access the necessary training for these positions and impossible for some women (due, among other reasons, to family responsibilities) to be available for the travel the positions require.
- Even for groups that have members who have learned to harvest, lack of protective gear has meant continued dependence on BNP.
- BNP is first and foremost a business. While it recognises the poverty within its producer population and the poverty reduction possibilities the enterprise offers, it puts its own economic needs as a viable business before the challenges and needs of its suppliers, women or men.

Lessons learned and future directions

So what is the future of women in beekeeping in Uganda and what role do women have in plans for the expansion of the apiculture industry?

If the Government is to achieve its targets for increased production and export, several hundred thousand farmers will have to be attracted to the industry, which will only be possible with the increased participation of women. For this expansion to contribute significantly to poverty reduction in rural areas, women must be able to enter the industry at all levels in the production chain – including those that yield higher returns. Thus, strategies are needed to enable thousands more women to become involved in beekeeping enterprises and to participate in both high and low value activities.

As has been seen in the case studies, there is every reason to believe that this is an achievable objective. While earlier income-generating projects implemented by NGOs and development agencies to involve women in beekeeping have had limited success, newer strategies involving civil society and private companies offer more opportunities for the expansion of apiculture in a gender-sensitive way.

The case studies point to two successful paths to sustainable growth with a more equal distribution of benefits between women and men farmers. These are:

1. Support for CBOs and socially owned businesses, such as KWBA, that supply a range of needed services to their members who are engaged in beekeeping (through links with governments or other support agencies);
2. Investment in private companies that contract supplies from the individual farmers, women's groups and beekeepers associations that are registered with them (the BNP model).

The common factors leading to success in each of these approaches are:

- Their imperative to promote beekeeping and encourage increasing numbers of farmers into the industry;
- Their ability to leverage available governmental (e.g. NAADS) and non-governmental resources and to link their members/suppliers with necessary sources of financial and technical support;
- Their ability to organise producers so that issues of quality and quantity of production, transport and marketing are taken care of;
- Their interest in modernising the industry and their ability to make innovations in processes and products so that returns to farmers, processors, traders and retailers can be increased;

- Their interest in developing backward linkages to local artisans who can manufacture hives, protective clothing and other inputs, so that rural employment is created with widespread benefits to the community as a whole; and
- Their provision of opportunities for women to participate equally with men in modern beekeeping by ensuring that they receive training in all aspects of the production chain and by creating opportunities for them to earn incomes through providing training and other services to fellow beekeepers.

These are all essential steps to increase production, initially for local markets and eventually for export.

There are, however, some noticeable differences between the two approaches. First, the BNP model is very much a top-down affair and although it represents a relatively quick way to provide income to farmers from the sale of honey, it does so without giving them a great deal of control over their participation. By contrast, the KWBA model is very much a bottom-up approach. This can be slower in reaching farmers but, once established, gives members a great deal of say and control over their own enterprises. The small enterprise/CBO model has also been characterised by a wealth of innovation at the grassroots level. This could be usefully shared among groups and associations if support was given to networking at the national level.

Second, with an increasing proportion of the expanded output of honey and other bee products aimed at the export market, issues of quality, cost, volume and timeliness of supply become much more important. The BNP model – because of its large-scale (600 metric tons a year capacity), its sophisticated processing and packaging equipment, and its mechanisms for quality control – is well suited to supplying such markets. In contrast, CBOs are smaller, quality control is more difficult and filling large orders in a timely manner is more complicated as it depends on collaboration. However, the social advantages of CBOs are sufficient to warrant paying serious attention to assisting them to overcome the constraints involved in competing directly in export markets. As was seen with KWBA, CBOs are more than capable of making their own international links, but support will be needed to allow them to federate nationally to deal with quantity and quality of produce, transport issues and negotiating power. Given that the Government sees expanded honey production not just as a source of economic growth and increased export earnings, but also as a means of poverty reduction (and given that women make up a large proportion of the poor), support to a network of women's beekeepers' associations would seem to be particularly important.

In practice, given the potential for growth of the industry, both paths will probably need to be followed simultaneously. Neither will succeed, however, without the countrywide support in terms of outreach, training and technical assistance that only government can supply through programmes such as NAADS. It is also essential to establish an overall policy framework that is conducive to the growth of output and exports, and to the equal distribution of the resulting benefits. Several CBOs look to TUNADO as the body best able to advocate for policy changes on their behalf.[49]

The policies and institutional support programmes to promote the expansion of beekeeping in Uganda are in place, and the case studies have shown that women can both contribute to and benefit from such policies and programmes when they are enabled to do so. The lessons offered by these individual cases now need to be fed into national strategies for increased production and export promotion, so that success can be achieved at the level of the individual women producer in the informal economy, the household, the community and the nation as a whole.

References

Carr, M, Nadelman, R and Siliman, S (2007). *Women, Honey and Money: Women's Role in the Expansion of the Apriculture Industry in Uganda*, SEEDS, The New School Graduate Program in International Affairs, New York.

Kasozi, J and Kato, J (2009). 'Honey Production: Uganda Yet to Fully Realise Potential', *The New Vision*, 27 January, http://www.newvision.co.ug/D/9/756/669465

Marshall, E, Schekenberg, K and Newton, A C (eds) (2006). *Commercialization of Non-timber Forest Products: Factors Influencing Success. Lessons Learned from Mexico and Bolivia and Policy Implications for Decision-makers*, UNEP World Conservation Monitoring Centre, Cambridge, UK.

Ministry of Finance, Planning and Economic Development (2000). 'Poverty Reduction Strategy Paper – Uganda's Poverty Eradication Action Plan: Summary and Main Objectives', Government of Uganda, Kampala, http://www.imf.org/external/NP/prsp/2000/Uga/01/

Nadelman, R, Siliman, S and Younge D (2005). 'Report on Women and Beekeeping: Opportunities and Challenges in Uganda', The New School Graduate Program in International Affairs, New York.

Shreckenberg, K *et al.* (2006). 'Commercialisation of Non-Timber Forest Products: What Determines Success?', ODI Forestry Briefing #10, March, http://www.odi.org.uk/resources/download/540.pdf

Wiegratz, J (2007). 'Case Studies of Lead Firm Governance Systems in the Context of Commercialization of Smallholder Agriculture in Uganda', dissemination workshop presentation, September.

Wilson, E (2008). 'Quest for Economic Development in Agrarian Localities: Lessons from West Nile, Uganda', ISS Working Paper No. 452, Institute of Social Studies, January, http://biblio.iss.nl/opac/uploads/wp/wp452.pdf

Manufactured Exports

www.toeholdindia.com
rading Places
New Delhi
India

21 Toehold in India: Women Artisans Exporting Leather Sandals

Madhura Chatrapathy

Background

A significant portion of export earnings in India – estimated at US$2.9 billion in 2004–2005 – comes from products such as curios, fashion accessories, household goods and leather footwear that are handcrafted by artisans in the informal economy. Traditionally, the production of any handcrafted product involves a whole family, with women and men performing different operations in the production process and with men managing markets and finance. Generally, traders control the producers, who fall into debt traps by borrowing from them and are then compelled to produce for a particular trader who has lent them money and accept the minimum price that person offers. The vicious cycle of a trader-dependent market situation is perpetuated and the producer families get caught in a downward spiral.

A number of initiatives have aimed at assisting producer families to gain more independence and develop community-based businesses serving export markets. However, as the role of women in the production process – despite being very significant – is often overlooked, these have tended to be gender blind, with skill-upgrading and other interventions aimed at men.

Ideally, interventions are needed that:

1. Increase competitiveness in export markets;
2. Enable producer families to take control of their own enterprise activities; and
3. Promote gender equality in access to resources/services, in decision-making and in distribution and control of income.

This case study looks at an initiative of the Asian Centre for Entrepreneurial Initiatives (ASCENT) in India that has successfully supported hundreds of artisan families producing traditional *kolhapuri* leather sandals to form their own collaborative organisation supplying domestic and export markets. The women in these families are the main stakeholders, while men also have access to benefits such as training. Whereas many other interventions implemented by NGOs and international agencies have been successful in linking women micro-entrepreneurs with global markets, they have tended to see women as the producers, with the NGO acting as the exporter and catering largely to fair trade markets. In contrast, the ASCENT initiative provides an example of a successful group enterprise model in which women own and manage an export venture that has been co-created with men as co-entrepreneurs.

ASCENT and Toehold Artisans Collaborative[50]

History and purpose

ASCENT is a social enterprise located in Bangalore that is committed to fostering wealth creation and an entrepreneurial culture in the society. It seeks to instil a spirit of enterprise, self-reliance and self-help in individuals and organisations; to foster a sense of self-worth in people, particularly women; and to enhance the quality and effectiveness of entrepreneurial ventures. ASCENT has implemented a number of projects and programmes in the area of exports and group enterprise, including export-led poverty reduction and export of organic foods from farmers' groups. In all of these, it believes that the entrepreneur, the enterprise and the environment in which they exist need to be addressed together and not in isolation.

In 1998, ASCENT proposed 'Project EnterPrice' – a process of transforming a large group of traditional *kolhapuri* artisans into entrepreneurs. The emphasis was on economic empowerment, with a focus on the artisan family and especially on women. *Kolhapuri* footwear is handcrafted from natural leather that is eco-friendly, being locally bag tanned using vegetable dyes. Athani and Nippani in Northwest Karnataka are the heartland of *kolhapuri* sandals and home to over 400 families or artisans with a rich legacy of this traditional skill. Footwear craft is their only livelihood.

Traditionally, the sandals would be bought from artisans by local traders and then distributed across the country. Up to the mid-1980s, dealers also undertook some exports of the sandals. However, market competition led to *kolhapuris* being marked down in price, in turn leading to lower prices to artisans. Most artisans were then forced to look for lower priced leather, which made for poor quality and even lower prices. The vicious cycle led to increasing poverty among the artisans, with many families having to give up the craft and find alternative employment. Consequently, craftsmanship suffered, with degradation of skills over time. Exports also underwent a severe setback when some shipments were found to be inferior in quality and standardisation, with the result that *kolhapuris* became informally blacklisted by buyers abroad. This in turn squeezed the demand further.

While some skill training and technology up-gradation was made available to artisans through various government programmes, these were generally inadequate to deal with the problems. In addition, even though women played an important part in the production process – fashioning the intricate uppers while men crafted the hardy soles – their role was largely ignored and the limited amount of assistance available was targeted only at men.

This was the situation that ASCENT's Project EnterPrice sought to address. The overall objective was to ensure that artisans got the right price for their handcrafted footwear and in the process were transformed, particularly the women, into entrepreneurs. The core focus was economic development through distance marketing, including exports, and the core principle was 'build, operate and transfer'. Careful attention was given to the balance between business and social objectives and needs using an equality, equity and inclusive approach.

The outcome of this project – which was implemented between January 1999 and December 2002 with funds from the National Leather Development Programme (NLDP) and United Nations Development Programme (UNDP), technology support from the Central Leather Research Institute, and infrastructure by the Government of Karnataka – was the formation of the Toehold Artisans Collaborative (TAC) in 2002 with its own brand, 'Toehold'. Two hundred women organised into 11 self-help groups form the basis of TAC. Some men have also joined the movement and set up their own self-help groups. A common facility centre provides for selective mechanisation and technical support, and a raw material bank provides access to quality raw materials. TAC was registered as a trust, but it is being converted to a Section 25 company to take care of all business operations, including collective marketing of the produce and development of the artisans as a leather cluster around Athani. While women own the business entity, men participate in all business operations along with them. Women and men receive joint training in design development, entrepreneurial skills and leadership. The project has also facilitated the artisans' direct exposure to international markets through trade fairs and other methods.

Progress

TAC's achievements

TAC is now a prominent player in the international market for ethnic footwear, supplying international clientele in Australia, Italy and Japan. A chief reason for this has been its insightful marketing strategy deriving 'high margins from small volumes', rather than 'small margins from high volumes'. It has delivered commendable business performance, with revenues almost quadrupling between 2001 and 2003. In 2006, export sales exceeded

US$100,000 and TAC received the Excellence in Export Award (2006) instituted by the Federation of Karnataka Chamber of Commerce and Industry. TAC footwear products have maintained a consistently high level of product quality and have reached designers and designer boutiques, as well as leading retail chains. To the amazement of buyers and critics alike, 200 decentralised home-based production units are able to meet both quantity and quality with minimal or no variations. Rejection rates are less than 2 per cent.

An advance queuing, business-to-business, web-driven model supported by the participation of the artisans has been established, and attendance at international trade fairs has taken *kolhapuri* footwear from obscurity to international fashion markets. The showcasing of over 450 designs through its web catalogue provides testimony to the design and quality capabilities of the artisans and builds confidence among visitors to the site. In addition, IT-enabling among low and zero-literacy women has exploded the myth that 'technology equals men'. The web catalogue is acknowledged as a model for digital bridging and in 2005 *http://www.toeholdindia.com* won the National Manthan Award for e-content in the business category.

Impact on artisans

Before 1999 the artisans could earn a net income of about Rs12–15 per pair of sandals. Today, this has gone up to about Rs40–50 per pair,[51] depending on the design and material. Earlier, they were making a maximum of three pairs a day. Today, they make about six pairs per day and they are occupied about 200 days a year, as opposed to 150 days before TAC was formed. In terms of wages alone, they thus earn on average Rs54,000 per year, as opposed to Rs6,000 before. Apart from this, they also receive a dividend at the end of the year. Forty per cent of the profits go to individual artisan families in proportion to how much they have supplied; 20 per cent goes to the self-help groups; and 40 per cent is retained by TAC for business development. This increased income is used to keep children in school or even send them to a better school. While previously girls were dropping out from the 7th or 8th standard, many more are now going on to higher standards and have ambitions for professional careers such as flight attendants. More than 80 per cent of artisan families now have gas connection and improved stoves, and telephone connectivity. Many have also been able to pay off long-standing debts to local traders and free themselves from 'bonded labour'.

In addition to these economic benefits, there have also been many non-economic benefits. The development of an entrepreneurial spirit within the groups has yielded a greater sense of self-worth among the artisans. They seem less fearful of authority and more courageous in taking control of their own destinies. For example, having saved money through their own savings and credit groups, the women have gained the confidence to approach banks to negotiate loans. The spirit of entrepreneurship has also fostered innovation among the artisans, who feel free to express their creativity in coming up with new and radical sandal designs. Direct exposure to export markets has increased their understanding of international customers and what is required in terms of quality, delivery commitments and design.

Lessons learned and future directions

Lessons learned

One of the determinants of TAC's success is its carefully targeted marketing approach. As noted above, the philosophy has been to derive 'high margins from small volumes'. It positions itself in the international market for authentic, limited edition designer footwear with the added value of being handcrafted, high quality and eco-friendly. In doing so, TAC has rejected the 'sympathy' or ethnic market and has entered a very highly competitive and discerning high-end international market that is design and quality sensitive. Commitment and contractual behaviour have brought special credit to the group.

Another determinant of success is the intense market exposure of the producers – both women and men. Artisan couples have participated in international shoe fairs at the national level in New Delhi and internationally in Dusseldorf and Shanghai. This, combined with the women's natural flair for design and increased opportunities to hone their skills, has led to international designers coming to their doorstep to work with them and offer co-branding.

Gender equality and women's ability to own and manage their own business enterprise has been promoted by ensuring opportunities for women in exposure and training in all aspects of the export business, including the use of ICT. This is needed to ensure that women (and men) artisans are conversant with the entire production and marketing chain and not just the production side. Similar initiatives elsewhere in India, while achieving outstanding export performance and noteworthy improvements in design and quality, have not brought about significant changes in gender relations as the projects have remained focused on men. The export benefits have accrued to the exporting company owned by the Government, while the artisans have remained a supply source and glorified wage earners. The main differences between the ASCENT model and the conventional approach to linking microentrepreneurs/artisans with global markets are outlined in Table 21.1.

Table 21.1 Conventional approach to export promotion versus ASCENT approach

Conventional approach	ASCENT approach
Product-focused	People-centred
Only craft/trade focus	Enterprise focus
Technical skill inputs	Technical and business skill inputs
Experts working the markets	Artisans and professionals working markets together
Limited/no market exposure	Intense market exposure
Skill training for individual male artisans	Skill training through groups of women
Men exclusive training activities	Women exclusive group, men inclusive training activities
No financial support, market and bank borrowing, resulting in defaults and bonding to traders, further lowering of self-esteem and confidence	Self-help group for savings and credit, freedom from borrowing and bonded work, better self-esteem and confidence
Welfare approach	Empowerment approach
Decision by external support system	Decision by artisans through participatory process
Absence of leadership	Growing leadership
Male domination issue not addressed	Women taking charge of institution-building process in equal partnership with men
Mass market, high volume, with low margins resulting in non-viable enterprise	Class marketing, low volume with high margins, resulting in more viable enterprise
Generic brand – identified as tough-wearing rough footwear	New own-brand image, design and comfort combined with tough wearing
Income generally from wages, occasionally from actual profits	Income from profits shared between artisans and Collaborative, in addition to factoring labour costs to artisan's credit
Artisans not much known to outside world	Artisans better known and drawing media attention

Specific measures are needed to ensure that the quality and delivery demanded in export markets are maintained and the brand name is protected. In the case of Toehold this was achieved in two ways:

1. Increasing the artisans' understanding of the need for quality control and timeliness of delivery through intense exposure to international buyers;

2. Training a woman from each self-help group, who acts as a quality monitor.

This unique model of enterprise, owned and run by the artisans through women's self-help groups, has taken the humble *kolhapuri* to 'couture' status in the trendiest mainstream international fashion markets. This can act as a learning model for similar efforts in other sectors/products.

Future directions

Plans for the future of Toehold are to:

- Enter the domestic market, especially high value segments. One of the challenges of domestic retail is that the business is on the basis of consignment sales. Normally, this means that payment is made when the goods are sold, with unsold goods being returned. This has major implications, such as having to accept back shop-soiled goods that have no value. Small artisans cannot afford this. To overcome these constraints, there is a proposal to set up Toehold's own retail outlets. This will require a large amount of capital and will be a major challenge.
- Enlarge the producer base and institutionalise people's organisations. As the market expands, more producers will be required to increase capacity.
- Expand the product range. This is a long-term plan and the details are being worked out with fashion designers and marketing experts.
- Build the Toehold brand through a variety of image-building initiatives, in addition to existing activities such as road shows and participation in trade fairs.
- Establish a skill development centre to improve processes and skills and build human capital.
- Target niche markets as an ongoing effort.
- Build the capacity of the next generation,[52] in both the craft and the business side, and strengthen the role of artisan women as business leaders.

brother

22 Stitching Local to Global: SEWA Trade Facilitation Centre

Reema Nanavaty and Mona Dave

Background

In developing countries, the informal sector is simultaneously associated with both poverty and growth. While producers and workers in the sector suffer disproportionately from poverty, they are also a primary driving force in the growth of their economies and are highly enterprising and productive, even when very poor. In India, they contribute 60 per cent of national income, over 54 per cent of national savings and over 40 per cent of national exports.[53]

All non-regular wage workers, both rural and urban, and virtually all self-employed people (except professionals and technicians) belong to the informal economy. Petty traders, small producers, micro-entrepreneurs, domestic workers, home-based workers and casual labourers – including shoeshine boys, rickshaw pullers, home-based garment workers, home-based electronic workers and street vendors – are all part of the informal sector. They work without technical or financial support and/or without minimum wages, assured work or benefits. Yet their persistence and ability to adapt to changing economic circumstances and make do with little or no infrastructure has been an essential component of the ability of developing countries to grow and manage transition in a globalising economy.

One large group within the informal economy is that of rural craft workers, most of whom supply very localised and often limited markets. In the case of rural women, a popular activity is the embroidery of clothing and household goods that are produced for own consumption, gifts for friends and neighbours or sale in local markets. Over the past several decades some of these products have reached Northern markets through government handicraft marketing organisations, NGOs and Fairtrade groups. However, this has been on a limited basis and has involved no more than a handful of the rural women artisans who engage in embroidery activities.

This case study focuses on an intervention implemented by the Self Employed Women's Association in Gujarat, India, building on the traditional embroidery work of rural women to develop a business enterprise owned by the women themselves, that aimed to supply embroidered products to export markets on a broad and sustained basis.

SEWA is a member-based organisation of poor self-employed women workers in the Indian informal economy. Founded in 1972, it has built up a membership of around one million women workers, making it the largest national women's organisation. SEWA's two main goals are full employment and self-reliance of its members in order to equip them in their fight against poverty by ensuring livelihood security. SEWA strongly believes in the Gandhian ideology of self-sufficiency, and therefore strives to build its members' own business enterprises; members of SEWA do not remain workers and users but become owners and managers.

SEWA Trade Facilitation Centre

The SEWA Trade Facilitation Centre (STFC) is a design, production and marketing facility for apparel, accessories and soft furnishings, with value addition provided by rural craftswomen. Hansiba, the STFC brand, is owned by the 15,000 women artisans from the impoverished Kutch and Patan districts of Gujarat who are its shareholders. The uniqueness of STFC is its innovation in marketing the skills of the rural poor, thereby ensuring that they have sustained work and income. Today it has become the primary source of income and livelihood for these artisans and has also relieved them from the drudgery and suffering of being forced to migrate to find work.

The aim is to place more and more income in the hands of the rural women artisans and bring them into the mainstream of India's emerging new economy. Hansiba is unique as it not only ensures livelihood security, but also addresses environmental issues by promoting organic cotton, *khadi* (handspun cloth) and natural dyes. Now in its fifth year of operations, and following significant restructuring of its business model, the STFC is poised for a significant retail expansion strategy that will help the organisation achieve commercial sustainability.

History and purpose of STFC

The STFC has its roots in SEWA's expansion in rural areas. As a union, SEWA's key first step was to organise. Furthermore, since the rural regions of Gujarat depend on agriculture as a main source of employment, yet are susceptible to droughts and other disruptions to the crop cycle, the generation of non-land-based employment is critical. Recognising the rich craft tradition among the women in the region, SEWA began to organise thousands of them on the basis of their artisan skills. Providing secure work and employment was an urgent need for the households and an effective organisational catalyst.

As the years passed and repeated natural disasters struck (cyclones, floods, extended droughts), the artisan base expanded. Soon, craft activity became one of the only sources of income and livelihood for the artisans and their households. Eventually, the demand for work among the artisans exceeded SEWA's capacity to provide it on a sustainable basis under the system they had developed. In particular, SEWA's role of facilitating access to raw materials and linking the products with the market needed to be expanded, restructured and professionalised. In short, SEWA had to explore ways of turning this economic activity into a viable business – to ensure the artisans' income security by bringing the work to them on a sustainable basis that they could own and manage.

Thus SEWA initiated STFC as a company where the artisans have a stake in the ownership and decision-making processes, with the support of professional management. The overall aim is to ensure that craftswomen in the informal sector have socio-economic security and full employment, achieved through the sustained, profitable and efficient co-ordination of the design, production and marketing of their products and services.

Due to its unique business model and value proposition, STFC has two mutually reinforcing sets of objectives: business and social (see Box 22.1).

STFC interventions

In support of its objectives, STFC has developed a package of interventions that have been implemented with varying degrees of success. These include establishing market linkages, developing its own brand and production centres, and training and capacity building.

Establishing market linkages

STFC has a well-designed marketing strategy working through a range of channels that is a judicious mix of dedicated retail outlets; institutional sales by way of business-to-business marketing; exhibitions in major and emerging cities in India, Europe, Japan, South Africa and the USA; and promotion of e-marketing through the STFC portal.[54] STFC gathers comprehensive market intelligence that includes market surveys for specific product categories, access to buyers' databases, information on tariff structures and non-tariff barriers, and identification of possible distribution channels. It uses this information to develop an effective sales strategy and to increase exposure of the artisans to the demands of export markets and the operating procedures and quality norms required to penetrate them.

Developing its own brand and production centres

STFC launched its own national brand, Hansiba, in order to increase market penetration. It is named after SEWA's first ever artisan member who, at 93

Box 22.1 The mutually reinforcing strategies of STFC

Business objectives:

- Develop a sustainable and profitable business model where the surplus is ploughed back into strengthening the business organisation and expanding the member/shareholder base;
- Achieve a commercial operating break-even point by fiscal year 2011;
- Develop a competitive product based on artisans' traditional skills;
- Make production management efficient, while integrating remote producers by achieving economies of scale, optimal product sales mix and more efficient utilisation of capacity/resources;
- Market effectively both domestically and internationally, with sales planned to reach US$1 million by fiscal year 2010.

Social objectives:

- Build the productive capacity of artisans so that they can compete in and be integrated into mainstream markets;
- Maximise the employment of qualified artisans at fair wages and with fair working conditions (with a target of 15,000 artisans by 2012);
- Ensure shareholder livelihoods through production co-ordination and market-driven strategies;
- Empower women artisans through the realisation of their potential, so that they engage in the development of their communities;
- Provide technical service assistance to strengthen similar organisations.

years old, is still inspiring others with her embroidery skills. The brand symbolises women's artistry and skills at every stage of the value chain – starting from cotton growing to the final product.

Merged into Hansiba are two earlier marketing initiatives, Banascraft and Kutchcraft, named after the districts in which the earliest women members involved in embroidery work lived. As markets grew and STFC started working with big buyers and entering the mainstream market, it recognised the need for one focused business organisation. There was also a need to promote embroidery and skills, rather than the region in which the women lived.

Vastralaya (common production centres) have been set up where SEWA members from different fields such as embroidery and stitching come together and make ready-to-wear garments. For this purpose, the women were given training from the National Institute of Fashion Technology (NIFT). The clothes embroidered by the members in the villages are cut, stitched, washed and packed in the *vastralaya*. In future this is where dyeing and printing of cloth will also take place and where the weavers will work. The *vastralaya* has a production capacity of 500 pieces per day and contains the latest equipment for garment making, washing, printing and finishing to ensure that products adhere to international quality standards.

Following market research carried out by STFC in 2003–2004, the strategy has focused on the Indian retail market, since it is growing rapidly at about 54 per cent in total sales. There are now three retail outlets in India under the brand name of Hansiba in Ahmedabad, Delhi and Mumbai, all in high-end shopping areas. In the international market, STFC works only with high-end designer labels such as Dosa and Adili.

Training and capacity building

STFC has introduced innovative solutions that help the artisans build their competitive edge in the market and has designed a set of training modules that aim to continuously upgrade and develop their skills. Other training includes orientation of the shareholders, quality checking measures, capacity building of the master craftswomen to run a common production centre, costing, business planning, production planning and micro-enterprise management. STFC has also collaborated with design specialists and reputable national institutions to help artisans develop their skills. In addition, STFC builds artisans' capabilities as managers to ensure efficiency at all stages of operations. These grassroots leaders are trained in all aspects of managerial training by the SEWA Manager's School, and linkages have also been established with the Indian Institute of Management in Ahmedabad.

Progress

STFC has expanded rapidly since its inception, driven by the competitive advantage of strong networks among the craftswomen, their distinctive traditional skills and the market potential for their crafts. The unique qualities and social impact of STFC's activities have been recognised and partially supported by the Ministry of Textiles, Government of India, and by international donors such as the Ford Foundation and the International Finance Corporation (IFC) of the World Bank Group. Under these programmes, the STFC builds marketing channels and directly sells the women's crafts.

The other production stages, such as design and procurement, are handled by SEWA or its partner organisations (i.e. district associations)[55] or are outsourced to third parties. Under these arrangements, sales have improved steadily, as can be seen from the 2007–2008 status of STFC shown in Box 22.2.

Box 22.2 Status of STFC (2007–2008)

Overview

- Annual turnover: Rs40 million
- Three outlets in Ahmedabad, Delhi and Mumbai
- Total employment generated: 3,500 rural artisans and 200 urban garment workers
- Provided an average monthly income of Rs1,500–1,800
- Business partnerships with large national organised retailers such as Shoppers Stop, Fab India, West Side, Life Style and Arna Clothings Ltd; international organisations; high-end designer labels such as Dosa, Adili and Hi Sister; and fair trade buyers such as Sevya
- Created a cadre of grassroots business managers to streamline the entire production process and establish a robust supply chain
- Technical partnership with the IFC to evolve a commercial business strategy
- Provided market access and business development services to grassroots artisan groups from the North-east, Bihar, Orissa, Rajasthan and other south Asian countries such as Bangladesh, Nepal, Pakistan and Sri Lanka
- Replication of the model of STFC in South Asian Association for Regional Co-operation countries and Afghanistan
- Constituted a core cell within the Ministry of Textiles to enable the formulation of pro-poor policy

Financial performance

Share capital:	Rs1,41,75,800
Income:	Rs3,01,75,956
Total assets:	Rs3,79,57,992

Undoubtedly, the rural women involved with STFC have benefited from the business. Sixty-five per cent of the sale price of the products goes directly to the women, and a monthly income of an average Rs1,500–1,800 compares favourably with the minimum wage of Rs40–60 per day. In most households, this represents the sole source of income available to the family. What this means to the women is best expressed in their own words. According to Gauriben and Puriben, master craftswomen and shareholders of STFC:

> We bring to you our story, which is our real life experience of building a company of the rural poor women, by the women themselves and for the women. The life of my family hangs by the thread with which I embroider.

Implicit in this statement is the importance not just of the regular source of income available to the women, but also of a sense of pride in the fact that this is their own company and all that goes with that – an increase in self-reliance and an increase in standing within their communities and households. As a result of their new empowerment, women who had never been out of their villages now go to the district and central offices. They go to government offices and take advantage of government schemes that are available to them. They even travel nationally and internationally.

The journey of these craftswomen or artisan women was not easy. When the project began, life for them was a struggle for survival and there were no alternative economic opportunities. They had to migrate in search of work in the absence of rainfall, agriculture or fodder for their cattle. Health, child-care and education of children was never a possibility, but always just a dream. Distress sales of the intricate embroidery and valuable cloths given to them as heirlooms by their mothers and grandmothers was common. These women say: 'We had never seen 100 rupees before, but the first pieces of cloth for embroidery brought 100 rupees, which created history and brought a major breakthrough in our lives'.

More importantly, artisans like Gauriben and Puriben are always referring to the benefits of regular income and a choice of employment: 'I can make the choice of laborious work in the field, migrating or doing embroidery at home – and I always choose embroidery'. They also point out that they are now known in the village by their own names instead of being known as 'wife of or mother of or daughter of'. The traders and money-lenders who were previously unwilling to offer loans are now pushing for their custom because they can see the women have regular work and income.

Extra income has been spent on the women's own development and that of their families and village communities. Money has been spent on educating daughters, on shelter, on agricultural inputs so that husbands and sons can get a job and on constructing rainwater harvesting and watershed development structures.

Transition

Despite STFC's obvious success at the level of the company and the individual woman artisan, by 2004 it had become apparent that the scale of operations was beginning to exceed the capacity of such a system to co-ordinate and optimally serve the craftswomen. This resulted in a partial breakdown in operations as the infrastructure struggled to keep up with continued growth.

SEWA and the district associations therefore decided to review the business model in order to reach financial sustainability and make their operations more efficient. With additional help from the IFC, the operational restructuring was based on several initiatives:

- *Consolidation of all craft activity under one entity* (the merging of two other brands into Hasiba).
- *Extension of the services offered to members*, including:
  - Market access and development – through establishing a range of both national and international market networks;
  - Product development – through developing a range of contemporary products in line with current trends, fashion forecasts, consumer tastes and preferences, employing the traditional skills of artisans;
  - Capacity building and training of artisans – through strategic alliances with specialised technical training institutions and building in-house training facilities;
  - Technical assistance – through establishing a centre for member artisans equipped with state-of-the-art machines and facilities to enable production of high quality and high value-added products;
  - Policy initiatives – through undertaking various policy roundtables to enable a bottom-up flow of the needs and demands of the artisans and translate these into policy measures.
- *Transformation from a selling-oriented to marketing-oriented company:* Earlier, when a business plan was made, STFC looked at how many artisans were available, how much work they needed and what STFC wanted to supply, rather than what customers wanted. Now, in order to reach the mainstream markets and high-end markets, it is necessary to become market driven and meet the requirements of the customers.

- *Operations re-engineering:* The products being offered to the market were having numerous technical problems. Hence, there was a need to do a lot of product engineering in terms of size, cuts, fabric testing, colour fastness and fit, together with product development and designing. Operations include an efficient production system and supply chain that ensures timely delivery of quality products to customers, which in turn ensures a more cost-effective company and more income for members.
- *Strengthening the management team:* Small companies such as STFC cannot afford market rates for CEOs and other managerial staff, but it is still important to have such positions in place to ensure proper facilitation, along with clear-cut roles and responsibilities.

Lessons learned and future directions

STFC has travelled a significant distance along the path of building a model, artisan-owned, sustainable business enterprise. Among the main lessons learned are:

- When forming an organisation such as STFC, the investment needed for future expansion should be included in the initial planning. STFC is still struggling with restructuring because this was not done.
- The fact that this is a business operation should be kept in mind from day one, but the social objectives cannot be ignored because income and work security for poor women is the main objective of the initiative.

STFC is now clear about its future journey. It needs to successfully communicate the unique selling proposition of 'hand embellishment'. It has gained experience in the retail market and feels that it is now time to focus on communicating that the STFC product is 'wearable art' instead of just a garment.

STFC plans to achieve 100 per cent growth in the business in the next three years. Its proposed strategy focuses on ethnic modern women's apparel, home furnishings and gifts and accessories in the high-end premium market, the mainstream fashion market and staple products market. It is entering the high-end premium market segment by co-branding with the labels and designers of design houses. The strategy is to market the embroideries and designs so as to get more remuneration into the hands of the artisan women.

23 Communications and Commerce: The Role of ICT in Linking Women Entrepreneurs with Global Markets[56]

Nidhi Tandon and Giséle Yitamben

Background

In an increasingly globalised and networked world, businesswomen need access to a range of information to enable them to make informed choices concerning their livelihoods, management of resources and income, and to understand and influence the policy decisions that have an impact on their business activities. The role of ICT in enabling women to access and analyse this kind of information cannot be underestimated. Despite much rhetoric around the diffusion of ICT in developing countries, the reality is that a widespread assumption still persists that women in general have no real use for or interest in ICT. This is often reflected in the ways in which business support services are designed and delivered.

This case study – based on a needs survey conducted with people in the clothing sector in Douala, the economic capital of Cameroon, from July 2005 to March 2006[57] – seeks to examine this issue. It looks at the personal initiatives taken by a small group of women entrepreneurs involved in ready-to-wear clothing design, manufacture and export to learn about and use the internet as a support tool for their entrepreneurial, creative and export initiatives. It then looks at the donor-driven experience of a Chamber of Commerce initiative to increase and improve women's use of internet services through a new high-tech multimedia centre.

Women and the textile and clothing sector in Cameroon

Anyone who visits Cameroon and its neighbouring countries cannot fail to notice the rich, colourful and diverse textile and clothing sector that is dominated by enterprising women who manage everything from cotton growing to design, stitching, transport and retail. Much of the cross-border import/export trade in fabric and clothing is also conducted by women. The sector can be roughly divided into industrial uniform production, ready-to-wear clothing and traditional made-to-measure tailored garments. According to an estimate by the African Development Bank (2005), women entrepreneurs own approximately 38 per cent of the 7,100 small and medium-sized enterprises (SMEs) registered in Cameroon. Typically, these SMEs in the region of Douala have between 10 and 15 employees.

The 1995 WTO Agreement on Textiles and Clothing established a quota system governing international trade in textiles and clothing. When this agreement ended in 2005, many developing countries, including Cameroon, faced more and more challenges entering or remaining in international trade in this segment of the market. With the renewal of the African Growth and Opportunity Act,[58] however, some textile production in member countries continued to be exempted from customs duties. According to the *Washington Post*, AGOA brought about an increase in the value of textile exports to the USA from US$600 million in 1999 to $1.5 billion in 2003 (cited by Afrik.com, 2004). Also in 2003, imports from 37 countries, including Cameroon, grew by 55 per cent compared to the previous year (ibid.).

Several programmes are being developed to further strengthen and support the capacity of clothing sector entrepreneurs to better organise themselves to penetrate the US market. Within these programmes, companies owned or managed by women are being specially targeted. The trade potential is quite substantial. African designs are attractive and certain American retailers specifically seek to obtain supplies from the continent. Market studies have shown that African Americans are interested in products that express or reflect their ethnic heritage. This market, estimated by the World Bank in 2003 as potentially worth between US$200 and 270 billion, is a promising niche for African exporters in the clothing sector (Biggs *et al.* 2003).

Potential benefits of the internet for entrepreneurs

A series of publications from the International Trade Centre (Knappe, 2005; Hirsch, 2005) has highlighted the advantages of the internet for entrepreneurs in the clothing sector of developing countries, which include:

- Monitoring goods that could improve the competitiveness of producers;
- Speeding up delivery, reducing costs and improving services;
- Integrating design and development of products through access to virtual prototypes of clothing and 'tests' in real time that can simulate the appearance and adjustment of a new model in two or three dimensions, considerably reducing costs of research and development;
- Developing solutions in collaboration with buyers or simply using their system;
- 'Internal security' and other customs protection;

- Receipt by manufacturers of data on outlets in an almost instantaneous way – they may start production and ship replacement stock without waiting for orders from the retailer; and
- Short delivery times and reduced inventory costs.

Use of the internet by women entrepreneurs

In a survey of members of organisations supporting women entrepreneurs, fashion designers and the women entrepreneurs themselves in Douala, most of the women interviewed stated that they knew about the internet. Jeanine, for example, said:

> *I know the internet very well, for at least five years my uncle* [a senior staff member in a private company] *had internet in his office. When I went there, very often, I found him busy reading or sending mails. I profited from consulting my mailbox.*

Of the 34 women entrepreneurs interviewed, 32 used the internet for social reasons and 17 used it for professional reasons. The social users wrote, edited and sent messages, chatted, and scanned and sent photos of family events to friends and parents abroad. All of them said that they used it to communicate with their relatives. For example, Yveline noted that:

> *I only use the internet to receive and send mails. I have family abroad, and as they have internet at their home, they have obliged me to get used to the Net. At times when they have things to tell me, they call and the telephone does not go through. It is in the cyber café that I consult or send my mails.*

Source of information and training

Those who use the internet for professional reasons were self-trained. They generally agreed that it could be of great use to them in their search for customers and access to sites communicating useful information for their market studies. Two of them said that it enabled them to become informed on current fashion trends and to improve their own creativity and competitiveness. Nicole, a fashion designer who exports to the USA, said:

> *The world of fashion changes often. Trends, colours, and styles change from one season to the next, from one country to the other. In my case, I have a varied clientele, in Cameroon, but also outside the country. So, in order to be up to date, I dip into the internet, I find out what's changed, and even about emerging trends. This allows me to be in phase with my clients.*

Women respondents also used the internet to search for information (on prices and brands of dressmaking equipment, fashion sites, fashion trends), to share information with foreign partners and colleagues, and to watch fashion shows. Esmerelda declared:

> *Through the internet, I have learnt to search for information on suppliers of sewing equipment and on the trends of fashion. I needed an over-sewing machine. As I could not find the brand on the market, I launched a search on the internet that enabled me to locate some suppliers abroad that were selling them. I contacted them at the same time that my sister stayed in that location. She put me in contact with the one in her location, and I negotiated and was able to acquire my machine. It is providing me with so much fame in my trade!*

Three women said that they had used the internet for training. Françoise holds a baccalaureate. She is married and has three children. Her passion for the internet was born during the course of her training:

> *I got to know the internet when I was still a student. When I started training as a fashion designer, I was pleasantly surprised to find on the internet some sites of foreign dressmakers and their designs ... I got inspired by them during my training, and I have designs that are very much appreciated by my customers, that I created with inspiration from these sites. I do not frequently visit them, but when I do visit I am prepared to give up some hours of my time. I get a lot of ideas. All that I regret is not being able to have internet in the house.*

Diane, who holds a First School Leaving Certificate, is married and a mother of five, and is a member of an association affiliated to the Chamber of Commerce. She took several training courses in entrepreneurship, and then took part in computer training provided by the Association pour le Soutien et l'Appui à la Femme Entrepreneur (ASAFE) based in Douala. It is thanks to her son, who always accompanies her to the cyber café, that she learnt to use the internet:

> *In the beginning, the internet was a real curiosity to me. But so long as I go there, I learn a lot from it. The speed with which I work with the internet is increasing. I know how to open my mailbox. I can download documents. I would not have believed it two years ago.*

Providing visibility for enterprises

Three women used the internet to create greater visibility for their activities by means of 'virtual boutiques'; four used it to communicate with their clients.

Rose, a fashion designer and married mother of two, was recruited after university to be a senior staff member in a local private enterprise. A number of years later this enterprise went bankrupt and she found herself jobless. With her severance benefits she decided to learn dressmaking. She originally learned how to sew from her seamstress mother and sewed dresses for her colleagues, who appreciated her talent. She went to Paris and a year later, on return to Cameroon, opened a dressmaking workshop. Since then she has been participating in fashion fairs at national as well as international levels, and has won several prizes. Rose said:

> *I am the proprietor of a website. It was created for me by one of my Canadian partners. During a sojourn in Canada, I participated in a fashion parade and fair. Thanks to this site, you can imagine, I was found by one of my best American clients that had for a long time had difficulties contacting me. The internet enables me to communicate with my customers. I have a lot of other customers outside Douala, and even outside the country.*

Ingrid holds a Higher National Diploma in Dressmaking obtained years ago. Based in Douala, she has opened shops at the airports of some European countries. She has participated in numerous fairs and fashion shows in Cameroon and abroad. Every two years she organises a fashion parade in which renowned fashion designers participate. Her reputation rests on the high quality of her products and on their originality. Ingrid said:

> *The internet has brought so much to me. It is a source of inspiration. When I visit fashion sites I get myself always versed with news in the domain of fashion, and that gives me a lot of ideas. Our sector is one of those that witness a lot of mutations. These trends change frequently, new designs appear while others eclipse. I make European fashion design in ready-to-wear. One must always be up to date in order to retain or win other customers. Often I have found patterns that I adapted to come out with original designs that have earned me awards. Today I have customers in all the provinces of Cameroon and in Europe. I have the good fortune of belonging to a dynamic association. We have a partner abroad that placed at our disposal a website where we exhibit our designs. I was recently contacted by an American trader dealing in ready-to-wear. Negotiations are under way and on course. I have hope.*

Two women said that they used the internet to communicate with their suppliers. Rachel, who has an export and import business, uses it in this way:

> *I don't always have the possibility of travelling. So, if I have an order to send, I send an email to my supplier and I specify what I want. Since I've*

been working with him for quite a while and we know each other, everything usually goes well. I'm glad that the internet is here.

On the other hand, Florence, another entrepreneur, specified:

I prefer to deal right on the spot because you are not always sure if what you buy through the internet will be good quality merchandise.

Constraints on women's use of the internet

While the women knew of the internet as a communication and information search tool, other services – such as discussion forums and the capacity to undertake collaborative work – were not known to them.

Moreover, despite the promising examples noted above, the internet still seems to be unknown or inaccessible to the large majority of women entrepreneurs in Cameroon. Like many other parts of Africa, the country has limited access to and use of the internet (Chéneau-Loquay, 2002; Tankeu, 2005). A 2006 report by the International Telecommunication Union underlined the lack of ICT infrastructure in Cameroon and the relatively high cost of bandwidth, as well as the lack of adequate local content, making women's participation difficult. Government action to encourage the use of the internet is embryonic and barely visible. Objectives in telecommunications and ICT have either not been achieved or are experiencing considerable delays. These objectives included making available to the public an offer of access to 2 megabytes in all cities with a digital centre before the end of 2007 and increasing fixed-line teledensity from 0.7 per cent in 2005 to 30 per cent in 2015. Currently, however, the internet is used by only 0.16 per cent of the population.

Improving women's access to the internet

In an effort to help local enterprises to compete in the liberalised international textile trade, the Chamber of Commerce, Industry, Mines and Crafts (CCIMA) started a multimedia centre with funding from several partners. Apart from providing entrepreneurs with services, including training, counselling and useful information on the socio-economic environment, as well as facilitating access to foreign markets, this centre places at their disposal an internet access space with a capacity of 30 machines and a bandwidth of 128 MB. A support programme for women entrepreneurs in the textile sector and clothing arena is being developed in the centre with a view to preparing them to supply to the North American market within the framework of AGOA.

Of the 34 women interviewed, 17 were members of the CCIMA. However, only six knew of the existence of the multimedia centre, and only two had used the internet there. When asked why they did not use this resource centre, they gave the following reasons:

- Lack of information, even from the CCIMA to its members, of the existence of this resource centre (which was put in place in 2001). According to Edith, 'I did not even know of the existence of this centre, and we hold regular meetings in the meeting hall of this institution. I would have at least visited it once to see. As I know of it now, if I have time, I will go there'.
- The fact that the centre is not centrally located within the institution, but is situated in a residential quarter with difficult access.
- The opening hours (8.00 am to 4.00 pm from Monday to Friday) are not convenient even for those who wish to frequent it. These hours correspond to traditional work and school hours. Claudia, a fashion designer, says, 'It is by luck that I learnt of the existence of the multimedia centre. I have been there twice. I found mostly students there. There was nobody there to help me carry out my research. Moreover, the opening and closing times of the centre are not to my convenience.'
- The fact that it has never organised sensitisation activities for women on the uses of the internet.

Moreover, the Chamber of Commerce did not offer any dedicated training on how to use the internet among its other training programmes.

Lessons learned and future directions

Using ICT is turning out to be a powerful business tool for these women. Learning through the internet has helped enhance the competence of quite a few of the respondents, enabling them to acquire knowledge for themselves and for their enterprises. E-learning and self-training can reinforce communication and computer competencies, media attitudes and self-motivation. It is therefore suitable for women in general, and particularly for women entrepreneurs who are creating their own businesses.

While the CCIMA multimedia centre dispenses important resources, these are unfortunately not used by all the members. The location of the project renders access very difficult, and its opening hours do not provide women with optimal access. The centre appears to have been conceived and put in place according to the recommendations of donors. The beneficiaries of the project were not consulted either during formulation or implementation. In other words, its objectives, strategies and basic principles did not take into account the specific situation of the local women entrepreneurs or their particular needs.

For programmes to be useful to women entrepreneurs in Douala, it is recommended that the programme designers learn from what the women have put in place already, taking note of their emerging internet knowledge and practices. Only when women are consulted about their needs and realities can internet support programmes be developed that will enable women entrepreneurs to enhance their lives and their contributions to the Cameroon economy.

Over the next decades, the world will continue to shift it focus from connecting people to connecting nodes of information that people can universally access, share and build upon. Developing efficient and effective ways to value and sustain information networks goes hand in hand with social and economic development. In other words, working in isolation is no longer viable. Developing spheres of trust, influence, goodwill, buy-in, collaboration and partnership and, above all, the sharing of knowledge are the fundamental foundations for women's economic and social empowerment.

In the long term, the potential of this new form of global production is that research and development costs can become localised, and producers and consumers can become more involved in the design and development of products and services. In other words, manual workers can upgrade their skills and do more creative, higher value-added work.

Increasingly then, women are developing their own professional and business networks, which play an important role in both the commercial and policy arenas. One example is Les Femmes Chefs d'Entreprises Mondiales (FCEM) (World Association of Women Entrepreneurs), which was established in 1945 and now hosts a website that links together members from 33 countries and boasts a marketing list of around 45,000 members. More recently established groups include the National Association of Women Entrepreneurs of Malaysia, which was formed in 1993 and now has 170 members; the Alliance of Micro-Enterprise Development Practitioners, a subsection of the Women and Enterprise group of WomensNet – a South African initiative; and the Organization of Women in International Trade, a special interest group that brings together women exporters from both developing and industrialised countries.

These networks range from marketing co-operatives and professional associations to international virtual networks of small businesses. As ICT opens up channels for communication and commerce, more of them take on a cross-border and international character, even if from initially small beginnings.

References

African Development Bank (2005). 'De l'entrepreneuriat féminin au Cameroun', Financing Project, Stean and Associates, Cameroon.

Afrik.com (2004). 'L'Agoa est prolongé jusqu'en 2015: l'Agoa III a été adopté par les sénateurs américains', 2 July, http://www.afrik.com/article7424.html

Biggs, T, Miller, M, Otto, C and Tyler, G (2003). 'Africa Can Compete! Export Opportunities and Challenges for Garments and Home Products in the European Market', World Bank Discussion Papers, World Bank, Washington, DC.

Chéneau-Loquay, A (2002). 'Modes d'accès et d'utilisation d'Internet en Afrique: les grandes tendances', *Africa e Mediterraneo*, 41, December.

Hirsch, S (2005). 'E-management: Suppliers Become Closer Partners', International Trade Forum, 3, http://www.tradeforum.org/news/fullstory.php/aid/924/E-management_Suppliers_Become_Closer_Partners.html

Knappe, M (2005). 'Get Connected', *International Trade Forum*, 3, http://www.tradeforum.org/news/fullstory.php/aid/925/Get_Connected.html

Tankeu, R (2005). 'Fracture numérique de genre au Cameroun: quelle ampleur?', Environmental Development Action in the Third World (ENDA)/ANAÎS), Dakar, Senegal.

Yitamben, G and Tchinda, E (2009). 'Internet Use Among Women Entrepreneurs in the Textile Sector in Douala, Cameroon: Self-taught and Independent', in Buskens, I and Webb, A (eds), *African Women and ICTs: Investigating Technology, Gender and Empowerment*, Zed Books/IDRC, London.

24 Lessons Learned from Part Two

Marilyn Carr

Although the experiences described in the ten case studies in Part Two are at the micro level, there is a wealth of information that can be analysed to give some indication as to what works and what does not work in terms of linking women with export markets. This chapter seeks to draw out the lessons learned from the case studies in terms of:

1. Economic and non-economic benefits for women producers and workers;
2. The factors leading to success, including the policy environment and the pros and cons of the various strategies used by different agencies to assist low-income women producers and workers; and
3. The extent to which these individual cases are sustainable and the potential for their replication by other governments and stakeholders in the Commonwealth.

Benefits

The women (and men) in these case studies have undoubtedly benefited from the initiatives described. The nature and extent of the benefits tend to vary according to the degree of ownership and control that the women have over the enterprise concerned. Benefits are derived at country level, at the level of the enterprise owner(s) and at the level of the workers/contracted farmers. At all three levels there can be direct economic, indirect economic or non-economic benefits.

At country level, all the initiatives have made contributions in terms of output, employment and export earnings. In most cases, they have also tended to be environmentally neutral; some, such as marula oil in Swaziland and body products in Fiji Islands, have directly contributed to environmental and/or cultural conservation.

At the level of the enterprise, most of the export businesses have resulted in significant profits or dividends for their owners. In cases in which women producers have full membership and involvement in the enterprise – Kuapa Kokoo, Swazi Indigenous Products, Kitgum Women Beekeepers Association, Toehold Artisan Collaborative and SEWA Trade Facilitation Centre – the owners and rural women producers are one and the same, and share in the dividends. Some receive indirect economic benefits such as premiums from fair trade sales (Kuapa Kokoo) and/or augmented earnings through organic certification (SIP). In the case of member-owned enterprises, women also experience significant non-economic benefits in terms of confidence building, self-reliance and economic independence – as well as increased stature within the community.

In cases where the enterprise is privately owned by individuals (cashews in Mozambique and India, Pure Fiji, and dry flowers in India), the entrepreneurs obviously benefit directly in the form of profits, but also have received widespread recognition and acclaim, including through prestigious business and export awards presented by government. The extent to which rural women and men benefit depends on the aims and orientation of the owners and whether they make the welfare of rural poor producers and workers a priority. In general, the greater the connection between the owner(s) of the company and the rural community, the greater the economic and non-economic benefits derived from the enterprise. For example, the links between owners and rural producers are very close in the case of Pure Fiji, with rural women helped to establish profitable businesses of their own to supply the parent company and assisted with education and infrastructure. In the case of Ramesh Flowers, the outsourcing system certainly provides rural producers with income, but there is no link between the parent firm and these producers, and so no further direct benefits can be assumed – although the parent company provides higher wages and much better working conditions for its factory workers than its less socially conscious competitors.

In general, rural women are more likely to benefit at all levels from export enterprises if they are the owners of the enterprise or linked to it through a very short supply chain. They are also more likely to benefit, especially in non-economic terms, if they are independent producers rather than workers. Ideally, there should be a 'win-win' situation in which the country, the enterprise and the producers/workers all benefit at all three levels so that export earnings can be expanded at the same time as rural livelihoods are improved and the environment is conserved. As several of the case studies show, this is entirely possible if the political will is there and the entrepreneurial spirit and rural skills exist to make it happen.

Factors in success

Policy and regulatory environment

As the case studies in Part One of this book showed, trade policy can sometimes present barriers to exports from developing countries in ways that affect women's livelihoods. However, as was seen in some of the case studies in Part Two, innovative thinking can often be used to turn these constraints to advantage. For example, in Ghana, protection of dairy and sugar products in EU markets was a factor in cocoa producers moving directly into the production of chocolate in Europe in order to overcome the ban on exporting chocolate. Trade policies can also be used by governments in support of processed exports. For example, Mozambique was able to argue for the raising of export taxes on raw cashew nuts to support the growth of local processing industries.

In most of the case studies, regulations such as strict quality standards in export markets, as well as the logistical problems involved in exporting, have been more significant than trade policy per se. For example, in Uganda, export of honey was an impossibility until the Government upgraded the structure for monitoring standards and was able to obtain a certificate for Ugandan honey producers to export to Europe. In Jamaica, the main obstacle to exporting organic coffee is not a specific policy, but the sheer amount of red tape involved in having to go through the US mainland to reach final buyers elsewhere. In niche markets also, Fairtrade and organic certification are difficult and costly to obtain without assistance of some sort.

More important than all this is that trade policy (including regulations) is only one of a set of economic policies and programmes that governments have to put in place to promote the equal distribution of benefits arising from increased trade. In both Ghana and Mozambique, the Government has offered support in terms of guaranteeing loans or providing low interest loans to the private sector to increase processing and/or export capacity. In Ghana, where the Government has only partially liberalised the cocoa marketing board, there is still a strong market support system that provides export marketing and quality control services to cocoa farmers. By contrast, Mozambique has a very weak market infrastructure that impedes the marketing of cashew kernels. In India, the Government of Karnataka has provided the infrastructure at the base of the Toehold Artisans Collaborative and in Swaziland the Government has given rent-free factory space to SIP for a four-year period. In Uganda, the governmental agricultural assistance programme, NAADS, has played a major role in promoting women's involvement in beekeeping through large and small intermediary organisations such as BNP and KWBA. However, Ramesh Flowers in India has received no government support and has blossomed despite this.

Organisation and production systems

One of the major lessons learned from the case studies is the vast number of organising structures and production systems that have been put in place in pursuit of the common aim of expanding export earnings (and profits), at the same time as maintaining the livelihoods (and independence) of rural women producers.

In general, there is a tendency for the larger and less personalised forms of production to offer the greatest potential for expansion of exports because of the ability to use more sophisticated equipment, ensure better control quality and provide the quantities needed in export markets. More decentralised and smaller-scale operations provide more potential for increasing women's empowerment, for building assets and for women's control over their own livelihoods, but they face constraints in meeting the rigorous demands of export markets. Several of the case studies show how these two extremes can be brought closer together and how, with proper organisation and management, there need not be a trade-off between export earnings and women's empowerment.

In the case of some of the larger, individually-owned enterprises, such as Miranda Caju in Mozambique, Pure Fiji, Bee Natural Products in Uganda and Ramesh Flowers in India, various ways have been tried to increase the benefits realised by the rural poor producers/farmers. For example, Miranda Caju was the focus of an attempt pioneered by Technoserve and other donors to introduce a system of small, decentralised 'satellite' units that would supply the parent company with good quality inputs, while at the same time providing local ownership and employment opportunities. Unfortunately, this was not successful, but it could work in other countries, in other circumstances – as with the system of production clusters in Tamil Nadu. In the case of Pure Fiji, there has been a deliberate attempt to establish small rural enterprises run by local women who provide needed inputs for the main export business. In Uganda, Bee Natural Products has made every attempt to give equal training opportunities to women farmers, to deal with cultural constraints such as those involved in wearing protective beekeeping suits, and in involving women in non-traditional support industries such as making beehives. And Ramesh Flowers has organised a huge network of farmers to supply plants harvested from the wild or agricultural waste products. It also has a very supportive programme to improve the working conditions of the 95 per cent of its workforce at factory level who are poor women.

At the other extreme, Kitgum Women's Beekeeping Association is a small association that has shown it is possible to reach out to export markets through dynamic leadership. However, the prospects of supplying large amounts of exports from small groups like this are severely limited unless they are federated in some way. The Uganda case study suggests that forming a Network of Women's Beekeeping Associations might be one way of doing this.

In between are the community-owned businesses that are both more socially oriented than the privately owned businesses, and also larger than the small producer/marketing groups. These include SIP, Toehold and STFC. These have had remarkable success in exporting high quality products either from central processing centres or, as in the case of Toehold and STFC, from hundreds of small, decentralised units. As mentioned in the case study, Toehold has surprised critics with its rejection rate of only 2 per cent.

The global value chains through which producers and workers are linked with global markets are spelled out in more or less detail in the various case studies. Some of these are quite elaborate, involving many layers and many types of people at various levels. In general, women have traditionally tended to be at the bottom and lower-paid end of the chain, with little power to exert any influence in what are essentially buyer-driven chains. As has been seen in the case studies, most of the initiatives have attempted to increase both returns and power to these women.

Strategies have included the introduction of more appropriate technologies to enable greater value to be added at the grassroots level. For example, new cashew nut processing factories in Mozambique have turned to the use of semi-mechanised labour-intensive technology imported from India. This enables more people to be recruited in remote rural areas, but also results in fewer breakages and produces more whole nuts than larger-scale technology. And in Fiji Islands, the use of new small-scale oil expelling technology enables processing to be done in village level enterprises, while still producing at a sufficiently high quality to compete in export markets. Strategies also include those that give rural women greater control over the supply chain and greater access to more distant and lucrative markets.

Marketing strategies

Several different marketing strategies are illustrated in the case studies. One is fair trade. Kuapa Kokoo in Ghana markets a proportion of its cocoa as fair trade products in collaboration with its chocolate company, Divine, in the UK and USA. Although the market for fair trade goods is relatively small, it is growing and is influencing consumers in the North to think in terms of more fairly traded goods (which focus on returns to producers without necessarily having Fairtrade certification). In Jamaica, women coffee farmers are also trying to get Fairtrade certification, but they are finding it difficult because they are isolated and do not meet the qualification of belonging to a group or co-operative. In Swaziland, SIP has been marketing bulk oil to export markets through commercial channels, but is now considering arrangements with the Body Shop International plc, which already imports 'community traded' marula oil from the PhytoTrade Africa affiliate in Namibia. Fairtrade certification brings with it the benefit of a premium of US$150 per tonne for cocoa that, in the case of Ghana, has been used to build schools and wells, buy grinding mills and set up women's rural enterprises such as soap making.

Another popular strategy has been to target the market for organic products/goods or other niche markets for natural-product based goods. Examples of this are coffee in Jamaica, marula-oil based products in Swaziland and natural body-care products in Fiji Islands. A problem with supplying the organic market is that it is very complicated and expensive to gain organic certification. However, the benefits to producers are well worth it in terms of increased prices. In Swaziland, for example, where SIP has obtained certification with the assistance of PhytoTrade Africa, suppliers obtain approximately E128 per litre for organic marula oil versus E114 for conventional marula oil. There is, however, the middle way of marketing a 'natural' product (as opposed to one which is organically certified) and still appealing to special markets in the North.

Finally, there are the mainstream markets that enterprises described in the case studies are trying to reach either through specific export promotion strategies implemented by governments (e.g. the Apiculture Export Promotion Strategy in Uganda) or on their own through their own contacts and initiatives. For example, SIP has developed a network of commercial distributors for Swazi Secret products through visitors who used these products while staying in hotels in Swaziland. Ramesh Flowers has built a network of well-known retail outlets through contacts with the consulates of various countries. And Toehold has extended its markets through visiting international trade fairs, its website and exposure in the media. Toehold has stayed away from the fair trade markets and deliberately focused on the highly competitive and discerning high-end international market.

In most of these enterprises, a brand name has been very important in maintaining international buyers. These include 'Divine' for Kuapa Kokoo's chocolate; 'Swazi Secrets' for SIP's marula-based products; 'Pure Fiji'; 'Toehold' for ASCENT; and 'Hansiba' for STFC.

Another important aspect of marketing has been the use of the internet. The case study on the Cameroon focuses on the many ways in which women who run small ready-made garments businesses have used the internet to break into export markets. However, the enterprises in many of the other case studies – especially Divine chocolate, Pure Fiji, Ramesh Flowers, Toehold Artisans Collaborative and STFC – have also built up their export businesses partly through their websites.

Reliability and sustainability

So what of the future? Can the individual models outlined in the case studies be replicated or scaled up, and are they and the markets they are linked with sustainable?

Replicability

There is every indication that replication is already underway in a number of the initiatives. Community-based enterprises similar to SIP have been successfully established through PhytoTrade Africa in other southern African countries, and there is no reason why it could not be replicated throughout the region with marula oil and with other natural products. The technology on which Pure Fiji's cold-pressed oils is based – direct micro expulsion – has already been transferred to other countries in the Pacific, where it has been used by rural women to process oils for use in beauty products that are then exported.[59] In Uganda, private companies, community-based enterprises and women's associations are all successfully expanding their numbers or helping to replicate themselves through the government programme, NAADS. In India, STFC has obtained funds from the World Bank and the Indian Government to help women's organisations in other countries to replicate its model with necessary adaptations.

The one case study in which replication has not taken place successfully – even though replication was built into the original project – is that of 'satellite' cashew nut processing units in Mozambique. This seems mainly to have been because of lack of financial viability, combined with inadequate managerial skills.

Sustainability

Replicability is one thing, but are these initiatives sustainable in the long term, both economically and environmentally, given all the changes taking place in world markets and in the global environment?

In the case of economic sustainability, there is the important question of maintaining competitiveness. Most enterprises described in the case studies have adopted various measures to keep their hold on the market. These include upgrading technology (as with honey producers in Uganda); diversifying into new products (Pure Fiji); and establishing better infrastructure for use by rural producers (Common Facility Centre and Raw Materials Bank at Toehold, and common production centres at STFC). Many of the enterprises also use various methods, including the internet and international trade fairs, to keep abreast of market developments. It appears that nothing succeeds like success – and most of the enterprises in the case studies have experienced significant growth over the years. Even in Mozambique, where the 'satellite' units have not proved to be financially viable, the parent company Miranda Caju and the other 17 similarly sized private firms operating in the country are all doing very well and look likely to continue to do so.

Questions do need to be raised as to the effect of the world economic recession on the markets for some of these products. Both Pure Fiji and Ramesh Flowers specifically mention this as a new challenge, but most of the enterprises featured in the case studies will experience some effects. The impact is likely to vary according to which type of market is being supplied. Surveys indicate that products supplying both fair trade and organic markets are more likely to hold their own during the recession than are those supplying conventional retail markets. Many people are unwilling to put aside their concerns with poverty and the environment even during a downturn, so that although sales to fair trade and organic markets are likely to slow down significantly, there will still be some growth (Demont, 2009; Scott-Thomas, 2009).

Environmental sustainability has particular relevance in the case of natural product/non-timber forest products. In Swaziland, SIP has had a very positive environmental affect by increasing the value of the marula tree economically and preventing the trees from being cleared for agricultural production. In Fiji Islands, the traditional uses of many trees and plants are being revived, again with better care given to them by rural populations. In India, dry flowers are more environmentally friendly than fresh cut flowers because they use plants harvested from the wild or agricultural waste rather than agricultural land that is diverted from food crops. And even the shoe and garments case studies in India are environmentally friendly through their use of organic cotton, natural dyes and manual equipment.

References

Demont, P (2009). 'Fair Trade Products Hold Their Own During Recession', *CBC News*, 15 May, http://www.cbc.ca/money/story/2009/05/11/f-fair-trade-canada-recession.html

Cretney, J and Tafuna'i, A (2004). 'Tradition, Trade and Technology: Virgin Coconut Oil in Samoa', in Carr, M (ed.) *Chains of Fortune: Linking Women Producers and Workers with Global Markets*, Commonwealth Secretariat, London.

Scott-Thomas, C (2009). 'Organic Growth Freezes But Will Thaw, Says Mintel', *Decision News Media*, 23 February, http://www.foodnavigator-usa.com/content/view/print/237387

About the Contributors

Marilyn Carr is a development economist with over 30 years experience working in Africa and Asia. She was Senior Economist for the Intermediate Technology Development Group (now Practical Action); Chief, Economic Empowerment, UNIFEM; and founding member and Director of the Global Markets Programme, WIEGO. She holds a DPhil in Economics from the University of Sussex and has been a Research Fellow at the International Institute for Environment and Development, London, the International Development Research Centre, Ottawa, the Radcliffe Institute for Advanced Studies at Harvard University and the Institute of Development Studies, Sussex. Her recent publications include: *Lightening the Load: Labour Saving Technologies and Practices for Rural Women*, Practical Action Publishing/IFAD, 2010; *Gender and Trade Action Guide*, Commonwealth Secretariat, 2007 (with Catherine Atthill, Sarojini Ganju Thakur and Mariama Williams) and *Gender and Non-timber Forest Products: Promoting Food Security and Economic Empowerment*, IFAD, 2008.

Madhura Chatrapathy is Trustee Director, Asian Centre for Entrepreneurial Initiatives. She set up Food Associates, Bangalore 26 years ago and it has grown to become a renowned customised dehydrated food ingredient manufacturing company. She has been working in the field of entrepreneurship development for over 25 years as the progenitor of ASCENT, pioneering the concept of group enterprise. She has spearheaded the movement of women entrepreneurs. Her particular concerns are micro-enterprises and technology. She is committed to fostering entrepreneurial initiatives in both the social and commercial spheres.

Itai Chibaya is a social ecologist with more than five years experience working in forests and wildlife management. Currently, he is Research Associate (Monitoring & Evaluation) with PhytoTrade Africa. He is responsible for co-ordinating all activities at the Harare Office in association with the London Office. He has conducted work in Liberia and several other African countries and has worked for the Centre for International Research (CIFOR) and the Zimbabwe Parks and Wildlife Authority. He has a BSc (Hons) in Forestry Resources and Wildlife Management (NUSY-Zimbabwe) and is completing an MSc in Social Ecology (University of Zimbabwe).

Yves Conze holds a PhD in Economics from the New School University of New York and has served as Economic Adviser to the Minister of Finance and the Ministry of Planning of Haiti, the Minister of Finance of Rwanda and the Head of Civil Affairs in the Peacekeeping Mission in Croatia. He has also worked as a consultant for the UN Secretariat, UNDP and USAID in the areas of capacity building, export promotion, monitoring and evaluation, and trade and macroeconomic policy. He is currently a trading instructor at Prism Trading Group LLC. **Mona Dave** has worked with the Self Employed Women's Association for 18 years and was elected as its Vice President in 2009. Currently, she is also Chief Executive Officer of the SEWA Trade Facilitation Centre and a Trustee in SEWA Gram Mahila Haat (both of which she co-founded) and Senior Co-ordinator of Rural Organising in SEWA. In addition, she is a member of the Association's core management team and is responsible for its future path. During her years at SEWA, she also founded the Kutch Craft Association and the Mahila Vikas Mandal (district level organisations of poor self-employed women). She has worked with many national and international agencies on various projects and participated in the Seventh World Summit of Young Entrepreneurs organised by UNIFEM and the Institute for Leadership Development (ILD), where she was given the Best Entrepreneur in Social Responsibility Award.

Pramod Dev is a researcher based in New Delhi with interests in issues related to the political economy of development, trade and the environment. Until recently he was a Policy Analyst at the Centre for International Trade, Economics and Environment (CITEE) of CUTS International, India, where he was engaged in research and advocacy related to trade and development issues, and trade and the environment. He has also contributed to the development of the CUTS International Trade and Gender Programme. He holds an M. Phil. in South Asian Studies and read Economics and International Relations for his Bachelor's and Postgraduate degrees, respectively. He is currently researching the impact of European ecolabels on garment exports from India for his doctoral thesis at Jawaharlal Nehru University, New Delhi. He is also a part-time documentary film maker, focusing on environmental and social issues.

Sanae Ito is Associate Professor at the Graduate School of International Development at Nagoya University, Japan. She conducts research on issues related to poverty and globalisation. Her publications include articles on the shrimp industry and microfinance practices in Bangladesh and Cambodia. She is currently working on the implications for small farmers in these countries of integration in agribusiness value chains.

Paul Kamau is a Research Fellow at the Institute for Development Studies (IDS), University of Nairobi. He holds a PhD in Development Studies, University of Nairobi; MSc. in Economics from University of Zimbabwe; and BA in Economics from University of Nairobi. His research interests are international trade and industrial development in sub-Saharan Africa, with particular emphasis on the textile and clothing industry. He has conducted research and published on trade, innovation and industrial development in Africa.

Nazneen Kanji is based in London, working for the Aga Khan Development Network (AKDN). She is director of a research programme on the 'quality of life', designed to inform AKDN's programmes in countries in Africa, south and central Asia and the Middle East. She has worked extensively on gender, livelihoods and social policy and has research, teaching, consultancy and field experience, mainly in Africa and Asia. She lived in Mozambique in the 1980s and in the United Republic of Tanzania in the mid-1990s. As a senior research associate at the International Institute for Environment and Development (IIED) from 2000 to 2006, her interests focused on trade, gender and livelihoods, including a study of international value chains in cashew nuts, and on land and livelihoods in Africa. Most recently, she has co-authored a book entitled *Non-Governmental Organizations and Development* (Routledge, 2009) that provides a critical overview of this wide-ranging field.

Maideyi Kutambura is a young environmentalist currently studying for an undergraduate degree in geography and the environment focusing on ecosystem management and sustainable development at Midlands State University, Zimbabwe. She is also an intern at PhytoTrade Africa. Her interests include the environment, climate change, sustainable livelihoods, corporate social responsibility, forestry, gender, HIV and AIDS, and food security.

Amit Lodha completed his studies at St Xavier's, Calcutta, pursued chartered accountancy unsuccessfully and then tried a stint at collecting dried flowers from Nepal, which was an unexplored area at that time. He moved to Tuticorin, South India in 1995 to work for Ramesh Flowers. He was appointed Director of Sales in 1998, a position that he still holds.

Rachel Nadelman is a Social Development Specialist with the Sustainable Development Department (Latin American and Caribbean Region) at the World Bank. In this role, as well as through her prior work with organisations such as GROOTS International and American Jewish World Service, she has focused her fieldwork and research on community-driven development and women's economic empowerment. She has worked in central and south America, the Caribbean, east and central Africa and the USA. She has a BA from Brown University and an MA in International Affairs from the New School University.

Reema Nanavaty was elected as General Secretary of SEWA in 1999 and in this position she helped to double the association's membership to over 500,000, making it the single largest union of informal sector workers in India. Currently, she is managing a US$6 million programme of economic activities for SEWA through a federation of 100 co-operatives, nine district associations of artisans, salt farmers and forestry workers, and a direct outlet of 12,000 artisans. She initiated and negotiated the first ever NGO-Government of India-IFAD loan to rebuild the lives of 60,000 earthquake-affected SEWA members and is running a post-conflict reconstruction package for 40,000 members affected by the 2004 riots. She sits on various government and multilateral agency committees, and is expanding the activities of the SEWA Trade Facilitation Centre in Afghanistan and the entire South Asian Association for Regional Cooperation (SAARC) region, with the aim of making women's voices and contributions central to world trade decisions and collective brand-building and marketing.

Carol Narcisse has over 25 years of experience in fields related to human, social and organisational development. She is an accomplished educator, broadcaster, trainer, social policy researcher, analyst and advocate. Her collective experiences express her passion for the empowerment of children and disadvantaged groups, and for sustainable human and social development. Carol is a graduate of Columbia University's Teachers College and holds a Master's degree in Education.

Nontokozo Nemarundwe is a sociologist with 17 years experience in rural development, mainly in southern Africa. She holds a PhD in Rural Development Studies from the Swedish University of Agricultural Sciences. Her specific area of focus is on socio-economic research using both qualitative and quantitative methods, project/programme design, monitoring and evaluation, social and environmental impact assessment, gender issues in community-based natural resource management (CBNRM) programmes and institutional development using participatory methodologies. She has worked on consultancies for numerous international agencies and is currently the Impact Monitoring Manager at PhytoTrade Africa. Her work involves monitoring the socio-economic and environmental impacts on rural harvesters and processors of the development of the natural products industry in southern Africa.

Dorienne Rowan-Campbell founded Rowan's Royale – an enterprise that produces Jamaican Blue Mountain Coffee, one of the most expensive and sought after coffees in the world. Her organic enterprise sets a model for communities in Jamaica, as well as highlighting environmental issues and the role a small farmer can play in combating climate change and environmental degradation, and contributing to disaster mitigation. For the past 30 years, she has been an international consultant on gender, human resource development, training and environment and is currently part of a team running ICT and organic farming workshops for women farmers in the Caribbean. She is a qualified organic farm inspector and runs a community 'greening project' in her neighbourhood, which has the first regular recycling collection service in Jamaica.

May Sengendo is a lecturer with the Department of Women and Gender Studies at Makerere University in Uganda and also plays a leadership role in the private sector, including as the Vice Chair for the Federation of Uganda Exporters Associations. She has worked on gender mainstreaming in the trade and industry sectors of the National Development Plan for Uganda, participated in engendering the National Export Strategy for Uganda with the International Trade Centre, UNCTAD and the Uganda Export Promotion Board, and worked on preparation of the gender content for WTO negotiations and COMESA and East African Community trade policy planning. Her published studies include *Searching for International Markets: Market Access Information Provision and Needs for Female and Male Exporters in Uganda's Horticulture and Fisheries Sectors*, funded by Gender and Economic Reforms in Africa.

Sarah Silliman co-ordinates programmes for two global civil society networks focused on building women's economic empowerment: the Women and Governance programme for GROOTS International and the MDG3 Accountability Initiatives for the Huariou Commission. She holds a BA in Economics from Antioch College in Ohio and an MA in International Affairs from the New School University. She specialises in the areas of strengthening democratic governance at the local level, increasing women's influence in decision-making and resource allocation and building women's leadership skills.

Nidhi Tandon is Director of Networked Intelligence for Development at www.networkedintelligence.com. Originally from East Africa, she works on local grassroots issues in the context of globalisation and increasing disparities between peoples and nations. She has been specialising in digital media, information and communication technologies and applications that enhance women's livelihoods since 1995. She designs and runs workshops for women's organisations, small businesses and farmer communities in east and west Africa and in the Caribbean, enabling women to organise and articulate their priorities around sustainable development. Much of her work revolves around the relationships between women and water, energy, natural resources and political agendas. She has published critical articles on climate change and its varying impact on women's land use options.

Pauline Tiffen is a London-based consultant who has worked with farmers and artisans developing export capacity and marketing strategies for more than 20 years. She is a business and organisational advisor to Kuapa Kokoo and a Non-Executive Director of Divine Chocolate. Pauline currently works for Light Years IP, a Washington-based NGO promoting the use of intellectual property rights by low-income producers and artisans in Africa to raise export revenues by capturing a larger share of the intangible value of their distinctive and unique products (see http://www.lightyearsip.net).

Lucy Welford has 17 years of experience in environmental management and community development. She has worked for the Department of National Parks in Zimbabwe and the Food and Agriculture Organization of the United Nations where she specialised in appropriate media and communications for rural development. She has an MPhil in Environment and Development, specialising in ethnobotany and a doctorate in community-based natural resource management in Zimbabwe, both from the University of Cambridge, UK. She has been heading

up PhytoTrade Africa's marketing and communications since 2003.
Mariama Williams is an economic and trade consultant, a Research Associate with the International Gender and Trade Network and a director of the Board of the Institute of Law and Economics, Jamaica. She is also a consultant adviser on gender and international trade to the Commonwealth Secretariat, London, a consultant on gender and climate change financing with the Global Gender and Climate Alliance (GGCA) and a member of the International Working Group on Gender, Macroeconomics and International Trade (IWG-GEM). She is currently a member of the Board of Trustees of the Dag Hammarskjöld Foundation, Sweden, a Member of the Board of the Center of Concern, Washington, DC and a member of the UNDP's Civil Society Advisory Committee. She is the author of *Gender Issues in the Multilateral Trading System* (Commonwealth Secretariat, 2003) and co-author (with Atthill, Thakur and Carr) of *Gender and Trade Action Guide* (Commonwealth Secretariat, 2007).

Giséle Yitamben is an economist by training and the founder and President of the Association for the Support of Women Entrepreneurs, a non-profit enterprise. She is a member of the World Economic Forum's Global Agenda Council on the Gender Gap 2009, one of the intellectual drivers of the Global Redesign Initiative, an international, multi-stakeholder and multimedia dialogue that aims to develop a 21st century vision of global co-operation. Since 2007 she has also been a member of the Reference Group for Sustainable Development set up to provide expert guidance to UNESCO. In addition, she initiated street football in Cameroon – her team ranked 8th out of 48 countries represented at the 2007 Homeless World Cup (HWC) in Copenhagen, Denmark – and presented a female team in 2008 HWC in Melbourne, Australia. She is the recipient of many national and international awards.

Notes

1 That is, welfare decreases despite economic growth.
2 All figures are from CIA (2008) unless otherwise stated.
3 This agreement between the ACP countries and the EC, signed on 23 June 2000 in Cotonou, Benin, transformed what had previously been a non-reciprocal preferential trading arrangement into a reciprocal arrangement. See Commonwealth Secretariat (2004).
4 Jamaica's Safeguard Act is compatible with the WTO general safeguard agreement. Article XIX of the General Agreement allows a GATT member to take a 'safeguard' action to 'protect a specific domestic industry from an unforeseen increase of imports of any product which is causing, or which is likely to cause, serious injury to the industry'. However, this is a complex mechanism that many developing countries do not have the legal or institutional framework to handle.
5 Thanks to Ann Weston and Dorothy McCormick for comments on earlier drafts.
6 Flexibility in labour use may be obtained either through employment flexibility or through the development of functional flexibility among the workers.
7 The size categorisation of garment manufacturing firms draws from McCormick *et al.* (2007), who use the number of workers to classify firms as micro (1–9 workers), small (10–49), medium (50–99) and large (100 or more). Given the very low threshold for large firms, another category of 'very large' is used here to include firms with 500 or more workers.
8 These included the virtual removal of price controls and liberalisation of imports through the removal of import and foreign exchange licensing, and rationalised tariff regimes.
9 For more information about AGOA see McCormick *et al.* (2006), Kamau (2007) and Weston *et al.* (2008). See also www.agoa.gov
10 Vijayabaskar (2002: 67) also finds the same in Tirupur, India, where trade unions seem not to play any role in the garment industry.
11 Unless otherwise noted, all information in this section is from the AGOA website, www.agoa.info; Malie (2001) and Government of Lesotho (2008).
12 See http://www.agoa.gov/
13 Expanded and updated from a case study by Lera Pascal, see http://www.thecommonwealth.org/gtinformation/164419/164437/164427/banana_production_in_st_lucia/
14 European currency unit (ECU), the precursor of the euro.
15 See http://news.bbc.co.uk/1/hi/world/americas/4737473.stm
16 See http://www.fco.gov.uk/en/about-the-fco/country-profiles/north-central-america/st-lucia?profile=all
17 The Windward Islands – so called because of their exposure to the north-east trade winds – include Grenada, Martinique, St Lucia, and St Vincent and the Grenadines.
18 Approximately US$15 million.
19 Approximately US$1,124.

20 ANZCERTA: Australia–New Zealand Closer Economic Relations; NAFTA: North American Free Trade Agreement; CARICOM: Caribbean Community.
21 This case study is a follow-up to Sengendo and Tumushabe (2005).
22 These include the IDEA project, famine and early warning systems, IITC, International Institute of Tropical Agriculture, Market Information Service and Food Network.
23 Argentina, Brazil, Egypt, India, Indonesia, Namibia, Philippines, South Africa, Tunisia and Venezuela.
24 Free on board means that the price quoted by the supplier includes delivery of the goods to a specific destination (e.g. on board a ship) without extra cost to the purchaser.
25 For a detailed history of Kuapa Kokoo and its progress up to 2002, see Tiffen *et al.* (2004).
26 Asante tribe symbols found everywhere in Ghana, most often stamped on cloth, that are often linked to proverbs or folk tales.
27 It is notable, perhaps, that David Croft, formerly with the Co-op Food Group, moved on in 2005 to work first as Ethical Sourcing Director and then as Global Director of Conformance and Sustainability at Cadbury Schweppes.
28 In 2000, there were allegations of widespread slave labour, including child trafficking, in the cocoa industry. While mainly relating to Côte d'Ivoire, rather than Ghana, these allegations resulted in campaigners putting pressure on large companies to address the problem promptly and brought about concern that formalising accountable commercial relations with millions of individual cocoa farmers would depress the prices they received because of the high transaction costs involved in monitoring.
29 The ripe fruits of coffee shrubs that contain the beans.
30 Just before this book went to press, the CIB gave Rowan's Royale permission to register to be licensed to produce, sell and export organic coffee.
31 US$600 at JA$72 to US$1 at the time of writing.
32 Quote from Prior Notice customer service after a package was detained in Miami Customs for five days because of questions as to place of origin. All documents had been filed with the FDA, FedEx and JAMPRO and all stated, in detail, the place of origin.
33 See http://www.Fairtrade.org.uk/
34 The workshops were co-organised by JOAM and Networked Intelligence for Development (NID), an NGO based in Canada, to provide women farmers with exposure and training in the use of ICTs to enhance their organic enterprises. For reports see http://www.networkedintelligence.com/index.html
35 This chapter is adapted from Kanji (2004). This in its turn draws on collaborative research carried out in Mozambique with the University of Eduardo Mondlane and in India with the Centre for Development Studies in Trivandrum and the Madras Institute for Development Studies. For a longer version of the Mozambique case, see Kanji *et al.* (2004). For a longer version of the Indian case, see Eapen *et al.* (2004).

36 PhytoTrade Africa, established in 2001, has members in Botswana, Malawi, Mozambique, Namibia, South Africa, Swaziland, Zambia and Zimbabwe.
37 See http://www.swazisecrets.com/index.asp
38 Emalangeni is the currency used in Swaziland; at the time of the fieldwork it was 7:1 against the US dollar.
39 Specific company names cannot be cited because of market confidentiality.
40 Information supplied by Pure Fiji except where otherwise stated. Further information is available at http://www.purefiji.com
41 A crore is 10 million rupees or around US$205,000 (US$1 = Rs48.78).
42 For more information on Ramesh Flowers see http://www.rameshflowers.com
43 Research for this case study was underwritten by the SEEDS Pamphlet Series. A full-length pamphlet featuring the research will be published as part of a two-part series on Africa in 2009.
44 The revision to the PEAP in 2000 included increased emphasis on, and sensitivity to, gender issues.
45 For more information, see http://www.naads.or.ug/
46 The Lord's Resistance Army (LRA) has destabilised the northern part of Uganda since 1989, ostensibly fighting the Government while killing, torturing, raping and abducting civilians, including large numbers of children.
47 The data for the years after 2005 is based on Wilson (2008) unless otherwise indicated.
48 2005 prices. At the time of writing, USh2,100 = US$1.00.
49 In 2005, TUNADO had already helped in acquiring a licence to export honey to the EU by promoting a more co-ordinated approach to honey production in the country.
50 For more information on ASCENT and Toehold see: http://www.ascentasia.org and http://www.toeholdindia.com
51 About US$1.00.
52 There is generally concern about succession, with doubts expressed in some quarters as to whether the younger generation will continue the trade.
53 Based on SEWA estimates in 2006.
54 http://www.sewatfc.org
55 District associations are registered associations that organise women workers in various social and/or economic activities and employ the staff at the common production centres. They operate independently – both financially and administratively – although they maintain very close links with the Central SEWA Office in Ahmedabad.
56 Adapted from Yitamben and Tchinda (2009).
57 The survey was conducted by local consultants Giséle Yitamben and Elise Tchinda. The real names of those interviewed have not been used.
58 For more information, see http://www.agoa.gov/
59 For the example of women-headed co-operatives using this technology in Samoa and exporting through Women in Business Development Incorporated (WIBDI), see Cretney and Tafuna'i (2004).

Index